on the wild side

experiments in new naturalism

on the wild side

experiments in new naturalism

Keith Wiley

Timber Press
Portland • Cambridge

To Ros,
without whose unwavering support and understanding
this journey would not have been possible.

Published in 2004 by
Timber Press, Inc.   Timber Press
The Haseltine Building   2 Station Road
133 S.W. Second Avenue, Suite 450   Swavesey
Portland, Oregon 97204, USA   Cambridge CB4 5QJ, UK

Designed by Hilton/Sadler, London

Printed through Colorcraft Ltd, Hong Kong

Library of Congress Cataloging-in-Publication Data

Wiley, Keith.
  On the wild side : experiments in new naturalism / Keith Wiley.
    p. cm.
  ISBN 0-88192-636-1 (hardback)
  1. Natural landscaping. 2. Native plant gardening. 3. Natural
gardens. I. Title.

SB439.W5445 2004
635.9'5--dc22   2003018259

A catalogue record for this book is also available from the British Library.

Contents

Foreword

In 2001 my partner Robert Jones and I designed and installed, with the help of our staff at Heronswood, a display garden at the Northwest Flower and Garden Show, Seattle. Our garden, titled 'On the Eaves of the World; In the Footsteps of Wilson', was our intent to re-create a slice of mountaintop in southwestern China as it might have appeared when plant collector E.H. Wilson had trekked there a century earlier. Of course, the palette of plants we used to create the illusion of wildness was in fact much richer than Wilson would ever have encountered. With that said, we did not primp and prime the space as one would a prototypical garden, and even made artificial snow leopard scat to further pile on the reality.

Although we earned a gold medal for our efforts, it was more than obvious that our 'garden' did not cater to the mainstream show attendees, who were primed for primroses, forced delphiniums and splashy fountains laid out in formulaic patterns. 'Who's responsible for this mess?' was one of the more notable critiques heard from the herd as they trod past in a trance-like state.

Keith Wiley, however, would have assessed our garden with a more radical and worldly set of criteria while, hopefully, appreciating our under-cooked yet complicated portrait of a Chinese wildness. In this book, Keith has issued a clarion call to embrace the intricate, often elaborate, examples of planting design from untrammelled places of our planet. And if the proof is in the pudding, what has resulted through his efforts at the Garden House is not only unparalleled, but would hush even the harshest critic.

In Western horticulture at least, retreating to the original garden for inspiration was first championed by William Robinson and Gertrude Jekyll at the turn of the last century. They successfully sedated the uptight rigidity of the horticultural establishment by the use of irregular and pliable swathes of perennials replicated through their borders. Their approach was a fundamental shift from the contrived and kaleidoscopic bedding-out schemes fabricated from annuals, tender perennials and lots of money. The formalized informality they popularized has remained in vogue for more than a century of garden-making on both sides of the Atlantic, settling down to a long nap of horticultural inertia.

This approach was carried further by Reginald Farrer in his attempts to re-create the essence of an unalloyed, though still highly artificial alpine meadow. There is an important distinction to be made, however, between that which Farrer so passionately advocated and Keith Wiley's equally waggish observations. Farrer, it might be argued, was simply using individual words in his reconstruction of nature whereas Wiley suggests that we re-create, or reinterpret, entire conversations.

In this book, the voices of Thoreau, Leopold and Huxley are as attendant as the past and present horticultural mentors Wiley has listened to throughout his career. His nascent take on what gardening might be is the result of that inevitable collision between the human need to order the universe, in part through the manmade landscape, with the relatively recent understanding of ecology and natural community. Once we had begun to appreciate fully the complexities found in any ecosystem, to imitate anything less in our gardens would seem irreverent, if not foolish.

More than anything, it is this godly reverence for the natural world that shines through the pages of this book. Romanticizing the natural landscape is a perfectly righteous concept if it results in both pleasure and a greater connection to the whole. Keith's writing accomplishes both. This is a work of intimate study as well as loud and colourful strokes, begging with the same eagerness of Farrer a change of direction in our approach to gardening without losing sight of either the inspiration or the end. If what Keith Wiley predicts in *On the Wild Side* is true, that a revolution in gardening is about to occur, then he has with this book issued a well-aimed volley that will be heard around the world.

Dan Hinkley

OPPOSITE *Ursinias form part of the massed displays of native annuals at Kirstenbosch Botanic Gardens in Cape Town, South Africa.*

Preface

Around the world, a trend for putting more emphasis on the importance of our natural landscapes and wild flowers has been gathering pace for some time. I have been interested in the wild landscapes around me for as long as I can remember, but over the years I have increasingly thought it strange that the way we grow plants in our gardens bears little resemblance to the way these same plants grow in the wild. A much-respected, much-travelled horticulturist recently admired a naturalistic area of my garden in Devon and remarked that he could show me any number of areas in northern Italy that looked just like it. As he is someone who has seen more plants in their natural environment than most of us ever will, I wanted to know why he thought nobody had really tried to emulate these natural plant associations. His reply, that he believed nobody thought it could be done, was interesting. What I hope to show in this book is that it can be done, and that by doing so we take the lid off a vast, untapped reservoir of gardening possibilities. I firmly believe we stand on the edge of perhaps the most exciting period in gardening history for maybe the last hundred years.

Although I allow my own inspiration to come from any direction, however unlikely, be it roadside verge, suburban front garden, city-centre flower bed or hotel car park, over the last twenty years I have become totally convinced by the concept of taking gardening ideas from natural landscapes, both on my own doorstep in southwest England and from further afield. It seems to me that we have all but ignored the biggest single source of gardening ideas on the whole planet—the countryside around us. Cast your mind around the subtle variations of natural flora you may have already seen and then reflect on the literally countless variations around the globe. Hardly any of them have been adapted to garden situations. Now consider that in every group of people looking at the same landscape, each and every person would interpret what they see there differently, as the members of any group of artists would each paint it differently, and you begin to imagine the endless possibilities open to you.

The more you travel around the world the more you see the incredible range of habitats many of our garden plants call home, with the seemingly most inhospitable environments occasionally capable of the most spectacular floral displays. Given that the majority of us have only one type of soil in our gardens and are generally limited by a single aspect, be it north or south-sloping for example, it is little short of staggering

LEFT Papaver orientale
var. bracteatum *brings
an early summer touch
of brilliant scarlet to an
otherwise green oasis at
the Garden House. The
immaculate lawn and
ancient wooden seat
induce a sense of calm
and restfulness at the
core of the Walled Garden,
an invaluable antidote to
the narrow paths and
flower-filled borders that
make up the rest of this
part of the garden.*

that we bring home plants from our local garden centres whose natural homes are all these amazingly diverse habitats and expect them to thrive in the one set of conditions we have. The fact that they usually do survive speaks volumes for the resilience and tolerance of many plants.

The particular set of conditions in which we garden are different for all of us. Factor in the experiences we each have had and our personal tastes, and our gardens, if they truly reflect these things, will be unique. This book is written to show how my experiences and preferences have influenced the naturalistic gardening style that

has developed in the garden here at the Garden House in Devon. By showing how the ideas evolved I hope to help others to release the potential within their own sites and from within themselves. One of the sublime beauties of this style is that there are no rules, with parameters being set only from the limitations of our own imaginations, experiences and memories; what suggestions I make are rough guidelines only. This is Wild West, seat-of-your-pants, pioneering gardening where you are never quite sure what is coming from year to year, so hold onto your hats—I know how exciting the ride can be.

Introduction

I am a Somerset lad, from the county in the south-west of England renowned for its cider and home to the world-famous Cheddar cheese. My family lived in the north of the county, equidistant from the sprawling metropolis of Bristol and the beautiful Georgian city that is Bath. No one really famous emanated from this quiet rural backwater and the countryside, though pleasant enough, is not spectacular. Nonetheless, we were fiercely proud of our cidermen ancestry.

North Somerset then was a landscape of rolling hills, tree-shouldered valleys and small fields where ox-eye daisies and other wild flowers still bloomed. Around the field margins grew tall hedges, predominantly hawthorn, which were rarely cut and even more rarely laid, and in the corners of many of these fields were small dew ponds, each seemingly with its own resident pair of moorhens. At irregular intervals along the hedges grew 25 m (80 ft) tall elm trees, with the occasional one marooned in the middle of a field. I would spend countless hours wandering these field edges looking at all things natural, but in particular for birds and their nests. The towering elms were home to very little in the way of bird life and so the oak trees were more interesting to me. These were not very numerous as the soil was alkaline and, as a result, they never appeared to be in great health. Strangely one never saw them as young trees, just as ageing, often hollow, hulks—like stranded, skeletal shipwrecks. Often these rather sickly examples of oak had dense thickets of young shoots sprouting

directly off their main trunks, providing perfect nesting sites for a whole range of different birds.

This landscape of my youth has all changed now—in fact the change was very abrupt, occurring in my teenage years in the 1970s when Dutch elm disease arrived and, within a very few years, took out all of the elms. It seems to be a fact of life that we do not really miss anything until it is gone, but it is still hard to convey the deep-seated loss this engendered in me. At a stroke, our landscape was altered. It was also a time when grants were available to farmers to drain ponds and take out hedges to facilitate the more efficient use of ever-larger machinery, including the single piece of equipment that for me most changed the landscape—the much-hated flail that mutilated my beloved hedges. In the space of ten years the countryside of my childhood had completely gone, to be replaced by the nearest approximation to prairie farming that our local farmers could manage. When I eventually found a soul-mate at college who had a shared passion for the countryside, and took

ABOVE *The stone walls of Borrowdale in the English Lake District are reminiscent of the Mendip walls of my childhood, only less tumbledown. If they were transferred to a garden setting, these grass verges would look fabulous planted with a range of natural-looking herbaceous perennials.*

PREVIOUS PAGE *Dusk falls over St Andrew's church in Buckland Monachorum and the Devon hills in the view from the Garden House.*

her proudly home to show her the country of my origins, her obviously profound disappointment at this singularly uninteresting stretch of landscape crushed my rose-tinted spectacles for ever.

Looking closely

Even as a young lad, scarcely tall enough to see over an ox-eye daisy, I became completely immersed in the countryside, observing every nuance and detail, even though I was largely unaware of doing this at the time. The reason, in a couple of words, was 'bird's nesting'.

Now, of course, it is severely frowned on, and quite rightly too, but forty years ago this activity was considered by country-folk to be a perfectly healthy and legitimate pursuit for a young person. Almost any youngster who had a love of the countryside would go bird's nesting every spring, in the same way that we would pick bunches of primroses and wild violets for Mother's Day—it was almost a rite of passage.

To be honest I was good at it, having devoured the contents of a wonderful book called *British Birds* by Kirkman and Jordain, in which the paintings managed to convey not only the birds themselves but also the essence of the habitat in which each lived—no small achievement as far as I was concerned. The result was that I felt I could walk into virtually any natural landscape and instantly produce a mental short-list of the bird species that might live there. I became acutely conscious not only of obvious variations in landscape, such as marshy ground, ponds, woods, hedges, barns, streams and so forth, but also of the minutiae within each of these habitats, such as the species constituting a hedge, the density of its growth and the type of plants at its feet. When I saw a barn I noted whether it was made of wood or stone, how it was roofed, if ivy was growing up the walls, and whether it was on the edge of an open field or in wooded country. All of these details had a profound effect on the bird species likely to be found there. Many years later, these early forays into studying landscapes closely would help to formulate the cornerstone of my whole gardening philosophy.

Very occasional holidays (we were a big family and were content, by and large, to stay within the confines of our few acres) might take us to the sand dunes of Brean on the Somerset coast, or the larger version, further to the south-west, at Braunton Burrows, in Devon, or to the wonderfully rich green steep valleys and glorious rocky coastline of that same county.

On the way back home we would often pause by Chew Valley Lake, with its unfamiliar water birds, or pass by the reed-fringed dykes of the Somerset Levels, or dozens of other locations, all looking wonderfully exotic and exciting to a young boy. I loved it all, and it instilled in me a lifelong addiction to the close study of natural landscapes that has become a key characteristic of the way I now garden.

A trip to the nearest coast always took us over the Mendip hills, close to our home. Here, stone walls had been built in lieu of hedges, as on many upland areas of Britain. Most years, in early summer, we would have one trip down to Cheddar, where, on the southern slopes of the Mendips, early strawberries could be bought. On the return journey—it is funny how in your memory it was always a golden, sunlit evening—we would often stop on a quiet little lane to eat some of our newly acquired bounty. This gave me a chance to explore the surroundings and I remember, as if it were yesterday, the lichen-covered stone in the tumbledown walls that were nearly always set back by at least a yard, sometimes much more, from the road, with the intervening space filled with wild flowers growing amid the grass. There might be stonecrop and harebells growing in the cracks in the walls and there would invariably be

a pair of anguished stonechats, flitting from bush to bush in an attempt to distract me from their well-hidden nest (they were always successful as I never managed to find one). Whether it was the setting, the beautiful evenings, the stonechats or the strawberries, this image has haunted me ever since. I went back recently, criss-crossing the Mendips, hoping to illustrate my words with a photograph of a similar little lane, bordered by walls, stretching downhill towards the Somerset Levels with the two or three scrawny-looking ash trees of my memory, but I could not find one.

Maybe the roads have all been widened now, so I shall have to make do with the sepia-stained image in my head. Not that I need a photograph personally as it is exactly such haunting images, collected from around the world and etched into my memory banks, that form the basis of my garden designs.

ABOVE *The Garden House itself is partly obscured by an enormous Rhododendron arboreum, which is of a similar age to the building. Dating from the 1830s, this was the vicarage to the church seen on page 11 for nearly another hundred years.*

The grand scheme

Like so many people I fell in love in my teenage years for the first time, but not alas in my case with a young woman nor, I hasten to add in this enlightened age, with a young man, but rather more mundanely with gardening. During this period, my father was busy turning a 0.8 ha (2 acre) field into a garden, and he was more than happy to receive any physical help he could get from his children. I was able to design and build rockeries, stone walls, heather gardens and whole pond systems to my heart's content and I loved every minute of it.

My father was one for the big idea and he never did anything by halves, other than, I am afraid, only ever half completing anything. His plans for creating a water garden would have made Capability Brown blush with conservatism. Needing stone for a rockery he was contemplating building, he persuaded a local haulier to drop off a load or two of rock from the foundations of the supermarket being built in the nearest town. The result was that 50 tons of huge boulders blocked our driveway completely for several years. One year he decided he would naturalize daffodils in a 100 m (109 yd) section of this new garden and so went off and bought over 500 kg (10 cwt) of them. My brothers and I planted out seven or eight bags before crippling muscle spasms and boredom set in, and the remaining bags stayed where they had been dumped, valiantly flowering the following spring through the netted sides. The rider to this story is that those we did plant out gradually faded away because the bulbs were suffering from something like narcissus eelworm, almost certainly the reason they were so cheap in the first place.

However, occasionally these big ideas did work out and then the effect he created could be quite staggering. I remember one occasion when he planted out a huge bed of mostly dark red wallflowers, interplanted with daffodils and all the gaps between filled with self-seeded, blue forget-me-nots—an effort worthy of a Dutch

LEFT *The granite boulder-strewn slopes and atmospheric woods of Burrator on the southern edge of Dartmoor, England, have an enchanted feel in the evening light. You would almost expect the wood elves to appear if only you could sit still long enough.*

municipal park, and the sight and smell of it was truly memorable. The excitement and enthusiasm he generated in me and himself over the latest new plan, and sheer bravura of his potential schemes, instilled in my developing consciousness of gardening a deep-rooted pleasure in witnessing plants growing on the grand scale, which is reinforced only by seeing them in the wild—and absolutely nowhere and no one does the massed effect of flowers better than nature. Absolutely nothing comes close to the euphoria, with spirits soaring into the stratosphere, that I experience when I am privileged enough to stand in front of a particularly spectacular display of wild flowers. Not for me the snail's pace of a botanical trip, gripped by the presence or otherwise of hairs on a plant bearing a remarkable resemblance to a rabbit dropping, when behind you the whole landscape might be a sea of orange daisies. Personally, I blame my father for this predisposition of mine for the grand scheme.

When I arrived at my first job after leaving university in July 1978, it was a massed effect of flowers of an altogether more subtle kind that stoked the fires of my enthusiasm. Here, on the lowest terrace of a walled garden, protected by the embrace of the encircling 3 m (10 ft) high walls and under the watchful, almost brooding eye of a 16th-century tower, was the most wonderful display of herbaceous plants I had ever seen. Frothy filipendulas in shades of pink jostled with lilac-blue *Campanula lactiflora* (see page 238), spires of elegant soft pink sidalceas and vivid blue delphiniums, yellow daylilies and the exquisitely graceful dieramas with pink bells hanging from under arching wands. Astrantias, rodgersias and astilbes all added to the picture. In one place that most superlative of umbellifers, *Selinum tenuifolium*, with its lacy, filigree foliage, raised its statuesque grey-white flower heads above a sea of pristine, dazzlingly white *Malva moschata* f. *alba*, the latter almost taking off from the efforts of hundreds of honey bees. Wafting in from nearby came the heady scents of many large bushes of flowering mock orange, *Philadelphus* hybrids, such as 'Belle Etoile' and the similar but

slightly more refined 'Sybille', a 1 m (3¼ ft) high bush that could be smelled at a distance of 20 m (22 yd) or more.

All of this was grown to perfection and assembled with consummate colour-coordinating skills. In my lunch-breaks and after work I would sit on the flagstone paths soaking it all in, listening to the birds and thinking I had found heaven. This was the Garden House, in south Devon, and here I was with a garden blessed with a wonderful setting and climate, a deeply ingrained love of natural landscape, a passion for the massed effect and an inherited preference for the big scheme. Throw into the equation my better half, with her artistic flair and overwhelming instincts for all things natural, and you have a cocktail where inspiration from nature was not only likely but almost a certainty.

The garden of the Garden House had been created by Lionel and Katharine Fortescue, who had come here in 1946 after Lionel's retirement from teaching at Eton school. The site they bought was an intriguing space, with perhaps 1.8 ha (4½ acres) of small paddocks around the house and a 0.8 ha (2 acre), 16th-century walled garden surrounding the entrance tower of a similarly old vicarage. In addition, there were numerous outbuildings and a 2.4 ha (6 acre) field to the west was an added acquisition a few years later. The whole property is on the north-facing slope of the small Lovecombe valley, which seems to me a slightly strange site to have chosen in the first place for the vicarage with its sheltering walled garden. Since the glebeland at that time totalled at least 16 ha (40 acres) and occupied most of the valley, it might have been expected that the vicarage would be built on the southern slope. Still, there are advantages to growing ornamental plants in a garden on this north slope, with a generally deeper soil, cooler aspect and more opportunity to view the flowers with the sunlight behind them.

The evolutionary process of taking inspiration from natural landscapes had become almost a gardening philosophy for me. What had begun with the subconscious analysing of landscapes

while bird's nesting and been modified by my father's visionary predilections had become entrenched after walking in my student days in the gloriously unspoilt upland scenery of Wales, Scotland, the Lake District and other national parks. After arriving at the Garden House I spent the best part of fifteen years tinkering with and modifying the walled garden and making small garden excursions into the field to the west of the main garden. The first winter we were here, though, was very significant, as it was the coldest we have experienced, with temperatures dropping to −14°C (7°F) for three or four nights and prolonged periods of −12°C (10°F), all with no snow cover. Quite a number of the Fortescues' established and cherished shrubs died or began

an inexorable decline over the next ten years. As these gaps appeared I took the opportunity of simplifying the design and opening up mini-vistas where possible. I cannot profess to planting naturalistically at this stage, although this style did develop in these areas subsequently. One such area eventually suffered the loss of two large *Eucryphia* × *nymansensis* 'Nymansay' trees from the effects of the cold that first winter, and sad as the loss was, it did mean a whole section of garden could be reworked; I created a snaking woodland path flanked by hostas and *Euphorbia griffithii* 'Fireglow' (see above), which proved to be a great success. The hostas made phenomenal growth, but it was some years before I attributed this to the presence of the adjacent septic tank.

ABOVE *A path snakes between bold clumps of hostas and the orange-flowered* Euphorbia griffithii *'Fireglow' in the old walled garden.*

ABOVE *Pink purslane,* Claytonia sibirica, *carpets the dappled shade of thin woodland in the gardens of Threave in Scotland. The mushroom-shaped summer house seen in the distance seems to emphasize the fairy-like qualities of these natural plantings.*

Call of the wild

In retrospect, although head gardener from the beginning, I was really serving my apprenticeship during this time. My fellow gardener, Tom, and I were kept very busy but that was not the only reason I tended not to visit many other gardens. Of those I did visit, the parts I liked most were more often than not the wilder areas, where plants more usually seen within the confines of a tightly controlled flower bed had been allowed to throw off their shackles and spread themselves where they wished (see above). I found myself appreciating the technical skills and expertise of the gardeners and owners, and admiring many an individual plant, but if I came away with one different creative idea I would consider I had had a good day. In contrast to this, the more I saw of plants growing unhindered in the wild, the more inspired I became.

Just think for a minute of the way plants grow in nature and it will not take you long to realize that it bears no resemblance to the way we grow these same plants in our gardens. For a start, gardeners tend to grow the different varieties of plants with a small exclusion zone around each of them. This traditional method certainly makes it easier to manage, plan and label any new bed. Finish planting the bed, follow the cultivation manuals and with a bit of luck you will know what will come up in any given space year on year on year. In other words it is reasonably safe, but it can be a bit boring after a while.

The walled garden at the Garden House was planted in this way, with blocks and clearly defined drifts. Any seedlings outside of their allocated block were rigidly removed. That does not mean that the effect was not beautiful, but when you can go around the garden in your head of a winter's evening and know what will be coming up in every square foot of the entire 0.8 ha (2 acres) throughout the season, the magic has been lost somewhere along the line.

Cretan lessons

Now let us study a wild planting. I am not talking here about stands of aggressive species, such as creeping willowherb, foxgloves or creeping mats of buttercup, which all seem hell-bent on colonizing the entire planet with a monoculture of just themselves, but instead of stable, flower-rich communities of plants.

Crete is especially blessed in these flower-filled ecosystems and my trip there seemed to pile lesson upon lesson. Not that the flowers were everywhere in Crete; farming methods are slowly changing, and although the olive groves can still produce rich pockets of native flowers, there are nowhere near as many as in the past before herbicides and the marauding flocks of goats became prevalent, both of which seriously denude the local flora. Nevertheless there were enough areas still, and few enough cars, to make driving slowly with the windows down very productive. After a week I developed what someone with an experience of daffodil-hunting elsewhere

in the Mediterranean had aptly dubbed 'narcissus neck' from looking sideways at the road verges for unusual plants—excellent if you are not feeling energetic enough for a long walk, and also indicative of the number and variety of wild flowers here to make this practice worthwhile.

One such hunting excursion took me along mile after mile of unmetalled road up through the mountains. The map indicated this to be quite a reasonable road but it seemed to be getting smaller all the time and I started to become worried when villagers looked on incredulously as I drove by. However, near the top of the pass, when the car seemed on the point of expiry, I found clumps of paeonies, drifts of *Arum creticum*, and *Euphorbia wulfenii* growing in very exposed conditions.

Discovering *Euphorbia wulfenii* on the top of a windy mountain pass was not the only thing this trip to Crete taught me. I have subsequently seen all of the following lessons repeated time and again wherever I have travelled and have come to treat them as the building blocks for the way I now garden.

◆ Observing the way plants grow in the wild helps you understand how to care for them better at home. That *Euphorbia wulfenii*, for example, was a revelation to me as for years I had been cosseting this plant in sheltered spots in the walled garden. After this experience I came home and immediately planted it in the windiest place I could find. The result is that it has now self-seeded all over the place and is in danger of becoming a weed itself—a pretty fair indicator of a very happy plant.

◆ Brought up on traditional gardening lore that suggests that any soil type that is not a rich, medium loam needs improving, I was surprised to find the greatest displays of flowers on improbably inhospitable soils. This has resulted in my increasing use of adding a variable amount of coarse sand to parts of the garden where I want to encourage diversity of species and to help encourage self-seeding.

◆ The flowering displays I saw in Crete were often centred around rocky boulders or stone walls, more as a result, I would guess, of farmers clearing stones to the edges of cultivated land rather than any evolutionary preferences of the wild flowers for this particular habitat. It is more likely that these field margins are simply the only available land left for the plants to grow in. This has implications for myself as gardener in that there becomes a natural connection between some plants and their stone backdrops. Certain plants just look right when they are viewed in conjunction with stone.

◆ The overwhelming majority of plants I saw growing in Crete were also clearly adapted for growing in the stony, poor-looking soil—ground that was obviously free-draining. Now whenever I am faced with banks of stone and quarry waste, I make absolutely no attempt to remove this material, but try instead to choose plants whose natural home is of a similar composition.

◆ Many of the plants were growing in open sites without tree cover of any description, thereby receiving maximum light. In a heavily treed and hilly landscape such as Devon, finding a site with the biggest sky possible is an important factor when growing plants that originate from these sunny locations in the wild.

◆ On the coasts and in the mountainous areas where I spent much of my time looking at the flora there was very noticeable constant air movement. Even on calm days I could feel a slight breeze and I wondered if this might not be an important factor in the successful cultivation of some plants, maybe warding off fungal infections, which are certainly more likely under still, damp conditions.

RIGHT *Wild flowers in Crete are often found near stone walls, as this is where agricultural cultivation is not possible. In this instance, although the flowers are mostly white and pink in colour, if you look closely the species diversity becomes more apparent.*

OPPOSITE *In an English bluebell wood, the bluebells provide the main wash of flower colour (and scent), but the white stitchwort and pink campion are important secondary players, and all are set off by the lush greenness of their foliage, as well as that of other plant species.*

ABOVE *The field to the west of the Garden House before development began in early 1992. Tom and David can be seen taking down the fence to join the meadow to the garden. The bamboo canes across the field delineate the rough lines of the putative Long Walk. Similar views photographed seven years later can be seen on pages 213 (below) and 222.*

◆ I was struck by the incredible diversity of plant species in any given space, a lesson which would be reinforced immeasurably by visiting South Africa. Plants growing in the wild can produce wonderful massed flowering effects which are often dominated by one, two or three species. Within these dominant types are much smaller numbers of many other different species.

◆ Another important lesson from Crete is that the density of plants growing in the wild is nearly always infinitely greater than gardeners are accustomed to in their tended beds. Can you imagine, for example, any gardening book ever encouraging you to grow your plants at 5 cm (2 in) intervals in places? The judges at any flower show would splutter over this, yet with a tolerance of self-seeding this is exactly what I found I could re-create.

◆ One of the most important general principles I work with is the concept of having the plants in a single area of the garden all flowering together, instead of trying to make each section flower for as long as is humanly possible. This means that single areas, whether they are small or large, are organized in such a way to have their flowering synchronized, producing a spectacular if at times relatively short flowering period. Experience has proved that with a little careful thought, each separate zone can have at least a six-week flowering bonanza, and usually much longer. Of course, the peak flowering time of each area will occur at different times of the year, with areas past the blooming stage allowed to die back gracefully, and very often there is a subtle beauty even in this process. It seems to me the potential effect of such planting during the flowering period can be truly breathtaking and memorable, rather than merely good. Think of bluebells—a single bluebell is pretty but the sight and smell of a wood of them is something else. Flowering in the wild, anywhere in the world, is very seasonal. If you want to see the orchids flowering in Crete, for example, or alpines in the mountains, you will visit at a very specific time of the year, which may be of very short duration—perhaps of just a few weeks. It makes sense to me that if you want to create truly spectacular, naturalistic planting in your garden you should be prepared, if necessary, for a similar relatively short main flowering period, although, as I hope to show through this book, this is not always the case.

The trip to Crete was crucial, coming as it did a year after we had included a 1.6 ha (4 acre) field within the garden's boundaries. The rationale behind this extension was very simple. The Fortescues had generously donated the house and gardens to the control of a charitable trust, the Fortescue Garden Trust, in 1961, but money was tight for the Trust, which was very much dependent on visitors through the gate to survive. As numbers slowly rose, as they had to, wear and tear on the narrow grass paths of the walled garden inevitably increased and it was decided to expand the garden into a neighbouring field in order to ease this pressure.

In 1993 work began and, after a few short months, green field it no longer was. Thousands of tons of soil were moved to make car parks, access tracks were built, a small quarry was opened and virtually all of the levels within the site were altered. In the process of gaining this area of new garden we had to forego 2023 sq m (½ acre) of the original Japanese cherry paddock, which by this time had reached an age where the trees were starting to die anyway.

Working with what you have got

The whole approach to soil management and plant feeding in ornamental gardening owes its origins to the historic practices involved in growing vegetables. In these, double-digging to improve soil-depth and drainage, liming if necessary to create a standard soil pH and applying as much farmyard manure or other organic matter as possible are the traditional norms. The aim

here is to grow the vegetables to as large a size as is possible to achieve. As ornamental gardening gathered pace these ingrained habits were simply transferred, becoming the accepted bible of the new discipline.

These doctrines are well entrenched and many of us, myself included, are moved by deep feelings of envious lust when standing in front of the 3 m (10 ft) high luscious delphiniums that can be found at a flower show. I now feel sure that this longing for the prize specimen is simply my traditional core speaking and over the years I have modified my perception of what constitutes beauty in a garden specimen. I believe there is even more pleasure to be had in a single spike of delphinium just 1 m (3¼ ft) high if it is part of a community of plants forming a harmonious picture. In other words, the community of plants together is more important than any individual within it. I am certainly not against the pursuit of the perfect specimen and avidly follow this route in much of the garden, but in the wilder areas,

ABOVE The soft pastel shades of predominantly evergreen azaleas adorn the upper reaches of the older garden and show that the effect created by these shrubs need not always be garish.

RIGHT *The Skilpad Nature Reserve, Namaqualand, South Africa. Shrubs with silver and dark green foliage form the architectural framework among which wild flowers flaunt their extravagant colours. In a garden setting, the orange could be replaced with pastel pinks, blues or pale yellows if these colours are more to your taste.*

BELOW *Illinois valley, Oregon, USA. Sunlight and shade, strong vertical and horizontal lines and a textural mulch of needles and bark that is home to a varied range of plants all suggest this would form the basis of a very fine garden. With bulbs below the trees, the ground becomes marshy beyond, where it is home to shooting stars, camassias and fragrant azaleas.*

LEFT *Kynance Cove, Cornwall, UK. Yellow-flowered gorse, heathers and grasses form a low-growing matrix on this wind-swept clifftop. The rock outcrop in the distance supports many alpine plants, with spring bulbs coming through the rabbit-mown turf that surrounds them. With a little modification, could this be a template for a wind-challenged site?*

BELOW *Near Kamieskroon, Namaqualand, South Africa. The key element in this breathtaking display of annuals is the way in which the colours blend, with drifts and ribbons of blue, orange and white winding through the all-embracing wash of yellow. The rock outcrop and the dark foliage of the trees provide a low-key structural element to the composition.*

RIGHT *The tower of*
St Andrew's church in
Buckland Monachorum
dominates the view from
the Garden House offering
a quintessentially English
landscape of rolling hills,
patchwork fields and
woods. In the garden that
subsequently developed in
the foreground of this
photograph, the outline of
the hills was echoed in the
shapes of new, low, stone
walls, and shrubs were
trimmed to mimic some
of those distant woods.
With naturalistic planting
between these structural
elements, the boundary
between garden and
landscape becomes
blurred and our
definitions of 'what is
a garden' questioned.

and where I am attempting to create naturalistic effects, I try not to let it become the holy grail.

Instead of the determination to create a single soil type that is worth while and probably essential if you want to grow vegetables, there is an argument, if you want to grow ornamental plants, for being more relaxed about your soil and going with the flow. If you have a sandy soil, embrace it, and grow plants from all over the globe that love just such soils; after all, some of the best wild-flower displays in the world are growing in seemingly nothing but sand.

Would it not be good if, instead of the costly and back-breaking efforts required to transform our stony, well-drained banks into something they are not, we could just go along to our garden centres and nurseries, or read our reference books, and find out about all the wonderful plants that grow in very similar conditions in the wild? Learning directly from nature in this instance would be of really practical help for all gardeners, irrespective of whether they want a more natural-looking garden or not.

One of my general philosophies on life itself is to make the best use out of whatever difficulties are put in front of you. The same philosophy has become a cornerstone of my whole approach to gardening; when problems surface, as they inevitably do when something new is attempted, I constantly try to turn them to my advantage. Occasionally it does not work, but it is amazing how often this can lead you off into exciting avenues of creativity.

Planning and planting

As a practical gardener, much of what I have tried has been based initially on looking carefully at nature before a cocktail of instinct and a certain amount of artistic eye kick in to progress the idea. Looking closely at nature takes practice and honing one's observational skills undeniably improves them with time. Maybe it is easier said than done, as are most things in life, but with a little effort the rewards can be enormous.

When seen at a distance, natural landscapes are primarily composed of a few major elements with a larger number of secondary features helping to make up the overall picture. It is the same principle, albeit on a larger scale, that you see time and again in plant communities in the wild. Even in a very fussy, complicated view, such as the one from the Garden House over St Andrew's church in Buckland Monachorum (see page 27) there are the major elements, including small woods, fields, hedges and the church tower, and the secondary elements, such as small barns, houses and isolated trees. Viewed from afar, the various species go largely unnoticed in the context of the overall composition, but they become highly significant when you get in close and walk among them. In wilder views than this, the major elements are even simpler to identify and I have found that the fewer elements you introduce into your garden design (you can repeat them freely), the more likely you are to succeed in creating a wild, natural-looking garden. When I introduce these repeating elements to the garden I call them the foundation plantings.

This is not meant to imply that you have to sacrifice diversity in the detail—far from it, even in the foundation plantings—just as long as these primary elements have a unity about them when they are seen from a distance. By this I mean that the different individuals appear to be the same species, thereby appearing as a single unit, and thus do not distract the eye with their individuality. Take, for example, one part of the garden here where I have used witch hazels, *Hamamelis* varieties, as a repeated foundation shrub planting to the African garden because they bear a strong similarity in leaf and in habit to the British wild hazel, *Corylus avellana*, which means they sit very comfortably in an English landscape view. Rather than limit myself to one variety I have planted a considerable range, but since they are all but identical when out of flower this results in an effect for most of the year of just a single species of background shrub bringing unity and harmony to the neighbouring, summer flowers. Come late winter to mid-spring, at witch hazel-flowering time, the variety becomes wonderfully apparent as each individual changes to a different shade of red, yellow, orange or coral.

In this same part of the garden, and overlapping with the witch hazels to a certain extent along the Long Walk, are the birches. These trees are another primary element, giving unity once again to the overall composition, but as you progress along the Long Walk the difference between the twelve or more different birch species planted becomes obvious.

Key elements

Once you have accurately observed the major and secondary elements of any particular landscape the next thing to look at would be the overall balance of trees to shrubs, perennials and grasses; the balance of sunlight to shade; the general topography and undulations of the land itself; the colour and texture of the ground's surface; the colours and textures of the plants and the combinations, colours and shapes of any flowers. This may all seem a tall order but the more you do it, the more it becomes second nature. Occasionally these key features, or *leitmotivs*, are almost instantly apparent to you and at other times they may gradually insinuate themselves into your consciousness. So addictive can this become I sometimes subconsciously analyse sections of landscape to the detriment of simply enjoying the view.

You do not have to attend a symposium on prairie planting, for example, to re-create the illusion of a prairie on your own land, provided you know the key elements that conjure up images of a prairie for you. When looking at any piece of scenery or plant grouping the trick is to decide what the key elements are for you, because by emulating those in your garden you will trigger an automatic recollection of the original in your own mind.

The powerful link between memory and the sense of smell should not be overlooked either at this point; it is amazing how a single smell can instantly transport us to a time and place we associate with it. For me, the sweet, distinctive smell of *Daphne* × *burkwoodii* will always remind me of the Chelsea Flower Show because my wife, Ros, and I were in close proximity to it for many a long hour at the exhibits we staged there in the 1980s, while the resinous scent of pines immediately takes me back to the woods of the Mediterranean or Bryce Canyon in Utah. Smell does not just trigger a particular line of thought, it has the capacity to slice through time. Capture a distinctive smell of a wild landscape in a garden reconstruction and you will already be over half-way to reminding yourself of the original.

In this way I have been able to make parts of the new garden here at the Garden House blend seamlessly with the beautiful natural landscape surrounding us, look spectacular in their own right and yet still remind me of wonderful wild-flower combinations I have seen in different places around the world. Nor are those vivid memories of the scenery of my childhood, with their little snatches of a now-lost landscape, forgotten either. The new garden here is for me like a collection of living postcards from many of the significant and most loved landscapes I have seen in my life, a living embodiment of the garden of my dreams.

OPPOSITE *A motel car park in northern New Mexico is separated from neighbouring land by a simple wooden fence. Made of heavy sawn timber, it is structurally more solid than normal wooden fences, yet lighter, and considerably easier to build, than a stone wall. A fence such as this would form an excellent contrast to a grass-dominated planting scheme, or it could be used as a structural element in a semi-arid garden design.*

part 1 The Plants

1 Bulb meadows and woodland floor

Many people will hold the view that of all plant groups, bulbs are the ones that are already used in many gardens in a naturalistic way. You need only think of drifts of daffodils or carpets of snowdrops or bluebells to reinforce that belief, yet I cannot help feeling that it is true only in so far as it goes. Undoubtedly we all know plenty of gardens where a single bulb species or, more rarely, two or three species together, have naturalized—and absolutely wonderful they look too. What I would like to explore in this chapter is the idea of taking this on a stage or two further.

I love bulbs, and the first winter and spring we were here remains to this day one of the most exciting periods of my time at the Garden House. As a student at university in Kent, I used to be the proud owner of two pots of *Erythronium revolutum* bulbs that we had bought on a rare excursion to Devon and kept in the prime spot on the conservatory windowsill of our rented house. After leaving college I took up the head gardener's job at the Garden House and at the end of that first winter here the ground in places literally heaved with the efforts of thousands of erythroniums pushing up through the soil, and not only pink ones but yellow and white as well. There were not just erythroniums, but also large patches of dark blue *Scilla siberica* and *Chionodoxa sardensis*, white *Anemone blanda* var. *scynthinica* and the white and blue forms of *Chionodoxa gigantea*. This being Devon there were also masses of pale yellow primroses (*Primula vulgaris*), which are so wonderfully colour compatible with the blues and whites of wood anemones (*Anemone nemorosa*).

Although every one of the named plants above is beautiful in its own right, it was the sheer volume of flowers that was so impressive. This was the massed effect of flowers on the grand scale again, this time in a colour range of soft yellows, white and vivid blues that was really quite exotic to me.

The massed displays of spring bulbs in our gardens and public places are most often associated with the municipal plantings of snowdrops, crocus, hyacinths and tulips that are responsible for spectacular splashes of colour to feast our eyes upon at a generally grey time of year. The Dutch are past masters at this and have become world-renowned for creating floral extravagances, but surely nobody could really call them refined. I had been brought up in a garden where my father thought bulbs hardly ranged further than the large-flowered Dutch crocus to 'Fortune' daffodils and back to crocus, so the subtle patchworks I found at the Garden House was something very different for me.

Subtlety, however, can only be viewed in the light of one's personal experiences, and groupings of bulbs I have since seen in South Africa make those early Garden House combinations look like a child's painting when held up against these naturally occurring Impressionist masterpieces. In one spot on a botanizing tour of the Western Cape, in a landscape seemingly inhospitable to plant life and strikingly similar to northern New Mexico, our mini bus had to screech to a halt as twelve botanists scrambled over each other to get out and photograph a display of mostly bulbs, the like of which I would not have previously thought possible. Growing no higher than 7.5 cm (3 in) was a fabulous

ABOVE *There is a brief time in late winter when* Crocus tommasinianus *and the similar, but slightly more robust,* Crocus vernus *'Vanguard' overlap their flowering to create a dazzling display in the short turf of the Acer glade.*

blend of peachy-pink oxalis, soft yellow moraeas and unidentified lilac-blue flowers, surrounded by a sea of the tiny white, pincushion blooms of cotula and all washed in the rapidly orangeing light of a sinking sun. Our tour guides' insistence for our need to move on and that strong yellow light almost makes a mockery of the resulting photograph (see above) but make no mistake, I saw my bulb heaven that evening.

Birth of a bulb meadow

In my early years at the Garden House, when Mr and Mrs Fortescue were still alive, there were very strict rules concerning what constituted a weed, especially within the confines of the walled garden. With the honourable exception of primroses they included just about every British native plant, but at least it made weeding very

easy—you just took out everything that had not been planted by human hand. Tom Hooper, the only other gardener at the Garden House, liked this and knew exactly where he stood. A bed weeded by Tom was a work of art; it was as if it had been steam-sterilized and no weed dared show its face for another six weeks or so. It took Tom a little while to adjust to my rather more *laissez-faire* attitude towards native plants.

The Fortescues were a little more tolerant of the areas outside the walled garden and were generally happy enough to indulge my liking for natural stands of native plants, such as celandines (*Ranunculus ficaria*), germander speedwell (*Veronica chamaedrys*) and lady's smock (*Cardamine pratensis*). The location of the garden is in a beautiful setting, blessed with wonderful views over the surrounding country-side, which the Fortescues, perhaps because of their advanced years or simply due to pragmatic commonsense, tended to ignore. They were, however, very happy for me to persuade them to open up previously hidden views and gradually allow the garden to encroach into a 2.4 ha (6 acre) field to the west of the main house and lawn.

There were still just the two of us to garden it all, so any new areas I kept deliberately simple, partly to make it easy to look after them and partly because this style blended effortlessly with the countryside. These initial tentative forays at enlargement tended to be shrubs and trees in small groups with plenty of grass in between. Anyone who has looked after a large area of grass, even it is not kept tightly cut, will tell you that it is amazing how much time is spent mowing.

One of my neighbours has about 1.6 ha (4 acres) of grass to cut in between and underneath the shrubs and trees in his garden and one of the sounds of summer is the distinctive hum of his lawnmower, which seems to be constantly in action. I have often wondered if he ever envisaged his retirement being spent in pursuit of a grass machine. Personally, as much as I enjoy cutting grass occasionally, I felt there were more rewarding things to be done, so when I heard my local city council was using a growth retardant on much of their grassed areas and it was saving them huge amounts of time and money on grass cutting, I thought I must give it a go.

Although this has been a great success in the longer term, initially it almost had disastrous results. Spraying instructions were that you should not apply the chemical in drought conditions. Well, there was not a drought when I sprayed a large area of long grass alongside the main lawn in late summer, but unfortunately one developed immediately afterwards. Six weeks later and all through the winter there was the embarrassment of a large grassless area in the middle of the garden. This was compounded further by newly turfed steep banks, sprayed at the same time, suffering in the same way. I had used turfs with rampageous couch-grass to help stabilize these nearly vertical banks and now they were starting to slump with the winter rains as there were no roots to support them.

There is a rainbow at the end of this story, for the following spring my decimated grass area became covered by drifts of lady's smock and celandines, which had been dormant when I sprayed the previous summer, and enormous patches of blue speedwell rushed in to take advantage of the lack of heavy grass cover, as did bluebells. The grass cover returned as well that following spring, and, as a bonus, less the majority of the couch grass. The relevance to this chapter is that I felt I could turn to my advantage this trait of the growth retardant to weaken coarse grass species by spraying areas where bulbs were to be grown. Another mini disaster gave me the opportunity to do so.

Almost dead centre of the extended garden grows an enormous horse chestnut tree (*Aesculus hippocastanum*) with a very wide-spreading habit, its branches almost sweeping down to touch the ground. It grows alongside the driveway, on the other side of which the Fortescues had planted all of their varieties of snake's head fritillaries (*Fritillaria meleagris*) in a monoculture bed. They certainly looked good in this elevated site, allowing you to admire in comfort their intricate markings, but they were not really thriving. In one of those wonderfully anarchic gestures that only nature can spring, the fritillaries chose to resettle on the rock-hard verges of the chestnut side of the drive, where they have spread and seeded prolifically. Under most of this tree's canopy nothing but ivy could grow, but on the southern edges other bulb species have taken advantage of the drainage afforded by the roots. In addition to the fritillaries, *Erythronium revolutum* has seeded among blue and white wood anemones and yellow celandines, thereby forming a perfect spring vignette.

One calm, still October morning there was a thunderous crack and a third of the tree fell to the ground, demolishing in the process many mature deciduous azaleas that grew beyond its northern fringe. When the grisly task of clearing up was finished, we were left with an area of about 170 sq m (200 sq yd) that was suddenly open to the sky. With mature magnolias growing all around, this was an opportunity to expand that bulb tapestry into a much larger area and the bulb meadow was born.

Strategic use of chemicals

Generally I prefer not to spray anything in the garden, if possible, and to evolve a policy of live and let live towards pests and diseases. However, I allow the occasional use of herbicides on non-sensitive areas such as paths, where they might save us time-consuming hoeing. The annual spraying of the gravel paths with a herbicide containing the active ingredient of paraquat burnt off the weeds and grass but generally left the moss unscathed, and it occurred to me that the strategic use of this herbicide might be justified to create an environment in which bulbs might flourish. Initially the infant bulb meadow was going to have native species such as celandines mixed with a limited number of the more exotic species, growing in grass kept in check by the single annual use of a spray. In this way, when the bulbs were finished, the ground itself could be first kept neat and tidy by mowing and then sprayed with paraquat to allow the bulbs to emerge each spring through a carpet of moss.

So much for the theory. It might have worked, too, if the whole site had not been infested with chestnut roots and also with couch grass, dandelions and rather too many celandines, which were not deterred by the paraquat. Instead of being in such a hurry I should have cleared the ground first of these perennial weeds by spraying several times with glyphosate (or, for organic gardeners, by covering the ground with black polythene, newspapers, carpet, or similar) for a season beforehand. Instead, I rushed in and planted, and then found myself for the next three or four years painstakingly weeding every spring. Even the wild celandines, which were to be a staple of this garden, proved too overpowering, and the ordinary yellow ones are now being removed as they flower. So many have I now taken out that their composted remains have made a mound 1.2 m (4 ft) high with a surface area of 8.5 sq m (10 sq yd), and the 'Celandine Mound' has become part of the structural fabric itself.

The tree roots were not so much of a problem because I landscaped the whole area into gently undulating curves, making up planting beds with additional imported compost if necessary above the tree roots to a depth of 15–30 cm (6–12 in). I

RIGHT *Winter-flowering heathers,* Erica carnea *varieties, are seen here growing with a late-flowering snowdrop,* Galanthus 'Straffan'. *The heathers, which flower for months, will later look equally good with other bulbs as well as filtering the wind at ground level to protect their more fragile neighbours.*

reasoned that by the time the chestnut's roots had monopolized these beds, the bulbs should have established themselves. These mounds and undulations help to hold interest in this area when all the bulbs have died down in summer.

New perspectives

Once the decision was made to be rid of the grass and to treat the whole meadow as one large flower bed to be weeded and mulched as any other, a completely different perspective was added to the planting possibilities. I could develop really quite complex groupings of desirable species without the worry of them being swamped by the grass or weeds. The diversity of species multiplied rapidly, from my original concept of about 20–30 taxa to the current number of about 250–300, and all in an area about the size of half a tennis court. With an increased

range of plants to work with, it is possible to have a very long flowering period for the meadow. Soon after midwinter the snowdrops start, followed by the *Iris reticulata*. Then, in late winter, the early daffodils, primroses, *Scilla siberica*, *Cyclamen coum* and crocus join the party. Early spring sees the main flush of daffodils, with chionodoxas, fritillaries, hellebores and early erythroniums, followed by the finale in mid-spring of the erythroniums, wood anemones, corydalis and magnolias. In early and mid-autumn the meadow flowers again with *Cyclamen hederifolium*, colchicums and autumn crocus, giving a grand total of nearly six months of flower from primarily bulbs with others as supporting cast.

Successional flowering

A few of the deciduous azaleas survived the fall of part of the chestnut tree and, together with

ABOVE *The tracery of naked twigs on one of the Dissectum Japanese maples adds a delicate counterpoint to the wealth of bulbous plants beneath. The seemingly vacant plots between the flowers are home to later-flowering bulbs or have been deliberately left clear to allow self-seeding to take place.*

ABOVE *Waylands Nature Reserve in South Africa is seen here washed in blue* Heliophila *and orange* Ursinia. *These spectacular displays are notoriously unreliable, so finding one is cause for thanks.*

RIGHT *Two weeks later in the same reserve as above, dark-eyed orange* Ixia maculata *flowers open on impossibly frail stems.*

hits of colour for specific periods in exactly the same way that nature does. More akin to my bulb meadow would be the effects created by mainly geophytes (bulbous plants) in the Waylands Nature Reserve, near Darling in the western Cape of South Africa. Here, among the sublime washes of pale blue *Heliophila* and soft orange *Ursinia* (see left), both of them annuals, I saw bulbs growing in incredible variety, lending subtle nuances of different colours to the overall palette. When I visited the same place two weeks later, the pale blue and soft orange of the annuals were beginning to utter their exit lines, the earlier bit players had left the stage, and a new set of leading characters were strutting their stuff in the form of the white *Sparaxis bulbifera*, orange *Ixia maculata* and the incredible blue of *Geissorhiza radicans* (see below left and overleaf). Two weeks later still, or two weeks prior to my first visit, it is possible that the whole colour effect might be different again. The real beauty of bulbs for the adventurous gardener is that many more colour effects can be created from a small space over a period of a few months than would be possible with either perennials or annuals.

Bulbs for woodland sites

The bulb season starts at the Garden House in midwinter with the snowdrops. Rather more years ago than I care to remember, I visited a remarkable lady, Amy Doncaster, at her home in Chandler's Ford in Hampshire. As a devoted fan of erythroniums, I had been told that I must visit her garden where they grew like bluebells, but it was other aspects that made the trip so memorable. She was in her nineties when I went, a tiny lady bent double with arthritis but with indomitable enthusiasm. The whole 1000 sq m (¼ acre) garden was a revelation, planted with ericaceous shrubs and every square inch underneath filled with woodland bulbs. If my memory serves me correctly, there were sixty varieties of dwarf daffodils alone, but they were not just any sixty varieties—they were the generally accepted

numerous weeping *Acer palmatum* var. *dissectum*, give sculptural shape and colour at other times of the year. It would be possible to extend the flowering period of the meadow still further by including plants such as the elegant, brilliant red *Tulipa sprengeri*, flowering here in late spring, or early summer-flowering rhodohypoxis, but having tried them I thought they were wasted among the rapidly browning foliage of the earlier bulbs, so I now aim to finish spring flowering in this part of the garden in mid-spring. The point here is that it is not necessary to feel obliged to have all-year-round colour from every section of your garden; it is more exciting to have controlled

ABOVE *This picture of Waylands Nature Reserve, South Africa, was taken two weeks after the main photograph on page 38. Great swathes of ground are now graced with the pristine white of* Sparaxis bulbifera *and the surreal understorey of* Geissorhiza radians.

best there were. The same could be said for many other genera as well, notably snowdrops. It was one of those gardens you walk around with your eyes glued to the ground, which was just as well in Amy's case because her arthritis had left her with no choice but to look downwards. It is the only garden I have ever 'walked' around literally on my knees so that I could more easily talk to her, an exercise that could be a very withering experience. On being asked my opinion on the classically shaped *Narcissus* 'Roseworthy', I volunteered that I was not particularly keen on the pink-trumpeted daffodils and was met by a riposte, delivered in the haughtiest of tones, that 'most people of good taste find it lovely', a reply guaranteed to make my knees ache a bit more after all these years. She was, however, very

generous and gave me one or two bulbs of some very lovely snowdrops that have over the years since become the core of the snowdrop displays.

Snowdrops

I like snowdrops and have a sizeable collection, but have not become an addicted galanthophile. They flower when the weather is too cold for me to spend long periods at ground-level gazing with rapt admiration into their beautiful upturned faces, so I prefer to admire them from my standing height. Varieties such as *Galanthus* 'S. Arnott' or 'Samuel Arnott' (but definitely not 'Sam Arnott' as Amy, who knew him, forcefully pointed out), and the similar but later *G.* 'Straffan', are excellent 'doers' and have far more garden effect than the wild species. Equally I love *G.* 'Atkinsii'

for its tall, upstanding habit and its garden distinctiveness rather than dwelling on any floral imperfections it may have. Other good garden snowdrops I would not want to be without are the tall G. 'Merlin' with its almost solid green inner petals, the graceful, long flower-stalked G. 'Magnet', which trembles in the faintest breeze, and the yellow-flowered G. *plicatus* 'Wendy's Gold'. If forced to restrict myself to just two doubles, I think I would be hard-pressed to beat Amy's recommended G. 'Hippolyta' and the smaller G. 'Barbara's Double', which both have immaculately formed centres.

Iris reticulata and companions

Following on the heels of the early snowdrops come the *Iris reticulata* varieties, which have been a revelation to me. I always thought they needed sun and drainage, perhaps because as a child I had seen them growing so often on rockeries and in those little beds atop double-sided walls so beloved of a certain type of suburbia. I tried them on my north slope, not only because I have always liked them but because they are very cheap to buy from the Dutch wholesalers. As expected they were lovely the first year and then, amazingly, have become even better year on year since. It would appear that they like quite a cool site and one of the nice things about these iris is that they mix so well with other early bulbs. All within a square metre (square yard) I have some planted with *Narcissus cyclamineus, Cyclamen coum, Erythronium dens-canis*, the vibrant orange *Crocus gargaricus*, lilac *C. sieberi* 'Violet

ABOVE *Lilac* Moraea tripetala *and white, pink-backed* Hesperantha *hover in exquisite harmony near Nieuwoudtville, South Africa. These* Hesperantha *flowers open only in the mid-afternoon, so if you wish to be privileged with such a sight, timing is crucial.*

Queen' and pristine white *Galanthus byzantinus*, all of which flower together.

One of the lovely things about many dwarf bulbs is that growing among them you can have other species that will flower later, giving you the chance to have at least two or three washes of colour from the same spot. This is mainly because many bulbs have narrow leaves that enable the light to reach neighbours still just pushing through the ground, and their generally rapid life cycle often results in these leaves dying back quickly. In this respect the dwarf daffodils with usually very neat foliage are invaluable and for community planting are much to be preferred to their taller and larger-flowered brethren.

Daffodils

Early spring is dwarf daffodil time at the Garden House, and there is nothing quite like them to give you those early spring carpets of flower. Crocus can, of course, but only if the sun shines and the mice and voles are kept in check. One of these factors is out of my control, and our ten cats are supposed to be in charge of the other but prefer to stay curled up in the warmth of the house at this early time of year, which means that crocus cannot really be relied upon here. However, daffodils nearly always can, even if the sun does not show its face much.

When I first came to the Garden House the only daffodil here was *Narcissus* 'February Gold', which starts in a normal season at the beginning of spring, flowering for some three weeks. The Fortescues had used 'February Gold' extensively because it is an excellent landscape daffodil, being both neat and compact at a height of about 38 cm (15 in) in flower as well as showy enough to make a good splash of colour from several hundred metres (yards) away. It is though a little too tall for the central area of my bulb meadow. By choosing species and varieties that are no more than 20–23 cm (8–9 in) high I can pack a much greater variety into the space available. There are now over fifty different dwarf daffodils in the bulb meadow, some of which are very slow to increase and others which constitute a major

part of the spring display. There are not very many daffodils that will self-seed in this garden, but among those which do, *N. cyclamineus* and *N. bulbocodium* are especially lovely.

It does not seem very many years ago that I would conscientiously count how many flowers the diminutive *Narcissus cyclamineus* had produced, it being part of my annual routine, like noting the first frosts or the first changing leaves of autumn. For years the number stayed pegged at around twenty, which made them especially vulnerable to being lost to local children in the early spring, a Mother's Day assault from the public footpath that passed close by. This was at a time when I believed unquestioningly what I read in books, and all the literature said that *N. cyclamineus* is one of the best species to establish in grass. That is true, but vital information is left out—for example, what type of grass sward. Obviously anything but short grass is going to be a waste of time with a plant that flowers at 15 cm (6 in) high, but if the grass is too thick the tiny seedlings get no light and die. Following advice and planting in thin grass with 50 per cent moss, which should give the damp conditions the daffodil desires, I found that they still did not seed. It was at this point that the chestnut tree was resized and I started experimenting with the growth retardants on the grass where these narcissus were planted. The result was that the grass and moss sward became more compact with a depth of only 5 cm (2 in) instead of the 12.5–15 cm (5–6 in) that previously existed. This, in turn, meant the seedlings could reach the light and at last the daffodils started spreading.

Over the next few years their numbers truly rocketed and I had to give up counting when the numbers got past five hundred each year. It is so obvious that it is almost embarrassing that I did not realize more quickly; if a plant is to seed around and naturalize then it must have space and light where it can grow. Many of these bulb seedlings are only 2–5 cm (1–2 in) high and are thinner than a needle in their first year, so it does not take very thick turf for their prospects of spreading to be seriously diminished.

LEFT *The hoop petticoat daffodil,* Narcissus bulbocodium, *looks wonderful flowering in the short turf. There are many different strains and forms of this species in the trade, some of which have small flowers and are rather reluctant to produce even these, so, if at first you don't succeed, try again from a different source.*

The hoop petticoat daffodil, *Narcissus bulbocodium*, looks wonderful in some gardens (see above), studding the ground with its bright yellow flowers 15 cm (6 in) high above a sward of emerald-green moss or thin grass, but it was even more pernickety about becoming established in the grass of the prototype bulb meadow at the Garden House, for several years just fading away. Amid the sheer exhilaration and wonder of seeing spectacles like these in other gardens I could not help sometimes experiencing tiny darker thoughts of envy as to why they would not do it for me. It was not until I took the decision to banish the grass altogether that this species started to recover and begin to self-seed in my bulb meadow. I think perhaps the pale yellow *N. bulbocodium* var. *citrinus* would top my list of favourite daffodils and, given the right conditions, is easy into the bargain.

I cannot leave the subject of daffodils without mentioning *Narcissus* 'Tête-à-Tête'. Many daffodils do have the occasional year when they do

RIGHT *The Californian fawn lily,* Erythronium californicum, *growing in northern California, USA. This species appears superficially to prefer damp conditions, but the roadside banks where we found it were actually very steep and stony.*

not flower, perhaps because the previous summer was not sunny enough. It is tempting fate to write this, I know, but 'Tête-à-Tête' has reliably flowered for me. It is not a self-seeder, but it is cheap, readily available and long-flowering. It is also very neat and pretty, creating solid blocks of bright yellow only 15 cm (6 in) high.

Erythroniums

Among the final flurry of bulbous flowers in midspring come my favourite group of any plants, the erythroniums. If any one species epitomizes the beauty, elegance and transient magic of spring flowering for me, it is this. From the moment of pushing the soil aside as they emerge there is the unmistakable hallmark of class writ large, whether in the form of the pair of arching, often marbled leaves, like exotic hostas, or in the elegant flower spikes topped by pagoda, lily-like flowers—all this in a package 15–45 cm (6–18 in) high. It is hardly surprising that these

plants are developing an almost cult-like following in the UK. Put me into a dentist's chair, an aeroplane seat or any other stressful situation and I will dream of these plants—my heaven will be carpeted with them.

Most of the species erythroniums will seed themselves about if they find the conditions to their liking, but only a few will do so reliably, the easiest in this respect being the pink-flowered *Erythronium revolutum*. This does not form tightly packed clumps, but spreads by seeding, ever widening the colony's boundaries while retaining a respectful distance between individuals. The result is that the flowers are never jammed together, giving the plant a refined, species charm. Bear in mind you need to be patient, or rich, to have a sizeable planting of this in your garden as it takes four years from seed production to reach regular flowering size, and in the first season after germination the frail grass-like seedlings need adequate light and air if they are

ABOVE *The pink fawn lily,* Erythronium revolutum, *growing in northern Oregon, USA. We drove nearly 3,200 km (2,000 miles) in search of this species, then climbed halfway up a mountain where it was supposed to grow, but all in vain. Then we saw it growing in its thousands by the roadside after we had given up all hope of finding it.*

to survive. I have found the ground underneath a magnolia to be an excellent place to sow erythronium seed, provided it is kept weed-free, both magnolia and erythronium requiring undisturbed soil. This was especially brought home to me when a neighbour who is a very good gardener wondered why the erythroniums did so well on my side of the valley and yet were failing in her herbaceous flower beds, which she lightly forked over each winter. I have found them to be easy provided you leave them undisturbed and realize they are basically antisocial to anything other than woody or bulbous plants and do not like any clump-forming plants growing on top of them. My self-confidence took a severe pounding one year when a large clump of one of my own hybrid erythroniums which had taken nearly ten years to bulk up was reduced in the course of a single season to a few scrawny individuals after I had allowed an annual *Impatiens* to occupy the same space through the summer.

Erythronium californicum will gently seed itself about, but also clumps up. It can vary widely in the degree of leaf marbling, in the shade of creamy white and in the number of flowers per spike, but always has white anthers with narrow filaments. The hybrid E. 'White Beauty' is very close to this species but does not set seed. Both are excellent easy erythroniums in a wide range of woodland conditions.

In recent years there has been an explosion of new erythronium species more readily available in the UK. It may well be that some of these new species will be just as amenable in cultivation once their basic needs are understood. The white *Erythronium multiscapoideum*, so distinctive with its flowering stems branching at or below ground level, grows in drier locations in the wild and certainly in my wet climate needs a better-drained site. I had already noticed how the only plant I had of this species had dramatically improved when it was moved into scree conditions after years of doing nothing in the damper garden positions. When I finally raised enough young plants from fresh seed I tried them out on the tops and sides of steep, shady and shaly earth banks and was rewarded within a couple of years with them self-seeding, a sure sign they are happy. I could have saved myself a lot of time if I had taken more effort in the first place to find out where and in what they were growing in the wild. *E. cliftonii*, which is usually considered a large-flowered form of *E. multiscapoideum* but starts flowering a month earlier, is the longest-flowering erythronium of all of those I grow. Once settled, this species can still be in flower towards late spring, an incredible two months after starting. I will keep my fingers crossed that this trait may be passed on to any possible hybrids this species may produce.

There are very few hybrids to choose from at the present time, a situation that I am certain will be remedied over the next decade or so as these newer species contribute their parentage. Some that I particularly like which are slowly becoming available are the impeccably neat, white *Erythronium* 'Jeanette Brickell', the pink and yellow 'Joanna', and two elegant selections that I have made, the pink and white 'Rosalind' and the pink 'Janice'.

The majority of bulbous plants feature strap-shaped narrow leaves and in any large area given over almost exclusively to growing bulbs one of the potential pitfalls is the 'sameness' factor. I have tried to avoid this by planting bulbs with bolder foliage in places, plants such as the commonly available, pale yellow-flowered *Erythronium* 'Pagoda', which within two or three years makes substantial 30 cm (12 in) high, hosta-like clumps. Similarly colchicums, which flower in the autumn, normally pilloried for their coarse foliage, are welcomed for their leaves alone in my bulb meadow. Coarse they may be if grown through tiny-leaved ericas, but handsome to my mind if mixed with daffodils such as *Narcissus* 'Dove Wings', 'Jenny' or similar *N. cyclamineus* hybrids and bold-leaved erythroniums such as 'Pagoda'. These bolder-leaved bulbs are also wonderful for blending the edges of the bulb garden with other spring-flowering herbaceous plants such as hellebores, epimediums, cardamines, *Pachyphragma macrophyllum* or primroses.

Cyclamen

I did not have many preconceptions about what was going into my bulb meadow, partly because I allowed the concept to evolve over time. I knew I wanted drifts of colour, and some of the most sumptuously rich colours to be had very early in the year can be achieved with big clumps of *Cyclamen coum*. We already had a sizeable colony alongside another section of drive looking wonderful under that queen of witch hazels, the sweetly scented *Hamamelis × intermedia* 'Pallida'. The fact the cyclamen's seedlings even managed to grow on the tarmac itself suggested that it should be no problem to grow, especially in what

I thought were ideal conditions of a semi-shaded north slope, but it has been stubbornly difficult to establish under the chestnut. I was less green-fingered and more green with envy when I saw this cyclamen flourishing in the garden of friends in Hampshire. Trying to fathom why they should grow so well in their wooded garden and not in mine was an interesting exercise which has repercussions when looking at plants in the wild. My current theory for the cyclamen is that they do not like strong winds buffeting their leaves through the winter, and the copious layer of dried leaves among which they were growing in Hampshire was in fact acting like a cyclamen-sized

ABOVE *In cultivation,* Erythronium *'White Beauty' is easy to please provided it is given a cool spot. Here it is growing alongside* Cyclamen repandum *in the light shade of rhododendrons.*

ABOVE *In the same garden in Devon, England, as the picture on page 47,* Cyclamen repandum *grows in a more naturalistic combination with* Fritillaria meleagris *and* Narcissus cyclamineus.

RIGHT *An enviable planting of* Cyclamen coum *in a Hampshire garden in England. The dried, crisped leaves in this woodland help to trap the air, providing insulation for the cyclamen tubers against low temperatures, and some protection against the winds for the new leaves and flowers.*

duvet and windbreak rolled into one. On the other hand, I, being for once Mr Tidy, was taking away my chestnut leaves every autumn and replacing them with a layer of leaf-mould; this was certainly very neat and nourishing but was not actually providing any wind protection right down at soil level. I am hoping that leaving the chestnut leaves over winter where the cyclamen grow will do the trick, otherwise that is another fine theory that did not work in practice.

In an attempt to lessen the effects of the Devon wind on my cyclamen I have also planted some winter-flowering heaths, *Erica carnea* varieties, in small groups among them and this has been a great success, at least visually. The heaths' small, richly coloured flowers consort beautifully with the early bulbs and look so much more natural than the more usual way of growing them with dwarf conifers. They are one of those plants that have become so ubiquitous that many serious gardeners tend to look down their noses at them, including, I am ashamed to say, myself. My salutary experiment with the heaths reinforces my belief that there are very few poor plants, just poor ways of using them.

Backdrops for bulbs

The question of the Devon wind focused my thought processes on mulches of all sorts and their relationships with plants. Nearly all bulbous plants, and dwarf bulbs in particular, have their flowers near the ground, so careful thought needs to be given to what is actually covering the ground surface and to their immediate surroundings if these plants are to be displayed as naturally as possible. By chance I had seen a photograph of an *Erythronium citrinum* growing in the wild in a natural bark mulch in a forest clearing. The beautifully marbled leaves of this classy woodland bulb looked fabulous against the mulch and it does not take too much of a leap of imagination to visualize other plants being equally enhanced with such a backdrop. The marbled leaves of other woodlanders such as the asarums, cyclamen and

hepaticas would look just fine with isolated clumps of crocus, erythroniums, trilliums and other bulbs coming up between. All I can say is that for myself, in a part of any garden where what is covering the ground is an important part of the design, I would generally want plants which have a strong architectural symmetry, and in miniature, many bulbs have this in trumps.

Nearly all of the plants mentioned to this point prefer growing in cool conditions, being woodlanders by and large, which is not surprising as my bulb meadow is placed on the north side of a very large tree on a north slope. The principle, however, will work just as well in a sunny site with a whole different cast of players.

Bulbs for sunny sites

The sand dunes of my African garden were laid out in the sunniest place I could find and are mostly dealt with in Chapter 2. They were principally made to accommodate annuals but I thought that introducing a few bulbs would lengthen the flowering period of this whole area, and give some colour in early spring at a time when some visitors considered the bare sand a bit too *avant-garde* for their tastes. Initially I tried a few tulip species, such as *Tulipa batalinii*, *T. bakeri* and *T. urumiensis*, more as an experiment than with any real hope of them looking good, but they did, possessing that indefinable glow that healthy plants exude. In retrospect I do not know why I was surprised at this, since the South African sands which had inspired this part of the garden in the first place were stuffed with bulbous plants. Encased in sand, these tulip bulbs were always going to be more likely to feel at home than in the moisture-retentive loam found elsewhere in the garden.

Some *Anemone pavonina* followed in various shades from soft mauves, pinks and biscuit to brilliant reds, and these too show every sign of settling down, self-seeding in their first year. In between these tulips and the anemones I planted *A. blanda*, hoping that it might naturalize and

RIGHT *Unusually, this clump of* Sparaxis elegans *was growing in full sun in rock-hard, stony soil alongside a road in South Africa. In this particular area this species generally preferred to grow in the semi-shade afforded by low bushes and grasses, a trait I copied with sparaxis hybrids in my own garden.*

carpet the ground in early spring with a wash of glorious blue, as I had seen in a photograph of it in a garden with chalky soil. Elsewhere in the garden *A. blanda* will grow, but more survives than thrives. Here in the sand it is looking plump and is self-seeding prolifically, and perhaps the similarities in the free-draining nature of the chalk and sand override the more obvious differences between the mediums as far as the plants are concerned.

Branching out with geophytes

My apprehension with all the bulbs in the African Garden was less to do with their ability to grow on sand than as to how they would react to other plants covering the ground above them all through summer and early autumn; knowing how plants are going to respond to the close proximity of neighbours is a vitally important factor in this style of gardening. Fortunately, most bulbs

are excellent community plants. Erythroniums and, to a lesser extent, daffodils will both happily grow with other bulbs but are less tolerant of smothering herbaceous plants or low shrubs. In the case of daffodils I always put this down to the covering foliage preventing the bulbs getting sufficiently summer-baked, an inheritance of the Mediterranean origins of many of them which can cause reduced flowering. This is why, whenever I am attempting a combination of planting that is unusual, I nearly always try first with something expendable, such as the tulip species mentioned earlier, which are all commonly available and relatively cheap.

Having tested the water with my guinea-pig tulips and the bulbous Dutch iris, I felt inclined to be a little more adventurous. If you have only ever seen the tall garden varieties of gladiolus, then meeting the scented, pale yellow *Gladiolus tristis* is a revelation. With narrow sedge-like leaves and only 75 cm (2½ ft) high in flower, everything about it is refined. At the moment it is doing beautifully in the sand, but its real test will come after we have had a hard winter, as it starts into growth in the autumn months. I planted *Roscoea cautleyoides* in the African garden more because its flowers reminded me of the many babianas I saw growing in South Africa than for any other reason. By rights this species should not like the sand, coming as it does from China with a penchant for cool, deep soil and light shade. I cannot even say for sure it is the deeper layers of compost that are responsible for its rude health, as it is planted in 20 cm (8 in) depth of pure sand. I used the bolder-foliaged, bigger-flowered 'Kew Beauty' and it looks just right.

On one visit to South Africa I was lucky to see the beautiful *Sparaxis elegans* in flower (see opposite) growing among small clumps of grass and low shrubs along the roadside. The commercial strains of sparaxis, commonly available from bulb distributors, are derived from several South African species and come in a wide range of colours with varying degrees of marking in the flower throats. Prior to this South African trip, I had bought five hundred of these hybrids, it being another of these relatively cheap bulbs to buy, with the intention of planting them through my South African garden. I had potted them up first to assess what they looked like in growth and had been slightly disappointed as their leaves were a bit weatherworn and torn at flowering time, which rather spoiled the effect. They remained in their pots, seeding around and bulking up prolifically and quietly becoming a bit of an embarrassment. Having witnessed where their ancestors chose to grow in the wild, I came home and immediately emptied out the pots, bulbs and all, around some low grasses and shrubs I had planted at the bottom of the acer glade. In this type of situation their foliage is reduced in importance, thus leaving their exotic flowers to drift and hover among the flowering grasses in early summer.

The genus *Dodecatheon* (shooting stars), like *Roscoea*, is not a bulb but shares the same growth

patterns and consorts well with them. On a trip to southern California that was full from start to finish with horticultural inspiration, the sight of acre upon acre of what we took to be *Dodecatheon clevelandii* subsp. *insulare* covering fields with its airy sprays of cyclamen-like flowers in every shade of pink and white was one of the

ABOVE Babiana villosa *set off by low-growing, silver-foliaged shrubs in the wild in South Africa.*

highlights (see opposite). Unlike many shooting stars, whose foliage to my mind is rather untidy, the leaves on this variety form a neat rosette flat to the ground, reminding me of *Lewisia cotyledon*. This dodecatheon seemed to be growing in soil that was quite ordinary at flowering time but would undoubtedly be dry throughout the summer months, conditions not particularly easy to replicate in Devon. I managed to track this plant down when I returned home and planted it in the sand of the African garden, where I hope the freer-draining conditions will take away the surplus moisture. It is still early days, but they are looking good so far.

Rhodohypoxis

Twist my arm behind my back and ask what is my favourite alpine bulb and I would have to say the little South African *Rhodohypoxis*. It is a plant that likes adequate moisture in its growing season and none at all when it is dormant. Since it grows through the northern hemisphere's summer months the first requisite is easy to fulfil if grown outside in a typical English damp summer. For some, the lack of a clearly differentiated centre to the individual flower counts against it, but I love the crystalline translucency of the petals

and the sheer exuberance of flowering created by this 5 cm (2 in) high power-pack. I wanted to grow them forming drifts as I imagined they might be found in their native homeland, high on the moist slopes of the Drakensberg Mountains in Natal, and consequently planted them in patches among creeping thymes on the newly excavated quarry banks (see page 55). In fact, I am sure that in their homelands they do not grow in such numbers and diversity as they do on my quarry banks, and they certainly would not grow among thymes, but romanticizing nature is what this style of gardening is all about. If the thymes are cut back hard every year immediately after they have flowered they do form very close carpets to the ground, enabling certain bulbous plants to come up through, such as *Allium pallens* (see above).

Rhodohypoxis are plants that do not like too much moisture around their roots when they are dormant. Many people grow them in containers so they can more easily keep the pots dry during the colder months by taking them inside their greenhouses. I prefer to cultivate them in the open ground, partly because I am able to grow more of them but also because they do not require summer watering grown in this way. The fewer plants I can grow in containers the clearer is my conscience should I have to leave them in the summer. Fortunately rhodohypoxis die down completely in the winter months and are very easy to accommodate in the open garden as well. All you need to do is remember to cover the ground as soon as the leaves have died away in the autumn with a weighted-down piece of polythene to keep all winter rain off them. In areas where winter temperatures drop below −10°C (14°F) it would probably be wise to spread a 5 cm (2 in) layer of chippings over the top of the polythene as an added insulating mulch. Remove

the polythene and mulch as soon as they re-emerge in the spring and gently cover them with a thin mulch of gritty potting compost, which both feeds the plants and gives them a little protection against late frosts in areas where these temperatures are a threat.

In my experience the species most tolerant of winter wet is *Rhodohypoxis milloides*, a marginally taller species with dark pink flowers. In the variety 'Claret', the leaves are large and dark green and the flowers are especially big and brightly coloured, being rather more reddish-pink than claret. I have left this variety out, uncovered, for several winters, one of which was exceptionally wet, and it has come through unscathed. It flowers in late spring at the same time as the equally large-flowered hybrid R. 'Picta' with its broad white petals occasionally tipped in pink, and I grow them together in one bed to good effect.

At the other end of the size scale is the diminutive *Rhodohypoxis thodiana*, barely struggling clear of the soil before opening its glistening white flowers almost flat on the ground. I love it especially as it is scented, even if you do have to grovel on the floor to smell it, but it is not one of the longer-flowering species, being early and relatively fleeting. *R. deflexa* is equally tiny but flowers a month later, producing its small pinkish-red flowers in early summer.

For most of my gardening life, the only readily available rhodohypoxis species has been *Rhodohypoxis baurii*, with flowers midway in size between the two species already mentioned and coming in a range of colours from white through pink to red. The species from which most of the named varieties have arisen, it looks fabulous growing with some of the smaller-flowered ones, their colours all mixed together. Very occasionally it produces small black seeds, but collecting them is a painstakingly slow process. The real bonus with this species is that it flowers for ten or twelve weeks, provided it does not get dry.

My various experiments with bulbs growing in a sunny, sandy site are still at an early stage but they have progressed far enough for me to realize how much potential there is for a dry-landscape bulb garden. The problem I have is that 150 cm (60 in) of rain spread relatively evenly throughout the year is not compatible with my dream, so I shall create my dry bulb garden under cover by joining a couple of 7 m (24 ft) polytunnels (hoop houses) together and leaving the sides open to give a 15 m (50 ft) square dry garden. Here, under cover, I can grow all my nerines, amaryllis, romuleas, moraeas and so many more of those wonderful South African and Californian bulbs and semi-desert plants with no fear of natural overwatering. I can indulge myself with drifts of

sugar-pink *Nerine flexuosa* complemented by lilac-blue autumn crocus such as *Crocus gouliymi* and the earlier flowering *C. banaticus*, and the naked chalices of colchicums with the candy-pink of *Nerine sarniensis* hybrids, all growing among the marbled leaves of autumn-flowering cyclamen and all protected from the elements that so often ruin their displays outside. It could be wonderful or it could be a mess, so perhaps prudence will dictate that I experiment away from the critical glare of the viewing public. But what the heck—I will have a fine time discovering which it is to be.

ABOVE *Drifts of rhodohypoxis join forces with clumps of* Dianthus 'Brymos' *(in the foreground) to form the basis of this early-summer display. Later these same banks turn purple when the creeping thyme comes into flower (see photograph on page 213).*

2 Deserts and semi-arid landscapes

I sometimes wonder whether it is human nature to appreciate most the things that have only a fleeting presence rather than those that are with you all the time. It would explain my fondness for bulbs as well as my current fascination with that ultimate of fleeting floral experiences, the unpredictable but magical blooming of a desert. Broadcast a television programme on a desert anywhere in the world and I will patiently sit through it in the hope that the producer will show images of the transformation that can occur after the rains, for a brief 'fix' of a few seconds' worth of haunting camera-shots of a waving kaleidoscope of fluttering flowers.

The majority of these flowering plants that fast-forward their growth cycles will be either bulbs or, more likely, annuals. Annuals are the masters of these marginal conditions and, because they tend to flower all together to cash in on this brief window of opportunity, they can create spectacular floral extravaganzas. Yet many serious gardeners tend to look down their noses at annuals, linking them with the massed displays in municipal parks of salvias, lobelias and alyssum that give pleasure to so many people. Some of the most exquisite flowers I have ever seen and some of the most sophisticated plant

combinations have been created with annuals, so perhaps it is time to look at these plants again.

As this phenomenon of massed flowering is so unpredictable there are only limited parts of the world where it can be relied on, and one such is the western fringe of South Africa. Here, especially in Namaqualand, south of the border with Namibia, can be found during most springs some of the best wild-flower spectacles in the world, where whole landscapes are transformed into sheets of colour. It took thirty years before the political conditions felt right for me to fulfil my ambition to see them, but the wait was worth it.

Inspiration from the wild

My first visit to a tiny portion of what is a vast country was aimed to coincide with the massed spring flowering of annuals in Namaqualand, about 725 km (450 miles) north of Cape Town, in late August. Even on such a short visit, the wealth of natural riches, both fauna and flora, was obvious, and the species count of plants alone is quite staggering. On one range of mountains which stretch southwards from Cape Town and the famous Table Mountain, for about 24 km (15 miles) to the Cape of Good Hope, there are more plant species than in the whole of the British flora. However, you certainly would not notice it from the sanctuary of your coach as you thunder by to join what by South African standards is almost a traffic jam heading towards Cape Point. In the early African spring of that time of year, much of the area bears a striking

resemblance to Dartmoor in winter, with low undulating hills covered in grey-green heath-like vegetation as far as the eye can see. It is not until you get out and start looking closely that you notice the astonishing variety. The flora around the Cape itself is called the fynbos and is a mixture of grasses, shrubs and a bewildering variety of heaths. A few years after a fire the fynbos can be quite colourful (see left), but to be truthful it is more of a botanist's paradise than a floral spectacle. Mass flowering in this part of the world is entirely dependent on exactly the right amount of winter rainfall—too little or too much spoils the party and Namaqualand that particular year had received very little, but around Langebaan and the West Coast Nature Reserve our party hit the jackpot. It is worth pointing out that on a subsequent visit this particular pattern was completely reversed; the flowers will be somewhere, but you may have to be flexible if you are to stand any chance of finding them.

Langebaan that first year, though, was stunning. Here, with the turquoise blue lagoon as background, soft white sand underfoot and unseen birds fluting rich, rhythmic melodies, lay a panorama a gardener would die for. Million upon million rainbow-coloured flowers fluttering in the breeze carpeted the ground in extraordinary diversity, stretching as far as the eye could see (see opposite and page 127). What I had not expected was the wonderfully good taste this profusion of colour had been assembled into, with drifts of pink *Senecio elegans*, acres of white *Osteospermum pluvialis* (the rain daisy) and great washes of gentian-blue, annual *Heliophila* weaving its patterns among them. Dotted through this were the colours of South Africa I had especially come to see, the yellows and vibrant oranges of *Gazania*, *Arctotis* and *Ursinia*—simply fabulous.

I had always professed that I borrowed ideas and gleaned inspiration from natural landscapes and 'enhanced nature' in my garden designs. At a stroke, faced with such a stunning show of colour-coordinated magnificence, this viewpoint seemed more than a little presumptuous. Here was nature that could not be improved upon and

ABOVE *A dazzling display of spring flowers near Langebaan in South Africa. Part of the West Coast Nature Reserve can be seen across the lagoon.*

LEFT *Ostrich, bontebok and egrets feed in the West Coast Nature Reserve among a background worthy of an Impressionist painter. Viewed through binoculars the flowers shimmer and dance, creating a quite magical experience.*

my arrogance (like my foot on many an occasion) disappeared down one of the numerous molerat tunnels that criss-crossed the whole area.

Across the bay from Langebaan is the West Coast Nature Reserve, which is opened every spring for its floral displays. Here 8 ha (20 acre) patches of land, cleared of scrub to allow for better grazing, become in most years a carpet of flowers. To see small herds of beautiful springbok, cape zebra or muscular eland feeding among a sea of multi-coloured flowers was like looking at an Impressionist painting, a living, shimmering Pissarro or Corot, and it was a life-enhancing experience (see page 59). The background of brilliant blue ocean and granite rock outcrops is just gilding the lily.

I remember one of Britain's most famous gardeners, Christopher Lloyd, telling me that you would not grow alpines if you had seen them at their glorious best in their natural surroundings, a sentiment I certainly did not agree with at the time, but for a while, confronted by this display at Langebaan, I understood exactly his sentiments. However, South Africa is too far away for me to visit as often as I would wish and I knew the temptation to try to catch some tiny essence of such splendour in my own garden would be too overpowering to resist.

Colour

These South African flower spectacles are all about colour, and colour is, of course, a key element in any garden, but not necessarily the be all and end all. Whole books have been written on the subject and authors have made their reputations on the careful colour grading of flowers, yet in nature there are no colour clashes, though colour mixes appear that would have some gardeners throwing up their arms in dismay. I think it is possible to have virtually any colours in a scheme if the planting is not just in traditional blocks. Clashes become a problem only when you have one solid block of a colour lined up alongside another block of an unharmonious

colour. The same two colours spread unevenly and dotted through the scheme can really make each other zing. By dotting and spreading colour in this fashion you can have every shade in the rainbow in a single area with not a single colour clash, although invariably one, two or three colours will be predominant.

How we view colour will often depend upon how reliably we can expect to see the sun. Desert annuals, for example, by their very nature have to be fertilized quickly if they are to set and ripen seed before dry weather conditions curtail all growth, so it is hardly surprising that many flaunt outrageously bright flowers to attract a pollinator as quickly as possible. For me, these colours still look fresh and vibrant even under the brightest summer sun and I love orange and red for this very reason. By contrast, the pastel shades so beloved by traditional Jekyll-schooled English gardeners fade into muddiness under the glare of a bright midday sun, only coming back into their own as the light loses its potency in the evening. Perhaps it is hardly surprising that the English love their pastel-coloured borders when we see so little sun in an average British summer. If your summer always brings bright sun or if you are a gardener who wants to enjoy your garden in the day rather than the evening, bright-coloured flowers are worth considering.

ABOVE *Part of the African Garden still under construction at the Garden House. The process of covering the compost with a thick layer of coarse sand is half complete at this point. Three months after this picture was taken, the area was a sea of vibrant orange, red and yellow from annuals sown direct on to the sand.*

OPPOSITE *Californian poppies,* Eschscholzia californica, *provide months of dazzling colour when grown in cultivation.*

ABOVE *Californian poppies growing by the roadside in California, USA. It is likely that the harsh conditions in which they were growing have stunted their growth, although you would almost think they was a different species if you compared them to those on page 60.*

The magic of sand

One of the surprising things to me about the habitat of these plants was that they appeared to be rooted in pure sand. There is clearly a very fine dividing line between an area of regular seasonal vegetation and of barren desert, based entirely on the regularity of rainfall, however minimal it may be. That may sound obvious but it does seem little short of miraculous that sand such as this can support one of the floral wonders of the world.

In South Africa many native plants bloom for just a short time, yet they will flower nearly all summer long in cool temperate British conditions. The vast majority of the spring display is of annuals and individually the plants are very spindly, providing a limited floral display before withering away. It is the sheer numbers of them that provides the visual feast. Likewise, *Cerinthe major* 'Purpurascens', from southern Europe, is rather a sad, fleeting, spindly creature on poor soil in its native habitat, but given a rich diet in full sun it is transformed into a sumptuous, long-flowering beauty with rich indigo-blue bells.

Fired up by such a floral extravaganza, I inevitably decided I would create a 'South African' part of the garden and I thought it might make sense to make up beds with masses of rich compost and then top them off with a layer of sand. In that way the roots would penetrate to the nourishing compost that would keep them plump and long-flowering, while the sand would provide surface drainage that might reduce the chances of mildews and rots underneath the foliage canopy. Choosing a sunny, open site, I made the beds slightly higher than the surrounding land to minimize any chance of standing water around the roots. Knowing that the main display would be from midsummer onwards,

I tried to shape the land into smooth, almost sensual curves so that at non-flowering times the area would still hold together as a garden feature. I have always reasoned that if you can shape the land into satisfying forms before a single plant is introduced then your chances of achieving a harmonious result throughout the year are greatly enhanced. Here, I wanted to create the flowing lines of sand dunes, a sculpture in sand which at certain times of the year would become a riot of colour and produce over a relatively long period what in the wild is an elusive occurrence—the magical blooming of a desert.

Planting in sand

The beds were made up with 23–30 cm (9–12 in) of compost and then topped off with 7.5–10 cm (3–4 in) of sand. I used a locally extracted, washed rock sand, because its grey-black colour matched the colour of our local stone. Beyond

checking there was no salt in it, I had no idea whether plants would grow in this sand, so I planted a few unimportant seedlings as an experiment. Within a week they had doubled the size of their rootballs, so pointing the way for full-scale seed-sowing. Some of the seeds I sowed were annuals I had bought in South Africa, but many species and varieties are available from seed firms internationally.

I appreciate that some people will feel more comfortable creating a natural-style garden if they are replicating as closely as possible a wild template. In that case they should welcome as much information as possible, from any source, of the exact conditions in which the plants are growing in the wild, but I am not of that school of thought. A straight copy of what occurs in nature is too restrictive creatively for my tastes and does not allow me enough flexibility to adapt a wild landscape to my garden conditions. I prefer to try

ABOVE *The way plants combine in the wild is very different to traditional gardening. In the picture on the right you can see flowers growing wild in South Africa. In the tiny area shown see how many different species are in flower and how they are randomly spread. The picture on the left was taken at the Garden House, and I discovered I could create the same effect by mixing the seeds of different annuals together before sowing them.*

to capture only the spirit of wild plantings and never attempt to replicate exactly any landscape or combination of plants I may have seen in the wild. Being realistic, many of the wild plants you admire in a different habitat from your own would not grow for you anyway, but that does not stop you trying to take the essence of any particular spot and emulate it in your own garden.

I am no purist and I have no qualms about using non-African plants to create an African feel. For example, I have always loved the vibrant orange of Californian poppies (*Eschscholzia californica*) and, given an open, well-drained, sunny position, they are reasonably perennial in Britain, so I knew they could form the easy-to-grow basis of this 'African' garden. Creating a more welcoming environment for these Californian poppies to seed into was one of the prime motivating factors for the whole exercise. Other Californians such as *Platystemon californicus*, *Camissonia* 'Sunflakes', *Eschscholzia lobbii* and *Phacelia campanularia* were sown with the seed mixed together and turned out to be a wonderful success.

Germination in the pure sand was extremely rapid, but subsequent growth was initially very slow. This was not surprising since the roots needed to get down into the compost layer before any real growth could be expected—it was lucky that my sand had been 'washed' since it meant no weed seeds were competing with the minute seedlings in these early stages of development. I found that overcoming this reluctance to grow required regular watering, and I took to using a fine spray twice on every day it did not rain right up until flowering started, which was about ten or twelve weeks after sowing. After the first year this strict watering regime became unnecessary, as the whole area had settled down into some sort of equilibrium.

Once flowering started I attempted to remove spent flowers each day, but after two weeks the sheer volume defeated even my enthusiasm. I justified leaving them by reasoning I was allowing them to set seed, which was partly true. It is, of course, obvious that annuals should be left to set seed if you want them there again next year

RIGHT *The Livingstone daisy,* Dorotheanthus bellidiformis, *growing in shingle found practically on the beaches near the Cape of Good Hope, South Africa.*

without the bother of reseeding, but it is also true that dead-heading undeniably extends the flowering season, so a compromise has to be reached.

The sand dwellers

About 20 per cent of the total area was planted out with summer bedding, notably arctotis and osteospermum, to help give an authentic African feel. This was religiously dead-headed in the first year, giving five months of unbroken flowering, although in subsequent years I have not done this dead-heading and I cannot say it has seriously diminished flowering. Cuttings are taken in the autumn and overwintered inside to plant out again the following spring. Surfinias, which are more often thought of as hanging-basket plants, seemed very happy growing on the flat on my dunes and were also long-flowerers, with the small-flowered *Surfinia* 'Million Bells' looking especially good.

However, the plant that encapsulates this whole experiment best is the old favourite mesembryanthemum (*Dorotheanthus bellidiformis*), or Livingstone daisy. As a young child I loved it for its vibrant colours and the sugar-crystalline translucency of its petals, but I had never gardened in a setting where I thought that it looked right. When I visited South Africa I found mesembryanthemums growing almost on the beaches, many among the fire-blackened remnants of scrubby shrubs, those beautiful, bejewelled flowers pressed flat against the soft white coral sand. Now, in my own dunes, placed amid driftwood, I have found a setting to show them off, not in such scrumptious sand or with views a patch on their native home, but my plants are at least happy and unfailingly take me back to that bewitching scenery of South Africa whenever I look at them.

Another South African succulent, *Bulbine frutescens*, has been a wonderful success in my sand dunes. From the moment I planted it out in early spring to the first real frost in late autumn it produced a constant stream of soft orange flower spikes, 45 cm (18 in) high, getting better and better as the season progressed. Its long, succulent leaves have a slightly exotic grassy look that seems just right in my African garden.

I must admit that in the first few months of this experiment I needed all the courage of my convictions to bolster the determination to carry on with it. There would not have been a problem if we had not had paying visitors coming in every day wondering what these strange burial mounds were. The sand too proved irresistible to children, and rather worryingly to many parents, who felt compulsively drawn to walk right through the middle of the dunes, which did not help with the growth of the tiny seedlings. Nor were the difficulties restricted to bipeds alone—our cats, numbering twelve at the time, thought this the biggest and best cat-litter tray ever. I was reduced to surrounding the area with wire netting to keep all and sundry off it until the plants started to make significant growth, and this was hardly in keeping with anybody's concept of naturalistic planting. Fortunately the problems did not recur in following years as autumn- and winter-germinated seedlings green a sizeable proportion of the dunes' surfaces, making it very obvious that these are in fact flower-beds.

Self-seeders

One of these overwintering seeders, the poached egg plant, *Limnanthes douglasii*, is also Californian. I introduced a couple of seedlings as part of the sand-testing process, but since this is one of the most prolific annual seeders you can grow in the British climate they have not been slow in colonizing. However, although it was not part of my plan, I cannot think of any other annual that will provide such a bright, cheerful patch of yellow through late spring and early summer, and it is worth growing just for the 'buzz' it gives the bees. By midsummer you can pull off the old stems and plant something in its place, secure in the knowledge there are already thousands of small seeds just waiting for the next wet spell to germinate. The patch of limnanthes we have in the African Garden includes the pure yellow 'Sulphurea' among the more usual white-edged form, which I think does help to give the group a

RIGHT *Here are two plants that would be strong contenders for my personal 'top ten' favourites: the pale yellow* Oenothera stricta *'Sulphurea' with the delicate wands and pink bells of angels' fishing rods,* Dierama pulcherrimum, *growing behind.*

more natural look. There are also pink and white forms available which I shall look forward to growing one day among the others.

Growing alongside the limnanthes and just as happy in the sand is yet another Californian annual, *Gilia achilleaefolia*. The pale blue, pincushion flowers start to appear at the same time as its yellow neighbour, but continue for months. It is a good, solid member of the community, without being one of its stars. It can create lovely patches of soft blue, but it is not so quick out of its starting blocks in the spring so can easily get swamped by the more aggressive elements among its neighbours.

As it germinates later in the year and then flowers earlier the following spring than the poached egg plant, it is a bit of a mystery to me why the much-loved forget-me-not *Myosotis sylvatica* is classified in my reference books as a biennial while the limnanthes is termed an annual. This highlights once again the difficulties that lie in categorizing plants. As far as I am concerned it is an overwintering annual that is unsurpassed for producing pools of good blue colour in positions where its rather coarse habit will not interfere with more special plants. I have not used the plant as much as I might because the obvious place to grow it is under the spring-flowering trees, and this is where I am already growing wood anemones and erythroniums, and I do not want to put at risk their continuing good health by introducing another plant.

Although normally biennial, *Oenothera stricta* seedlings, germinating in the spring, will easily be in flower by midsummer, thereby qualifying this beautiful evening primrose from Mexico as a bona fide annual. I love it, and could almost have included it as a key plant in any of my plantings, but it is among the sand dunes that it seems most in its element. Overwintered rosettes will send up their branching, elegant, red-tinged flowering stems to 1–1.2 m (3–4 ft) in late spring, open their first flowers during early summer, and then continue non-stop until early autumn. The pale yellow flowers of *O. stricta* 'Sulphurea' darken as they age to a peachy-pink and happily consort

with just about anything, but I am just as happy with the bright yellow of the true species.

With the passing years, other advantages to this approach of a 7.5–10 cm (3–4 in) top-dressing of sand have become apparent. In my heavy loam, many of these annuals are very sensitive to excessive moisture, which is a bit of a problem in a garden that gets 150 cm (60 in) of rain a year. Most self-seeding poppies, for example, except for *Meconopsis cambrica* and *Papaver lateritium*, disappear almost immediately. In the sanded areas, however, they seed themselves too prolifically and have to be rigorously thinned, a not too arduous task in the very easily weeded sand. The same vigour seems to apply to a lot of other plants in these sandy conditions, notably bulbs of all sorts (see pages 49–50).

Embracing semi-arid conditions

I have often wondered just why I have this fascination with dry landscapes and their indigenous plants. Is it a case of the grass always appearing greener on the other side of the fence? It certainly cannot get much greener than where I live, with its damp, mild climate. I have Japanese maples thriving here planted on piles of rock, stones and subsoil, with their roots just barely covered by good topsoil. The beautiful, ice blue-flowered *Primula whitei* will produce copious babies in its leaf axils, a trait it will not do in the marginally drier atmosphere of the nursery further east where I was given it . Surely I should just be grateful and strive to be as good a gardener as the very generous limitations of my climate allow, and yet . . . there is something about the creative possibilities of harmonizing stone, sand, rock, pebbles, wood and plants that I find irresistible, not to mention the gorgeous, over-the-top flamboyance of so many dry-climate plants. If you are not convinced, flick through a book of South African bulbs and marvel at the markings and outrageous colours of some of the moraeas, romuleas and sparaxis (see pages 68–69). I do

The diversity of species in southern Africa is truly staggering, with a bewildering array of flower shapes, colours and magnificent examples of plant mimicry. Alternatively you can simply enjoy them for their exquisite and intricate beauty.

CLOCKWISE FROM TOP LEFT Ixia lutea (there are 52 species of Ixia in southern Africa); Sparaxis elegans; Gortera diffusa ssp. diffusa; Moraea species (one of 49 in southern Africa); Daubeynia crinita; Romulea kamsbergensis (there are 73 Romulea species in southern Africa); Spiloxene capensis (there are 23 species of Spiloxene in southern Africa); Sparaxis grandiflora; Gladiolus alatus (there are 107 Gladiolus species in southern Africa); Romulea hantamensis.

not want to grow just a few of these plants in pots, even if I had the skills and knowledge of those amazing plantsmen and women who do. I want to grow them in the ground, surrounded by a little slice of landscape that encapsulates their natural origins and that, from a purely functional point of view, makes them easier to look after. So, until I can find that south-facing plot of land of my dreams, I shall have to make do with creating some of these experimental planting ideas under the protective canopy of that large polytunnel (hoop house).

The new green

Southern California is a treasure trove of ideas for giving your garden an arid or semi-arid atmosphere if you do not garden under these climatic conditions in actuality. I can almost hear a collective intake of breath from readers who think that is exactly what they do not want, and this does touch on a more fundamental question. To the casual observer, travelling around in these drier parts of California, as well as in New Mexico, Arizona, Utah and Colorado, it does seem that where gardens are produced for aesthetic reasons the overriding instinct of the creators is to make them as green as possible. You see sprinklers operating everywhere, even irrigating small areas of the roadside to support a sparse covering of vegetation. Around hotels and other buildings wanting to create a feeling of some opulence or horticultural enclave there are little green oases in a parched, sere landscape. Yet that landscape is so beautiful with its shades of buff and ochre, its bleached dried grasses, the wonderful rocks, the soft bluish-grey of the sage-brush and the evergreen trees and shrubs so perfectly adapted to the climate. If you put those ingredients together at Chelsea Flower Show and threw in a sprinkling of colour from flowering plants, especially if they were pinks and soft blues, people would be queuing up to say how sophisticated the planting was. The point I am trying to make is that gardens need not just be green. Even the lushest garden can benefit from having the occasional area that is more neutral in colour, perhaps

with the soft ochres and red-browns of grasses and stone, and such areas will accentuate the colour vibrancy of the entire garden.

The more I look at trying to capture that semi-arid feel to a garden the more potential I see. Think for a minute of the vast tracts of land surface of the planet categorized as semi-arid and the enormous variation that exists within these areas, many of them being very distinct. Obviously most of these will have very little vegetation of relevance to our gardens, but some, as in the

case of the Californian sage brush, most definitely do. It should go almost without saying that if you live in a very dry climate it makes much more sense ecologically and aesthetically to look for inspiration from your surrounding countryside and other parts of the world with similar climates rather than struggle to maintain a garden type not suited to your particular locale, provided you are prepared to make that quantum leap in acceptance that your garden for much of the year will not be predominantly green.

Gardening author and lecturer Lauren Springer, who lives in Colorado, grasped this idea years ago and with only 38 cm (15in) rain annually, 23 cm (9 in) of which come as snow, she has created a wonderful garden perfectly in harmony with itself and the surrounding landscape (see page 72). By drawing on her knowledge and colour preferences from traditional gardening, choosing plants that will tolerate her particular conditions and ensuring they complement the native plants, she has achieved an effect that is

ABOVE *With the Rio Grande in New Mexico for a backdrop, the dried grasses, sage-brush and dark pines combine to produce a palette of muted pastel colours in the foreground.*

far more sophisticated, artful and natural than any traditional garden I have seen and looks absolutely right for that setting.

Space and backdrop

The inspiration afforded by these dry landscapes is not just of relevance to those with gardens in such areas. Even for a garden in a damp climate such as Devon, there are lessons to be learnt from places such as the Mojave Desert in California. As in South Africa, plants in the desert tend to be well spaced, which has two advantages. First, you are able to appreciate the individual grace and form of a plant such the desert dandelion (*Malacothrix glabrata*) or the beautiful dwarf Californian poppies, the *Eschscholtzia* species. The thread-like glaucous leaves of these poppies, forming delicate mounds of foliage 10–15 cm (4–6 in) high, are the perfect foil and scale for the frail flowering stems rising to three times this height, all of which would be completely lost if the plants were overcrowded. There is a place for restraint and this is not necessarily an easy lesson for English gardeners to take on board as they are brought up with lush, exuberant flower borders. God forbid that that should be lost, but perhaps the occasional area of well-spaced plants, allowing their graceful form to be shown to full advantage, would accentuate the merits of both areas.

Secondly and just as important, open spacing gives you the opportunity to view the plant in conjunction with what it is growing in. The colour and texture of the sand can and should be able to complement and even enhance the beauty of the individual plant. There is no question that the lovely and varied sands in both South Africa and California are as much a part of the overall effect as the plants themselves, so we should try to incorporate the surface medium of the ground into the aesthetic equation.

Bearing in mind that I have seen relatively few examples, the one common factor with all the plants I have experienced growing in pure sand in the wild is that the sand itself is quite coarse—different colours and forms for sure, but always crystalline and granular and sometimes

LEFT *After a long, hot spell, Lauren Springer's garden in the foothills of the Rockies in Colorado, USA, still blends seamlessly with the surrounding countryside. Successfully gardening in harmony with nature, as Lauren has done here, means accepting the limitations imposed by the climate and local conditions and embracing plants that are happy in this type of environment. Her skills demonstrate that such a garden can look good, too.*

ABOVE *With just the right amount of previous rainfall, hundreds of acres of this part of the Mojave Desert in California, USA, were transformed into a vast flower garden. Desert dandelions and sweetly-scented camissonias formed the basis of this magical display.*

RIGHT *Also in the same part of the Mojave, the overhanging sun-bleached, spindly trunks of shrubs and the purple/blue of chia, Salvia columbariae, add structure and contrast to the wash of flower colour.*

nearer to grit. Really soft sand can tend to form a hard crust once it has settled, been watered and then dried, and this means any water, unless applied very gently, can run straight off without penetrating. The concept of water run-off leads on to another idea.

Water run-off zone

My visit to the Mojave Desert was about ten days too early for maximum flowering, but one thing clear was that many of the early flowers occur in the water run-off zones, either at the bottom of the rocky hills or in the dried-up flash flood plains. I was surprised to find such wide flash flood areas in such dry-looking country, and occurring everywhere rather than just on obvious watercourses. Judging from the incredible debris of boulders and dead trees left scattered about, they must be quite a sight in full spate. Although most of the water runs off, enough penetrates the ground to provide moisture for these early flowers and the result is masses of flowers growing amid the inevitable sand, some of which is formed into sand bars and little beaches, but with stones, pebbles, rocks and wood scattered about. The occasional living scrubby shrub or low cactus bush gives upright form to the composition.

All of these key elements would translate beautifully into a garden setting. The structural elements alone, before any plants are introduced, would look good all year, and the little flowering oases of plants, rotating in position around the site throughout the growing season, would produce seasonal colour. It could be both sculptural and artistic, a sort of extension of the beach garden at Dungeness in Kent that was created by the late film-maker Derek Jarman. With good soil or compost 15 cm (6 in) below such a medley of stone, sand and wood you could have a continuous eight-month display of flowers from early bulbs through annuals and grasses to autumn-flowering bulbs.

Succulents

I can see this same backdrop working well with succulents, which genuinely are adapted to more arid conditions. In Lauren Springer's Colorado garden, I was amazed to see quite a few succulents growing unprotected outside in what is a very harsh and extreme climate. Similarly, Dave Salman of High Country Nurseries in Santa Fe, New Mexico, who has a particular passion and encyclopedic knowledge of these plants, assures me that many are cold-tolerant provided they are kept completely dry during the winter. He suggests withholding water from these hardy types from early autumn onwards, so they are dry by the time the frosts arrive. Clearly, in a damp climate this is going to be difficult to achieve unless the succulents are covered with a cloche, which rather flies in the face of a natural approach. An alternative, if the succulent look is to be an important element of the garden design, is to grow these plants in containers and plunge them in the ground where needed, with the pots hidden below the soil surface. It is simple to lift the pots and take them under cover during early to mid-autumn. The beauty of this method is that by growing a range of succulents that flower at different times you can achieve a succession of colour in their allocated space in the garden by swapping the pots around after each has finished flowering. You may wonder, as I certainly would have done in the past, why you should bother. Having seen a bewildering range of them in South Africa, all I can say is that they can be staggeringly vivid or as subtle as any Jekyll-inspired michaelmas daisy border (see page 78), and there is nothing quite like them for capturing the spirit of arid and semi-arid landscapes. There is no question that these plants will feature strongly one day in my covered dry garden.

Out of context

The sight of familiar plants growing in a new environment is one of the pleasures of travelling. At Malibu Beach in southern California I came across an out-of-fashion but very well-known plant being used in a surprising way. This was a lilac-blue periwinkle (*Vinca major*), completely covering the 0.2 ha (½ acre) sloping front garden of a very stylish new house with patches of a

RIGHT *Taken 18 months on from the photograph on page 61, you can see in this picture that the African Garden has been extended and is ablaze in mid-summer with self-seeded annuals and a healthy smattering of planted half-hardy shrubs, such as argyranthemums, and more traditional bedding plants, such as brachyscomes, lobelias and nemesias. Around the edges the planting is more stabilized with perennials, including anthemis, hemerocallis, crocosmias and kniphofias.*

glowing purple-flowered *Lampranthus* growing among it (see above). Against the ochre stonework of the buildings and background hills I thought it was a master stroke of understated simplicity. Although in southern California *Lampranthus* is probably perennial, in one of these semi-arid type of gardens I would treat it as an annual and get it through the winter as cuttings.

A phormium and cordyline garden

Succulent plants would also contribute towards the semi-arid atmosphere in a garden created by growing the lovely grey and greyish-purple phormiums with the same colour cordylines planted nearer to the front and given space to show off their arching grace. Yuccas would look excellent among this, planted somewhere you could not accidentally step back on them and suffer the needle-sharp tips of their leaves. I have not actually seen a wild landscape that directly correlates with this idea, but it is very easy to imagine that somewhere in South Africa, or South America perhaps, there will be something

akin to it. There were certainly sections of the Karroo Botanic Garden at Worcester, in South Africa, where native African plants have produced a similar effect to how I envisage this cordyline and phormium garden might look. The site for this garden would have to be fairly sheltered in cool-temperate climates if the cordylines were to be grown outside all year, but it would be possible to grow them in containers plunged in the ground and then taken inside for the winter.

Cordylines and phormiums are such strong shapes that the spaces between them would lend themselves to any number of options—you could use rock, stone or large driftwood as architectural features, and plant drifts of many species. The grey and smoky-purple foliage colours of the main plantings would be a perfect backdrop for just about any flower colour combinations, with lilac-blues, pale yellows, soft pinks or vibrant oranges all being perfectly set off by such a backdrop. I can see such a garden looking good with penstemons and salvias, with stately eremurus, or undercarpeted with Californian poppies.

ABOVE *The west-facing garden of a new house at Malibu Beach in California, USA, has been given over entirely to periwinkle,* Vinca major, *and a purple-flowered succulent,* Lampranthus.

OPPOSITE *In Kirstenbosch Botanic Gardens in Cape Town, South Africa, borders dedicated to native succulent shrubs in the family Mesembryanthemaceae produce a display as good as any Jekyll-inspired late-summer michaelmas daisy border.*

Rich pickings from Crete

The Mediterranean is another rich picking ground for gardening ideas. The seasons in Crete, as in much of the Mediterranean, appear very polarized to those of us brought up with the seemingly non-stop rain of more temperate climates. In summer the island is almost completely devoid of any greenery, but when I visited it in mid-spring I was surprised how green it all was. I was also surprised by how familiar many of the plants were to me, with a number of native species bearing a superficial similarity to English wild flowers, albeit a bit bigger and brighter. Swathes of familiar garden plants were growing en masse in a larger-than-life setting not too dissimilar to England, and I kept discovering little pockets of plant communities that I knew would translate perfectly to an English garden. One such area was only about half the size of a tennis court, raised in the centre about 1.8–3 m (6–10 ft) above the surrounding countryside. Growing here and there was fennel, *Ferula communis*. Combining strength and grace, this magnificent plant made a 2.1–2.4 m (7–8 ft) arching yet upright mass of fresh green filigree foliage topped with impressive rounded flower heads of bright yellow in typical cow-parsley style. The combination of widely spaced rocks, asphodels, shrubby phlomis, fennel and the dragon arum, *Dracunculus vulgaris*, with a backdrop of gnarled olive trees and low rocky hills was a masterpiece of refined harmonized planting.

Under these taller plants were a whole series of smaller treasures, such as orchids or little pockets of scented *Cyclamen creticum*. Not long before I had been the grateful recipient of many bulbs of this arum from a local lady who believed the plant was the work of the devil and wanted

LEFT *It is hard to understand why* Ferrula communis, *seen here in Crete, is not grown more often in our gardens. Granted the flower spikes are quite sturdy and tall, but the fine tracery of the foliage would adapt well to many different types of planting scheme.*

no more of it. I suppose you could interpret its strangely mottled stems, dark leaves and large maroon red-hooded flower spathes, smelling of rotting flesh, as sinister, but in Crete's drier climate it appeared to carry no menace whatsoever, nor thankfully was its occasionally revolting smell so evident. Subsequently, too, I have been growing the fennel, and it still does not disappoint, though it does not seem to like winter wet and cold. It has also tended to be monocarpic, dying after flowering, in my garden conditions.

Apart from the example just mentioned, any number of mini-Cretan landscapes could be adapted to create a semi-arid 'feel' in a garden. Perhaps loosely based on scenery like that shown on page 80, it might be an area where *Phlomis fruticosa*, the Jerusalem sage, with its grey woolly leaves and whorls of hooded yellow flowers, is the main shrubby constituent. Some of the lower-growing cistus would also look good. In small groups or individually dotted around towards the back of this area I would plant the silver-leaved *Elaeagnus angustifolia* Caspica group. This is really a shrub but I would grow it as a small tree by restricting it to one to three trunks and pruning away the lower branches. Grown in this way it makes an excellent substitute for those stalwarts of Mediterranean landscapes, the olive trees. Again if gaps are left between these framework shrubs these spaces could be planted with countless different variations according to personal tastes. Personally I like the idea of a mixture of a few large rocks, some low grasses, bulbs, salvias and pink or blue annuals, such as consolida or phacelias. If your climate is mild enough, the South African bulbous nerines would make a fitting climax to the end of the flowering season.

Liberating patio plants

Planting tender perennials, such as bulbine, lampranthus and arctotis, and treating them as annuals, has spawned a whole host of other possibilities for planting in these 'dry' gardens. Many of these tender plants have been categorized as 'patio plants' by the marketing men, and I sometimes think we have become so accustomed to

seeing them growing in containers that we almost believe it is their natural habitat. In fact many hail from just such dry areas and they look really at home in open, sunny spots in the sand.

I have tried some of the smaller, more open-flowered pelargoniums grown on 'the flat' in the dunes of my African garden and they looked great. You could grow them in pots sunk in the earth and then take them indoors in winter, but I planted mine out and then took cuttings in the autumn. Next season I fancy planting some of the soft, salmon-pink diascias to run among and through the bright red pelargoniums. I have also tried various nemesias, brachyscomes, lobelias, argyranthemums and bidens, all of which are usually recommended for hanging baskets or containers and all, without exception, looked fantastic grown in this way. Any summer bedding could be grown in a more naturalistic setting, but I think it will be easier to pull it off successfully if you limit yourself to plants with single flowers that are not too large—in other words, plants which have a species look about them.

❖   ❖   ❖

THERE ARE OF COURSE MANY gardeners who have no choice other than to deal with a water-challenged climate as this is their reality, and it may seem strange, even slightly ungrateful, that I cherish dry landscapes and wish to emulate them occasionally when I live in a climate where lushness is the defining characteristic. Whether or not adequate water is a problem, there are many lessons to be learnt from these naturally occurring semi-arid landscapes, from the way plants adapt to these conditions to the increasing importance of non-plant materials in the overall composition and the lessening reliance on green as the only acceptable staple colour of our gardens. Of all the landscapes I have seen, these semi-arid conditions are the ones that excite me most creatively, and I know they will play an important part in any future garden of mine—if only as a counterpoint to the overwhelming greenness all around.

OPPOSITE *Succulents were not high on my lists of plant desiderata, but if you spend time looking more closely at them, they are undeniably beautiful.*

CLOCKWISE FROM TOP LEFT Dorotheanthus maughanii, Cheiridopsis cigarettifera, Delosperma sphalmanthoides *and* Titanopsis calcarea.

3 Mountain, coast and clifftop

Ever since I have caught this addiction to seeing plants in their native habitats I tend to ask anyone who has travelled, and who has an interest in plants, if there is anywhere they have seen they can especially recommend. It is surprising how often the reply is the European Alps. When my neighbours returned from a midsummer holiday in Switzerland enthusing above and beyond the call of duty, I knew we should put it off no longer. The next year we followed exactly in their footsteps, and stayed in the picture-postcard village of Mürren, one of the highest villages in the Bernese Oberland, situated about 24 km (15 miles) from Interlaken.

The village of Mürren is perched on a high plateau far above the floor of one of those gigantic, U-shaped glacial valleys that were scoured through the Alps during the ice ages. The spectacular views from the village are dominated on the opposite, northern side of this valley by the imposing triple peaks of the Jungfrau, Monch and Eiger. The village is almost completely car-free and can realistically be accessed only by railway.

As our train slowly trundled into the village we saw railway banks studded with orchids, the fairytale, snow-topped mountains opposite glowing in late-afternoon sunshine, and a black redstart, a bird I had always wanted to see, posing tantalizingly close before flying off. The omens were good.

Exploring alpine meadows

There are many wonderful walks in the area, all of them well sign-posted. Interestingly the signposts, and our maps for that matter, were marked not in kilometres, but in hours and minutes based on average Swiss walking times between points. Perhaps the Swiss are not interested in pastoral pursuits such as gentle walking and admiring the immediate surroundings, because our times were always 30–50 per cent longer than the signs, and we were not dawdling. We matched the given average route time only on one occasion, when we were anxious to get back to the hotel and have an early dinner.

There was a group of people staying in our hotel who must be quite a common sight in the

ABOVE *The snow-covered peaks of the Eiger act as dramatic background to this high alpine Swiss meadow, where the yellow-flowered* Anthyllis *species is the dominant plant.*

PREVIOUS PAGE *With the restaurant perched on its summit, the Schilthorn presides over a classic Swiss valley. In early July the meadows are awash with white* Ranunculus aconitifolius *and yellow buttercups.*

Alps at this time of year, a bit like migrating fieldfares or redwings arriving in our winters, or the snow geese in North America, and these are the botanizing groups—almost certainly British and with a top speed of next to nothing when they are in list-gathering mode. Each to their own, and I suppose this speed thing is all relative; to our ever-patient son, Tom, Ros and I must appear to drag along at a snail's pace, or perhaps more pertinently like a learner driver trying to master the clutch and accelerator pedals—jerky, fast or stopped—the latter as we suddenly see some new plant or photogenic composition. On one such pause in our progress, he asked what we were enthusing about. It was our first, and to us very significant, encounter with thousands of tiny, lavender-blue soldanellas flowering among the thawing, retreating snow. His comment, as

he resigned himself to yet another interminable wait on a nearby rock, of 'OK, so don't step on the little purple jobs', somehow put the whole exercise into perspective.

Floral diversity

Before you come here you know the Alps are going to be big, but it is still a surprise when you arrive to find a whole series of valleys, each as big as a Scottish glen, half-way up a much bigger mountain. Each of these valleys has its own character and, due to the vagaries of micro-climate, each may be florally very different. For example, some distance above Mürren, which is already perched on a plateau 213 m (700 ft) above the valley floor, open up three parallel valleys all heading on up into the mountains. Topographically they are of similar altitude and north-south orientation, but they are all different. When we saw them one was primarily a sea of white *Ranunculus aconitifolius* and yellow buttercups with picture-postcard Swiss houses dotted around (see page 85); the slopes of the second was covered with alpine flowers such as orchids, pulsatillas and anthyllis, which are usually associated with slightly higher pastures (see opposite); and the third valley was still under 6–9 m (20–30 ft) of snow in places, with the snow-melt soldanellas and crocus around the margins. In a single day, you can see plants in flower that in your own garden would be flowering over a six-week period. As a general rule, the flowering starts in the lowest valleys in early summer, and works its way up the mountainside to the high pastures in mid- to late summer.

Alpine meadows

To this gardener, and I suspect to many of us, the term 'alpine meadow' conjures up images of acres of low-growing plants that we collectively call 'alpines' growing on or among scattered boulders or rocks. We did find one magnificent area such as this, full of auriculas, gentians, orchids, pulsatillas and yellow anthyllis, which even in the dense mist was one of the highlights of the trip, but this type of meadow is only found on the much higher slopes. The lower areas vary widely, depending in part on the amount of grazing (the more accessible are grazed for longer and therefore receive more fertilizer via the cows) and also on whether the sward is cut for hay. In between these lower and higher extremes come a whole range of eco-systems, each with a different mix of species in bewildering variety and each with distinct possibilities for translocating into a garden setting given the right backdrop back home.

It is easy to see why so many British gardeners (including ourselves) become enraptured with the flowers of the Alps. Maybe for sheer spectacle they cannot match pockets of colour found in places such as South Africa, but perhaps the more muted colours of Switzerland more closely suit the English psyche. The Swiss flowers, however, are an integral part of a landscape that is

breathtakingly beautiful, and taken overall this marks them out, for this gardener at least, as firm championship contenders.

Although each one of these alpine meadow variations, and other areas such as the extensive limestone pavements, could make wonderful role models for different gardens, you still need a site in which to create these gardens that would capture the atmosphere of the original. I identified the key elements here in these alpine ecosystems as being the clear skies above, with considerable air movement around the plants. In addition, the natural location for many of the 'true' alpine plants was on steep, though not precipitous, slopes that almost by definition are well-drained, and, it almost goes without saying, are set among scenes of awesome grandeur. To re-create an authentic alpine feel back in our gardens we would need an open, sunny, preferably elevated and sloping site, and to really capture the essence of these high alpine meadows, the location would need to be blessed with extensive views. Cut down to these basics, many of us have land that fits these criteria, including myself when we first included the nearby field at the Garden House into the garden. In my case, the trees I planted initially on this new site for protection and year-round garden structure grew so fast that the open aspect which is such a key requirement to create an alpine meadow disappeared within a few years. Still, you win some, you lose some.

Sub-alpine meadows in the Rockies

At a gardening conference in Canada one of my fellow speakers showed a picture of alpines growing in the Rockies with the Indian paintbrushes, *Castilleja* species, looking wonderful, and I knew immediately that I had to see this scenery for myself. The following year, at midsummer, found us standing among these selfsame flowers at the top of Shrine Pass, near Vail in Colorado (see page 89). At a similar elevation

RIGHT *Red Indian paintbrushes, Castilleja species, dot a high alpine meadow in the Rockies, at Shrine Pass in Colorado, USA. This is a high meadow habitat comparable to that shown on page 86 in Switzerland.*

of over 3350 m (11,000 ft) above sea-level in the Swiss Alps you would be among the higher peaks with very little vegetation to be seen, but here the floral matrix was more akin to the vegetation to be found 1219 m (4000 ft) lower down the European slopes—except that Indian paintbrushes do not flower in Europe, whereas here they were magnificent. I knew they came in scarlet, but I did not expect to see them in pink, purple, yellow and orange as well. It is a great shame that to date their growability needle oscillates between the very difficult and next to impossible as I am certain that most gardeners would love to cultivate them. There is hope, though, as with an increasing awareness of native plants, some US nurseries are experimenting with growing paintbrushes. They have found that, since they are semi-parasitic, growing them among native North American grasses is proving quite successful, and that seed will germinate if sown directly among other native plants.

I must point out that my following comments are only from personal, very limited observations of how we saw plants growing in this southern section of the Rockies, and so probably constitute no more than generalizations. It seemed to me that above the tree line, which in this part of the Rockies seems to waver around 3500 m (11,500 ft), the vegetation tends towards being more tundra-like. With the best will in the world I cannot see how tundra has much, if any, relevance to our gardens, so we will quietly pass by that one. Below the tree line, as in the Swiss Alps, wherever the conifers grew the vegetation could change rapidly, large clearings tending towards the relatively short *Castilleja* matrix and then little patches of amazingly lush and tall herbaceous combinations around some of the streams, even at very high altitudes. In the *Castilleja*-dominated flora I loved the way the fire-blackened tree stumps studded the whole landscape, and together with the well-spaced conifers and distant mountain peaks, they form for me the leit-motiv of the whole region. It was also wonderful to see the bulbous *Zigadenus* and *Calochortus*, among many others, in their native

environment and the knowledge of where they were growing and what they were growing with has been stored on the imaginary paper-strewn floor of my mind's office for future reference. Of more immediate potential use to me were those lush stream-side plantings, not because of the actual plants involved, many of which may not grow in my climate, but because they can be represented by similar-looking plants which will. I would never have thought of growing *Aconitum* species in a mixture like this, and *Delphinium* species were filling the same role in other locations. Apart from the thrill of seeing these flowers in the wild in a lovely location, it reinforces a trend you see time and again of how plants grow in nature, but each time with subtle variations of colour combinations, textures and heights.

Coastal exposure

You do not have to go to the mountains, though, to see alpine plants growing naturally. Take a walk anywhere in the countryside where nature has the upper hand over the deadening effect of modern agriculture and is fully exposed to the elements, especially the wind, and there you will find plants adapted to the conditions. It could be a walk along coastal cliffs or any upland area, even on a smaller scale on the tops of some dry-stone walls or rocks with plants huddled tight into chinks and fissures to gain some small protection. I remember from my childhood little pockets of yellow stonecrop (*Sedum acre*) forming small communities with tiny dwarf ferns amid the maroon-stained foliage of herb robert (*Geranium robertianum*), miniaturized by the harsh conditions of its spartan lime mortar diet in which it grew atop the limestone walls alongside the lane where we lived. These plant groupings were on a perfect scale for the imagination of an enraptured seven-year-old boy. Forty years later I saw bigger, classier versions on rock outcrops in Swiss mountain valleys with brilliant blue gentians and pristine white mountain avens (*Dryas octopetala*) contributing to a tapestry of plants huddled into chinks for protection and creating a true, naturalistic alpine garden.

Inspiration from a Cornish clifftop

All too often, when faced with the challenging prospects of salt-laden winds and exposure, British home-owners of cliff-top coastal properties opt for the safe option of surrounding their houses with mop-head hydrangeas and conifers. If I see a white-washed bungalow surrounded by mop-head hydrangeas I almost involuntarily look around for the sea view, so synonymous have they become with coastal situations. Yet, with a little observation of wild plants adapted to these same conditions, we could open up gardening possibilities that are much more in harmony with these magnificent settings.

I saw several such bungalows with incongruous plants on a lovely part of the Cornish coast, at Kynance Cove. This part of the coastline is renowned for its fabulous rocky cliffs and secluded inlets, but we had come in late summer to see the heathland vegetation that grows on the cliff-tops. It is at this time of year that the Cornish heath (*Erica vagans*) flowers, covering acres with its pink and white flowers fading to rich russets. They grow mixed with yellow-flowered gorse, low shrubby roses and grasses, whose seed heads by this time are already bleached, with the whole lot kept low and compact by the constant battering of the Atlantic winds (see page 25). Among these low shrubs grows the sprawling bloody cranesbill *Geranium sanguineum* and every now and again a lichen-encrusted boulder will break the flatness. Occasionally these rocks form outcrops, populated by alpines and forming natural rock gardens (see page 92)—favourite haunts for rabbits, judging by the short sward that surrounds them. These little rabbit-mown lawns are repeated at irregular intervals throughout this shrubby matrix, and are only partially composed of grass, the majority of the sward being composed of low alpines growing on the flat with tiny bulbous plants coming up in between.

With the application of just a little imagination it would be possible to transform all of this combination (without the rabbits, it is to be hoped) into a very acceptable garden. Replace gorse with other more garden-worthy evergreen shrubs, such as low-growing *Cistus*, or *Berberis*, strengthen the grass element and widen the range of sprawling perennials, all the time keeping a similar balance to the original of rock, shrub and open space, and I can see a lovely garden emerging that would harmonize perfectly with its surroundings. Those open spaces could be expanded in places to create alpine lawns, forming rich spring and early summer tapestries of colour, and you could add interest and lengthen the flowering period by growing any number of bulbous plants to come up in between.

The grass theme could be strengthened by growing some of the graceful dieramas, assuming they will not mind the salty winds. If height is needed, wind-tolerant species such as sea buckthorn (*Hippophae rhamnoides*), mountain ashes (*Sorbus*) and tamarisks (*Tamarix*) could provide it while complementing the general theme. Before doing anything else you could landscape the ground into gentle slopes with occasional sheltered hollows where you could place your seats. In fact in many ways it would be easier to create this garden by clearing the ground to start with rather than attempting to exert control over an established cliff-top flora, but this would very much depend on individual circumstances. Far from being a problem site, it is a challenge I would love to face.

Hebridean machair

Creating a garden in an exposed, windswept location is always a challenge, but one way to overcome this problem is to follow nature's adaptation to this situation and choose plants that grow lower to the ground. Coastal locations are fairly obvious contenders for inspiration in this instance, and could produce some exhilarating gardening ideas. There cannot be many windier places than the Outer Hebrides, off the western coast of Scotland. The plants are, of course, adapted to these conditions, and this is home to a very special type of vegetation called machair.

OPPOSITE *Still in the Rockies in Colorado, but at a slightly lower elevation and in a damper location than the picture on pages 88–9, the matrix here is perhaps twice as tall, reaching 30–45 cm (12– 18 in). What consummate good taste the Almighty must have, with the pink paintbrushes here contrasting perfectly with the blue monkshoods, white bistorts and pink fleabanes.*

If you compare this photograph with that on page 135, which is of a meadow at a similar elevation in the Swiss Alps, there are obvious similarities, with different plants evolving very similarly on different continents to fill the same sort of ecological niche.

On exposed sections of parts of the islands the wind has blown limestone-rich sand, formed from shells, onto the strongly acidic peat-beds to create fertile meadows, rich in plant species. The incessant winds keep these plants low to the ground, often under 15 cm (6 in) high. In early summer these meadows form extraordinary tapestries of flowers, which vary according to the land management, and are favourite breeding grounds for many wading birds in particular.

In one manifestation, the machair forms a tight, grassy sward with daisies, white clover, eyebright (*Euphrasia*), wild thyme and orchids in countless number. In another, red clover, yellow violas, bright pink storksbills (*Erodium*), blue forget-me-nots, and violet-blue self-heal (*Prunella vulgaris*), join in the display. As it so happens, a very close copy of this mix, minus the orchids,

and substituting *Geranium sanguineum* for the storksbills, has fortuitously appeared in recent years, quite spontaneously, at the Garden House on the very fringes of the quarry garden where it abuts the Cottage Garden. I thought it was making a lovely natural grouping, without previously making any form of mental connection with these Scottish coastal grasslands. In other areas of the machair slightly lusher effects are created when the bright pink of *Erodium* species is joined by the blue-flowered green alkanet (*Pentaglottis sempervirens*) purple tufted vetch (*Vicia cracca*), red poppies (*Papaver*) and yellow corn marigold (*Chrysanthemum segetum*), all set off amid a haze of the rusty-red flowers of sorrel (*Rumex* species).

It is very easy to see countless variations of a machair-type vegetation working on relatively flat

BELOW A rock outcrop overlooks Kynance Cove in Cornwall, UK, with thrift or sea pink, Armeria maritima, and white sea campion, Silene vulgaris ssp. maritima, filling every available vacancy. These, together with the lichen-covered rocks themselves, make a very presentable natural rock garden.

sites in gardens near the sea. The principal feature in the evolution of the machair, notably the coarse sand topping off a fertile substrate, is exactly the same as the principle behind the South African Garden already discussed (see pages 62–4). However, without the dwarfing effect of those constant, coastal winds, it is possible that inland the rich soil or compost underneath the sand layer might make the plants grow a little too lushly, and therefore out of character. An alternative, if gardening away from the debilitating effects of such winds, is to increase the depth of sand and incorporate the fertility into the top (7.5 cm (3 in)). This would be especially useful on naturally occurring sandy soils where the poor fertility of the sand would help keep the matrix low and in scale.

I do not think you have to be gardening by the sea for the machair template to be a valid one, as even inland, this vegetation mix could make an inspirational garden in the right setting. This type of garden would work well in place of sizeable lawns that are open to the sky, creating an effect of previously mown grass returning to a romanticized natural state, and be much neater and more refined in the process than if the lawn were just left to grow untended.

Purely hypothetically, how would I go about turning a front lawn, like that at the Garden House, into a machair variation? Since our soil is a rich loam and it is essential that the plants do not grow too lushly, I would strip off the turf and probably 15 cm (6 in) of the topsoil as well, in order to reduce fertility. (If your soil is sandy there is no need to remove the turf, although you will still need to kill the grass by whatever method your conscience allows.) I would then spread 10–15 cm (4–6 in) of coarse sand over the whole site and rotavate this to incorporate the top 5–7.5 cm (2–3 in) of underlying soil. I would certainly spend some time trying to find a source of shell-sand, if possible, as not only would the limestone content neutralize the acidity of our soil, it would also show off the plants well.

Planting, as always, is a matter of personal preference. I would start by dividing the site into a central area where I intended to keep the sward particularly short, and the outer margins where it could be 2–5 cm (1–2 in) taller. In each case I would choose just four or five foundation plants to produce the main colour washes, and spread them unevenly to cover the area.

In the middle zone, I might locate various flowering shades of creeping thyme (*Thymus*), violet-blue self-heal (*Prunella vulgaris*), compact forms of *Geranium sanguineum*, white clover and *Sedum album* 'Coral Carpet' as the foundation plantings, because I know they work well together in other parts of the garden here. As an alternative to the geranium, that stalwart of exposed coastal locations, thrift (*Armeria maritima*), might produce an even better effect, so long as it stayed compact. I would leave sizeable gaps between these plants where I would plant smaller numbers of many other species, such as orchids and dwarf bulbs, and in places I would leave the sand bare. The foundation plantings alone would create a rich tapestry of lilac-blue and pinks in a multitude of shades during late spring and early and midsummer, with the secondary plantings extending the season to suit your own choice. What I would not plant, at least initially, is any grasses. This may seem a little strange as the machair itself is a grassland type, but, as is the case in many Swiss meadows, the majority of the sward is composed of broad-leaved species and not grasses. There is a practical reason for omitting them initially as well; they can spread so rapidly that the balance of the whole design would be very quickly lost, although I am sure that low-growing, tufted species would come in later in moderation when I could see where they would have most effect.

In the very slightly lusher marginal areas I might start with the yellow-flowered bird's-foot trefoil (*Lotus corniculatus*), purple tufted vetch (*Vicia cracca*) and rose-pink restharrow (*Ononis repens*), alongside *Geranium sanguineum* and self-heal which would help blend the two areas together. I would experiment with the first three before I planted them in any number to check they were not going to be too vigorous and get out

of proportion in the particular conditions of the chosen site. Any plant which derives its vernacular name from the capacity of its underground roots to bring a horse pulling a harrow to a halt, as is the case with restharrow, has to be treated with some caution. Once again, between these main plantings, I would leave gaps where I could experiment with a whole range of other plants, one of which for sure would be *Ranunculus gramineus* 'Pardal'. This southern European buttercup has low, grassy leaves, and in this form, open sprays of flowers reaching approximately 38 cm (15 in) high, rather like a large-flowered, dwarf meadow buttercup. This plant would be perfect for creating a yellow haze of gently swaying blooms whenever there was the slightest

LEFT *I planted these*
Geranium wallichianum
seedlings to run about
among the heathers and
soften their rather lumpy
outline. The grasses in the
background and Aster
sedifolius *in the front*
similarly help to soften
the overall effect, with the
dark green foliage of a
berberis kept clipped to
add structure. Later I
visited the Lizard
Peninsula in Cornwall,
UK, and saw these same
elements repeated in the
wild with native species
(see the photograph on
page 25).

wind movement. All of these plants, with the exception of the last-named buttercup, can be raised from seed and sown *in situ* if desired, but personally I would prefer to raise the seedlings elsewhere and then plant them out exactly where I wanted them. As far as maintenance is concerned, I can only say that the various elements of these combinations I have grown have needed little in the way of looking after, other than an annual tidy-up in early winter, with the removal of the old flowering stems. At this time, or in early spring, I also slip on my referee's hat to judge whether the balance of the community is being lost wherever self-heal, clovers and other rapid spreaders are involved and reduce their spread if necessary.

Heaths and grasses

Another adapted combination of plants for exposed situations, which I think would modify tastefully into a garden setting, can be found very commonly around the coasts of Britain, and is one I especially link with coastal cliff-tops. This is the place where grasses and heathers hunker down as low as they can, against the winds. I have seen a similar sort of grouping in places such as the New Forest in Hampshire, or along the margins of heaths nearly anywhere in the world, particularly where the heathers have been previously cut down. In the immediate years after this pruning, the heathers' regrowth produces neat, tight clumps of dark green foliage which contrasts superbly well with low-growing grasses, and it is this combination that I think would form the basis for a lovely section of a garden, especially if the soil were sandy.

Once again, I have planted little pockets of a similar type around the garden, but these combinations to date have been more by accident than design. I was thinking how good it might be to extend this into a much larger area, planting drifts and ribbons of heathers, interlocking and weaving their dark foliage colour among the grasses. The position for this garden might be on a sloping bank, or on the flat, as long as the site was sunny and open to the sky. As a garden feature, this heath and grass combination would sit very comfortably around the margins of the machair-type garden just discussed, having a coastal, edge of dune feel to it.

The key to this being successful, though, would be to use only one or two species of both grass and heather as the foundation planting, in order to give unity and coherence to the design. I would choose *Erica cinerea* as the heather. Its tiny leaf-size and dark, almost black-green foliage, together with the bright colours of its flowers, make it perfect as a foil for the dwarfest, daintiest-flowering grasses. For the grasses, I would be tempted to look among the festucas for possible candidates, as their blue-grey foliage hints at being wind-dried even before they come into flower. When the flowers of both heath and grass have faded they still consort well together, looking good for months, and this is before secondary interest and colour have been added with bulbs and low-growing herbaceous plants.

Borrowing from Barnsley House

Another idea for growing alpines in a naturalistic way was inspired by a visit to Rosemary Verey's garden at Barnsley House, in Gloucestershire. This mainly alpine collection was in a sunny position in the front garden. Here, she had an avenue of clipped Irish yew, *Taxus baccata* 'Fastigiata', planted either side of a path made of flat stones. Maybe the path had fallen into disrepair, or maybe she planned it from the outset (if so I take my hat off to her) but the gaps between the stones had been filled with low-growing alpines, notably rock roses (*Helianthemum*) in variety and the bronze foliaged, prostrate *Acaena microphylla*, with its red-tipped, burr-like heads of flowers. The red, yellow and orange flowers of the rock roses formed the basis of this early summer-flowering composition, and with the odd *Geranium sanguineum* variety growing among it created a wonderful effect in late spring and early summer. This is essentially a similar idea to the one I employed in the Quarry Garden (see pages 212–14), using rock roses instead of thymes as the core planting. Perhaps it worked as a naturalistic planting at Barnsley House because of the informality of the gaps and uneven stones and the use of a limited range of plants, not all of which are normally considered as alpines.

The principle of using just two or three species as the foundation plants is especially important with alpines in order to avoid a 'dotted' effect, but gaps between these core plants can be filled in any way your imagination takes you. They could be left plant-free, concentrating on the medium covering the soil, whether it be sand, gravel or rock, or, alternatively, the spaces between could be filled with an enormous range of different plants from spring bulbs onwards that will always remain secondary to the core plants. By that I mean these secondary gap-fillers should not be growing to the detriment of the main foundation plants or your main flush of flowering will be compromised.

I would like to create my own version of the Barnsley model, crossing it with the concept behind the Quarry Garden to create a hybrid with helianthemums, the more compact *Geranium sanguineum* varieties and creeping thymes forming the late spring and early summer flowering highlight, with early spring bulbs such as crocus and tulips followed by rhodohypoxis to extend the season. I envisage a wide, raised bed, elevated by 60 cm (2 ft) natural stone walls, so it would be easier for me to perch on the edge and weed as well as being able to appreciate the flowers more. To get a natural effect you do need to allow self-seeding to take place and the problem here is that weed species also take advantage of the relaxed seeding regime. Consequently I would not pave the whole area as once weeds get established among the cracks it would be difficult to get them out, but small areas of stones laid flat as a rock pavement with wide spaces between the stones would make a lovely height and textural contrast as well as providing a congenial home for prostrate plants like thymes and acaenas.

More structure could be provided by placing a few rounded large stones among the plants or by growing a few dwarf conifers. The advantage of dark-leaved conifers is the foil they provide to the flowers. As many a photographer or artist will tell you, sunlit flowers against a dark background is a proven winner. Top of the conifer list I would use would be the dwarf *Pinus mugo* or any of its varieties, whose scale would be in keeping with all but the smallest or largest schemes. I can see this working in an area as small as 8.5 sq m (10 sq yd) or as large as half a tennis court, in an informal, gently undulating bed or a formal raised one near the house. The key to the overall naturalness of this garden would lie in the core planting being restricted to a small number of species being repeated throughout the scheme—the smaller the site the smaller the number of species.

4 Impressionism with perennials

A garden that has its origins in a natural landscape should look natural at any time of the year, yet on the ground I am always more comfortable explaining the philosophy to a potentially sceptical audience when the herbaceous plants are in growth and preferably in flower. Without the benefit of the flowers in front of you, or, as a poor second-best, a photograph of them, some of the concepts can be a little challenging to explain. Perennials were the mainstay when I first experimented with the general ideas of a more relaxed planting style in the Walled Garden.

Part of my learning curve involved allowing self-seeding to take place and this meant reprogramming Tom Hooper, my fellow gardener, who had been working here since the garden's inception in 1946. 'Big Tom', as we called him, partly to differentiate him from our son of the same name, and partly because he was nearly as broad across the shoulders as he was tall, eventually came around to this different weeding regime and was a revelation. He could recognize every plant in the garden at the cotyledon stage of a seedling's development, but knew the name of none of them. He was happy to change from his old habits of removing every seedling, no matter what it was, to a selective system when he saw how self-seeded plants put themselves occasionally into the most wonderful places. Among the *Euphorbia griffithii* 'Fireglow' (see opposite), for example, *Tellima grandiflora* with its 1 m (3¼ ft) high spikes of tiny, frilly bells had seeded down from the terrace above and seemed quite happy to be completely overshadowed later in the season by the euphorbia as it continued to grow.

Controlled self-seeding

I allow some plants to self-seed within a limited area of the garden. The white-flowered annual

RIGHT *A medley of self-seeded plants colonize an out-of-the-way corner of the Garden House. The shuttlecock ferns, seemingly harmless in the background, are capable of totally dominating the planting if they are not carefully controlled.*

PREVIOUS PAGE *The tiny creamy bells of* Tellima grandiflora *lighten a clump of* Euphorbia griffithii *'Fireglow'. Even these casual combinations need keeping an eye on to keep the balance right, as, like the shuttlecock fern in the photograph on the right, the Tellima has proved itself capable of overpowering and killing the almost indestructible spurge by sheer weight of numbers—a flowery David and Goliath tale.*

honesty, *Lunaria annua* var. *albiflora*, and the pink, white or blue forms of the Spanish bluebell, *Scilla campanulata*, have all been allowed to spread unhindered under the shrubs on the tennis court level of the Walled Garden, but not on any of the other terraces. The Welsh poppy, *Meconopsis cambrica*, with its fresh green leaves, is allowed to put itself in either of its orange or yellow manifestations anywhere in the garden, but has never naturalized to the extent I saw it doing at Hidcote Manor in Gloucestershire. There, under quite a high canopy of deciduous shrubs, was a solid carpet of these delicate, fresh-looking poppies with that wonderful 'oranges and lemons' colour combination. At the Garden House, I have since been able to get the orange-red variety 'Frances Perry' to start spreading slowly but it is nowhere near as prolific to date as the paler orange and yellow forms.

The Sunken Garden is the lowest point of the Walled Garden and has always been slightly off the main visitor circuit, so with Tom and me constantly chasing our tails to keep on top of the weeds in more noticeable locations, it tended to get pushed down the weeding priority list. The result was that the dark blue *Aquilegia alpina* 'Hensol Harebell', purple *Geranium phaeum*, Welsh poppies, bright yellow *Hieracium maculatum*, bluebells and Jacob's ladders (*Polemonium caeruleum*) all introduced themselves by seeding (see opposite), growing among the widely spaced shuttlecocks of the fern *Matteuccia struthiopteris*. One of the few times we did weed this area was in the early spring to remove the smaller *Matteuccia* crowns, so on an annual basis the cleared, disturbed ground where they were taken from was clearly high-value real estate for these flowering interlopers.

This shuttlecock fern, to my mind, is much improved by removing many of the crowns, allowing you to appreciate fully the elegant vase shape of the emerging croziers. In the ensuing years since the photograph opposite was taken the ferns have crowded just about everything else out, so I must get back in there and thin them

out again. For many years, though, while the ferns were being annually thinned, the Sunken Garden was imbued with the feel of a community of plants in a stable, natural equilibrium, a state of affairs that I had only ever seen elsewhere in similarly semi-neglected parts of gardens or in the wild.

Tom's patience and eyesight were amazing. Spending a whole day painstakingly weeding New Zealand cress from a bed crammed with tiny rhodohypoxis roots, for example, takes both in large measure. I had to take what he said with a pinch of salt, though; he was very proud of his sharp eyesight and since he was aware that I was slightly short-sighted, I never knew whether to believe him or not when he said, for example, he could see an old dog fox with a black tip to its tail and a slight limp half a mile away.

One day I looked up and, seeing a strange vapour trail from a passing jet, shouted across to Tom to have a look. His reply of 'Yeah, it's got carburettor problems', from a man whose entire mechanical knowledge was limited to changing a spark-plug, was however a bit too much even for him. He loved every inch of the Garden House with a deep, unspoken countryman's passion, and once he had decided that he trusted my judgement he did so unreservedly through thick and thin, for which I am eternally grateful. He was a wonderful man and a rock upon whom we could all depend, who gave fifty-three years of his life to working here before he passed on in February, 2000.

You allow some plants to self-seed at your peril, as Tom Hooper was only too well aware. He knew that if you gave in to temptation with a plant such as *Campanula lactiflora* and left those cute little seedlings to grow for just a few months, their deep roots become very difficult to remove and those leafy tops can very quickly kill more refined neighbours by simply swamping them. It is a lesson I am currently relearning the hard way in the newer garden, where this campanula species has taken an especial liking to the sand top-dressing on the periphery of the African Garden.

Rapid runners

Spreading by seeding is vitally important for creating a wilder look, but increasing by underground runners can be very useful, too, at times. The spreading roots of the filipendulas are fine, creating bold clumps, but the plants really are quite anti-social, not wanting to share their patch of land with anything else during their main growing season, partly as a result of their large leaves preventing light reaching would-be neighbours. However, they do not start into rapid growth early in the year, enabling me to grow certain spring-flowering plants in the same space. Any plant that allows you to do this is thereby doubling the flowering season of any given spot and is especially welcome. Late-emerging hostas and rodgersias of all sorts are surprisingly good at this, allowing earlier-flowering bulbs and woodlanders to grow among their roots. I have snowdrops (*Galanthus*) and wood anemones (*Anemone nemorosa*) growing in the crowns of hostas such as *Hosta sieboldiana*, while blue wood anemones, and even the much taller Spanish bluebells, *Scilla campanulata*, look particularly good flowering among the bronze-copper young growths of rodgersias such as *Rodgersia pinnata* 'Superba' or *R. aesculifolia*.

The tall filipendulas, especially *Filipendula rubra* 'Venusta', also emerge from the ground in the spring with coppery-coloured leaves and produce a magnificent display every year with the massed flowers of the double white wood anemone, *A. nemorosa* 'Vestal', colonizing the same space. I look forward to this annual chance combination, admiring the anemones' opportunism and capacity to seize the moment, as this filipendula is a murderous villain with plants that hold their leaves later into the season, capable of overpowering almost anything.

There are not many plants that evoke in me such a strong sense of claustrophobia as I get right in among this filipendula to thin out its growth. It may also have something to do with the cloying, slightly sickly smell it emits when it is damaged. The large original clump of *Rodgersia pinnata* 'Buckland Beauty', whose leaves reached 1 m (3¼ ft) high, was all but obliterated in one season by this filipendula while my attention was focused elsewhere that year.

I think this doubling-up works with these perennials because they have fleshy roots, an arrangement that allows plenty of soil to remain between them. In contrast to this, an astilbe, for example, has a solid mass of roots that claims every scrap of moisture or nutrients available and brooks no companion plants. Compare this with a plant that most of us might have sleepless nights over, namely creeping willowherb, or fireweed as it is known in America (*Epilobium angustifolium*). This is most definitely not a plant

for our gardens on account of its impossibly invasive roots. However, its narrow leaves and widely running roots do allow other plants within the confines of its territory, even during its main growing season. This is not an option I would recommend to anyone with the ordinary pink species, but is certainly a possibility with the white variety *E. angustifolium* var. *album* and the two-tone pale pink variety *E. angustifolium* 'Stahl Rose', both of which will run about, happily popping up here and there among other plants. This is an extremely useful habit for helping to produce informal planting schemes. The trick to encourage it to flower well is to chop its roots, *in situ*, into smaller sections with a spade during the winter months.

OPPOSITE *Stately spires of* Lobelia tupa *grow together with one of the plume poppies,* Macleaya cordata, *out of an understorey of* Lysimachia clethroides.

BELOW *Late spring in the Cottage Garden finds aquilegias in full flower. Carefully choosing trees and shrubs and allowing wild flowers, such as campion and buttercups, to infiltrate the borders has blurred the boundary between garden and landscape .*

Another very gentle runner, *Lobelia tupa*, creates a rather more exotic effect. It is hard to imagine a plant that could be much more different to the little annual blue bedding lobelias so synonymous with hanging baskets. A native of Chile, *L. tupa* has grown up to 1.8 m (6 ft) with us on occasions, but is more often slightly less than this. The unnamed form we grow has dark red flowers (see page 102) and has been growing unprotected in this same spot for more than twenty years, though the taller-growing form with flowers more orange in colour is, I am told, not so hardy. Here at the Garden House I planted the red form near the *Macleaya cordata* and *Lysimachia clethroides* and the various plants grew towards and eventually into each other over a number of years. It was recurring fortuitous accidents such as this that I wanted to create deliberately when I extended the garden into our 1.6 ha (4 acre) field.

The inspiration for the Cottage Garden

With hindsight, the trip we made to Crete, ostensibly to see the orchids there, was both the catalyst and the coalescence for my ideas on natural planting for the Cottage Garden here at the Garden House (see pages 19–23). The view over Buckland Monachorum (see page 27) was the main reason I wanted to include the field in the garden in the first place. Back in 1979 I had persuaded Lionel Fortescue to allow me to extend an arm of the garden to include the Dell, a group of turkey oaks growing in the old infilled quarry, and it was from here that there was a marvellous view looking nearly due west into Cornwall. The Dell was, however, situated in a very quiet corner of the garden and only a tiny percentage of our visitors ever made the small walk over to see the view, so I was determined that in the new extended garden it would become our trump card, one that nobody could possibly miss. I planned it so that all of the new garden would revolve around this central view over the church in Buckland and

further onto the Cornish hills, but I needed a design that would harmonize with the landscape, so that wherever you stood you would not know where the garden finished and the surrounding countryside began.

Initially, I had not intended the borders surrounding the cottage to be based on Cretan wild flowers at all, as we had been sent a lot of seed from South Africa. These were mostly annuals, so my intention was to have more of a South African colouring to the area, with bright oranges and reds. This concept died a rapid death, first because these colours looked ill at ease in this site, and secondly as the lessons of our Cretan trip sank in I realized this was the place to attempt my Cretan experiment.

In Greece, wild flowers are very often found concentrated around old ruins, walls or piles of stones. The preponderance of wild flowers on stony ground or clustered around stone walls is almost certainly just a historical result of fields being cleared of rocks and stones to allow more productive cultivation to take place. This leaves the marginal peripheral areas for the wild flowers to move into and over the years to evolve into flower-rich tapestries.

Crete reinforced the idea that had been in my memory since my childhood forays into the Mendips, that flowers can look sensational against a backdrop of stone. I have always considered that abandoned buildings reclaimed by nature are exceptionally romantic, hinting of a quieter bygone age, and little stone barns were a favourite haunt of mine in my early youth. The area of ground where the Cottage Garden now stands overlooks a landscape dotted with small barns, and so it seemed a very obvious place on which to create my own 'ruin'—a logical way of linking the wonderful surrounding landscape with the new garden as well as reminding me of earlier happy days. Surrounding many little barns in my childhood were often areas of wasteland where farm machinery lay slowly rusting and patches of stinging nettles and brambles grew on the remains of long-forgotten dung heaps. Here was where the chickens always scratched and

the grass snakes would lay their eggs. Not ideal fodder, I grant, from which to base a garden design, but substitute shrub roses for brambles, a sea of flowers for stinging nettles, and perhaps a granite trough for that rusting machinery and a very different picture starts to emerge: one of an old building, worn down over countless years and reclaimed not by nature but by a natural garden—a romantic's paradise.

Highs and lows

The flower beds of this garden area were raised slightly with just about anything I could lay my hands on: old potting compost, upturned turves and, most significantly, our own garden compost. Properly made compost heaps are supposed to be weed-free, but not so mine, I am afraid. Our haphazard compost-making produces wave after wave of mustard-and-cress-type germination and just on the odd chance that something interesting might turn up we have always hand-weeded it. It was this compost-generated seeding and then the self-seeding of plants that I had put in, which initially included Californian poppies (*Eschscholzia*) and wild carrot (*Daucus carota*), that eventually gave this whole area its distinctive, natural feel. They were magnificent for a year or two when the beds were still quite new and the plants had plenty of air and light to encourage them, but as taller herbaceous plants increasingly seeded themselves around, the smaller species, including poppies of all kinds, were squeezed out. Having now seen these poppies growing in their native California I can see why they took exception to taller, overpowering neighbours, as in the wild they mostly grow on open hillsides alongside plants that are generally smaller than themselves.

ABOVE *This wide-angle shot shows the bones of the Cottage Garden in midwinter. The low walls, sparse planting of shrubs and gentle sculpting of the land itself provide a minimum of structural elements so that the summer flowers are not overshadowed by any 'tricksy' garden design.*

OVERLEAF *Different aspects of the Cottage Garden seen through the seasons.*

There was one low-growing plant that seemed to thrive between the taller members of the Cottage Garden, and this was *Viola cornuta*. I cannot remember now whether the lilac *Viola cornuta* Lilacina Group appeared of its own volition between the poppies coming up from seed from my compost, or if I planted the originals, but the effect was so good I was only too happy to let the viola continue spreading itself between them. Even when the poppies were squeezed out by taller plants, the viola continued to be content to understorey taller herbaceous plants. I was surprised by its persistence until eventually I remembered that several violas I have seen in the wild occupy just this ecological niche. How many times must I have seen the British native pansies *Viola arvensis* and *V. tricolor* under the canopy of taller-growing weeds or cereal crops without making a connection? In another corner of the same part of the garden, the white and lilac forms of *V. cornuta* seeded themselves side by side and grew into a wonderfully informal jumble of flowers with the small pink and white daisies of *Erigeron karvinskianus* scrambling among them—not easy to plan for, but lovely when it happens.

Ebb and flow

Still, gardening is all about swings and roundabouts. While the poppies have mostly gone, other plants, whose seeds had been lying dormant in the compost I had used to make up the beds, have come along and become mainstays. Tough plants, such as the 1.2 m (4 ft) *Campanula lactiflora*, have gradually squeezed out frailer species. Rather than dwell on the loss of a particular plant grouping I chose to go with the flow, and modify the effects created in this area by staying with those plants that seemed most at home there. Since I had tried nearly four hundred different types of plant in the Cottage Garden in the first few years from its inception, it was not any great hardship to wait and see which ones had the staying power to last the course.

In the earlier years, when the photograph opposite was taken, the main flowering period for the Cottage Garden was early summer onwards, perhaps peaking in midsummer, but over recent years this has changed slightly. The emphasis has very gently swung towards an earlier peak, mainly because of the double-flowered aquilegias, the columbines or 'granny's bonnets' which have become such a feature of this garden now in late spring. I had admired the flowers of double aquilegias for many years and had grown them in pots where they produced a few flowers to enjoy, but it was not until I saw them in Ray Brown's trial beds at his Plantworld garden and nursery near Torquay in Devon that I realized what fantastic garden plants they can be. Ray had been breeding and selecting aquilegias and had built up some wonderful fully double and pompom forms in lovely colours and with exquisite individual flower shape when seen at close quarters. Suddenly all the granny's bonnets we had in pots, and others we raised from Ray's seeds, were planted around the fringes of the Cottage Garden, keeping them as far apart from each other as we could so they would not easily hybridize with each other. There was no chance of stopping that from happening, though, as these grannies are decidedly immoral. However, I do not see how anybody could really complain when you see what their liaisons have produced.

Breaking my own rules

A general principle I had laid down for myself when I was planting this Cretan area was that because the view was so integral with this part of the garden, any plants I put in should have a general similarity to our own British natives. This part of the garden may have been inspired by the wild Cretan flowers and the habitats they grew in there, but it was obviously sited in an English landscape and needed to blend seamlessly into this setting. I hoped in this way to strengthen the link between garden and landscape. Consequently, I initially stayed clear of the big, bold

RIGHT *This picture shows the same area of planting as the photograph on the previous page, but taken from a different angle. The colour effect from this viewpoint is overwhelmingly yellow and blue from the efforts of* Anthemis tinctoria *and* Campanula lactiflora *respectively. By selectively cutting back some of the campanulas prior to flowering at various heights it is possible to delay their flowering, thereby extending the display period as well as breaking up the flatness of their structural outline, which is something that can become a problem when one species dominates.*

flowers of iris species, for example, but my wife Ros, who is an artist, was very enthusiastic about them and we could not resist buying a few bearded irises when visiting nurseries, even though I had no idea where I was going to plant them. The problem with bearded irises in our wet climate is that they need an open, sunny and well-drained position, which was not easy for us to provide at that time. One of the few places we had with such conditions was in the newly formed Cottage Garden, and since I knew these irises would look good against the low stone walls, I almost

It was only a short step to using another iris species, *Iris sibirica*, which would be more compatible with the overall planting themes of this Cretan area and rather less prone to the slug damage that had been inflicted on the bearded irises. The *I. sibirica* varieties are another reason for the increased flower power during late spring. This species has scores of them, ranging from some with flowers as big as side plates to others with more refined, delicate flowers. Of these, I prefer the more wild-looking and delicate varieties such as 'Southcombe White' whose white flowers touched with blue have beautiful falls pencilled with markings like the crazed glazing on old porcelain. Nearly all of them have narrow green leaves forming upright, gently arching clumps with the flowers held well above on graceful, self-supporting stems, and seem much more suited to mixing in with other generally upright perennials. The fact that *I. sibirica* bears a refined resemblance to our native flag iris, which can grow naturally in damp meadows, made me feel that I had not completely abandoned my original concept—not that it would matter if I had, as evolution is the name of the game with this type of gardening and rules, even self-imposed ones, are not what it is all about.

Colour domination

The slow introduction of the *Iris sibirica* varieties to join the aquilegias and natives such as pink campion (*Silene dioica*) and background buttercups (*Ranunculus acris* and *R. repens*) helps to provide the bulk of the flower interest in late spring and early summer, predominantly in the colour ranges of pink, white and blue. Later in the summer season the colour scheme from the same patch of land changes to mainly yellow and blue, with *Anthemis tinctoria* and native autumn hawkbit (*Leontodon autumnalis*) providing the bulk of the yellow, and *Campanula lactiflora* most of the blue.

These are not the only plants involved, as a glance at the photographs of the Cottage Garden

immediately broke one of my guiding principles. The bearded irises' grey foliage was not altogether convincing in this setting, seeming to me to belong better to a hotter and drier location, but the idea had been sown that iris flowers did not look at all out of place here.

RIGHT *The South American* Verbena bonariensis *is not reliably perennial, but seedlings germinating in the spring will easily be in flower by mid- to late summer. In the evening light, as is evident in this photograph; its flowers appear almost pink, yet most of the time they are more lavender-blue. Whatever the colour, it is a fabulous plant.*

will show, and they are not arranged in any conventional manner. Because we have become so ingrained with the notions of 'white gardens', 'yellow gardens', or 'hot-colour borders' there is a certain danger that saying the summer colour combination here is mostly blue and yellow will be interpreted as a statement that I have created a 'blue and yellow garden', when in fact it is anything but; there may at times be every colour in the rainbow present, but these secondary colours are spread throughout the scheme. Even the primary blue and yellow are dotted throughout the composition, sometimes aggregating together to form loose blocks and sometimes just dotted singly. I have found that the biggest pitfall to avoid when attempting planting like this is to spread the same plant out evenly over the space you intend it to occupy; you should aim instead for the way in which Impressionist painters may have applied their paints to the canvas. Colours mixed in this way do not produce colour clashes, and dots of what are considered to be tasteless clashing colours such as cerise and orange can produce instead a vibrant, zingy combination.

Planting for a 'dotting' effect

Suppose I am planting out a dozen specimens of a particular species, and want their flowers to drizzle through the entire scheme. Looking from the viewpoint I anticipate will be the main one, I start by putting the pots out in their intended positions, with perhaps a group of five placed where I want the biggest concentration of that colour to be, most likely slightly off-centre and towards the back of the bed. Then I will have a smaller group of perhaps three, offset to one side and to the front of the main group, with maybe two more positioned close together behind that central group but still visible from the main viewpoint. The remaining two I will put as singletons with definite daylight left between them and the central groups, and these will be placed almost as satellite moons might orbit their planets. The

effect I am trying to emulate is of a single plant in the wild that has gradually spread out from its original starting position (that is, the central group of five). Before actually planting any of them, I will walk around the whole bed and check that I have not placed them in too even a manner when viewed from any angle. If I have, I may need to squeeze the individuals in the groups closer together or pull the groups themselves further apart. The finished result will be of a loosely congregated concentration of that colour when seen from the main viewpoint, which changes to a more dotted, open effect from other angles.

This same pattern can be followed with other plants in the same area but with different numbers of individuals of any particular species, so that the overall scheme does not become too even. The different species will overlap and run through each other's territory, and by leaving some gaps unplanted to allow for self-seeding, or to allow for the introduction of very small numbers of completely different plants, we can start to achieve a natural effect. Creating 'randomness' takes a little practice, so if it all looks a little too even when you have finished, do not be afraid to change it. My usual mistake is not leaving big enough gaps between the groups of an individual species.

Summer indispensables

Other summer indispensables in the Cottage Garden are the violet-pink *Verbena bonariensis*, which changes colour depending on what time of the day you are looking at it. This is a fabulous plant for naturalistic plantings. It appeared in the new garden here of its own volition, coming up among the tomato seedlings in the compost used to make the beds, and quickly spread around, by self-seeding, in the gaps left between the plants I had deliberately introduced. Its thin, rigid, branching stems grow up to at least 1.2 m (4 ft) in height and are amazingly wind-tolerant and self-supporting, producing from early summer onwards a multitude of tiny heads of fragrant flowers, much beloved by butterflies and gardener alike. The joy of it for the natural gardener is its easy-going sociability, each individual taking up little ground space, but producing a transparent screen of violet-pink through which other plants can push their flower spikes. I have grown it to good effect in other parts of the garden with the slender, soft orange spikes of kniphofias, but there are not many plants that this stalwart will not complement.

The lacy white wild carrot (*Daucus carota*) also dots itself around by self-seeding and gives height and counterpoint lightness to the slightly heavy-looking campanulas. The flaw here of relying on the anthemis, verbena and carrot to hold things together during the summer is that they are all sensitive to excessive winter wet, and if we get an exceptionally rainy season these three mainstays can be all but absent the following year. In an attempt to minimize this potential loss I have started to introduce more grasses, notably *Stipa tenuissima*. This stipa is a wonderful grass that flowers in early summer but then hangs on to its bleached flower heads right through to the following spring, allowing you to use this neutral colour as a foil to other flowers that would otherwise tend to merge with their background.

Last year I planted the purple-leaved *Angelica sylvestris* 'Purpurea' with its cow-parsley heads of dusky pink flowers near the stipa, close to where a pale yellow evening primrose, *Oenothera stricta* 'Sulphurea', had seeded, and it was a terrific combination. The angelica unfortunately is biennial, so seed needs to be saved, but it is a plant I do not intend to be without in the future. The same could also be said about the oenothera, which is definitely on my list of favourite plants.

Another subtle purple-leaved plant is *Cryptotaenia japonica* f. *atropurpurea*, whose branching yet upright form looks lovely jumbled in with other plants like the bright yellow-flowered *Oenothera fruticosa* 'Fyrverkeri' ('Fireworks'), or coming up among pink campion. Although the tiny mauve flowers are almost insignificant, its purple leaves look scrumptious during early

summer and indeed the Japanese grow it as a vegetable, albeit in the green-leaved form.

The planting in the Cottage Garden on slightly raised beds is an adaption in our high rainfall area, with 150 cm (60 in) each year, to drain surplus water away from the plants which may well not be necessary in many other areas. However, allowing the soil fertility to diminish is likely to be universal. Although the beds were initially made up with good, rich compost, they have not been fertilized since and it is noticeable how the overall height of the plants is gradually getting lower. This, believe it or not, is a good thing as it makes individual plants less robust, so allowing more light to reach a greater surface area, which in turn promotes a richer, more varied flora. It is not by accident that the florally richest areas of the world have poor soils.

Managing the wildness

Although the overall effect of this Cretan area still retains the key elements I had identified from the original landscape (see pages 19–22), it may give the impression to some people of throwing handfuls of seed in the air and trusting to luck for the desired result. The reality is a little more mundane. Careful and time-consuming hand-weeding by knowledgeable practitioners is needed in the spring until the foliage canopy closes over. Aggressive, non-sociable species such as foxgloves (*Digitalis*), creeping buttercup (*Ranunculus repens*), dandelions (*Taraxacum officinale*) and native grasses are completely removed. Weeds, such as pink campion (*Silene dioica*), that we do allow and other prolific self-seeders such as *Anthemis tinctoria*, *Alchemilla mollis*, *Lychnis coronaria* and *Achillea* are thinned into selected areas. All other plants are left, irrespective of how close they may be growing together. In the autumn everything is cut down and the same weeding regime as in the spring is followed in order to create space for the winter-germinating species to develop. The end result is that for these relatively short periods of concen-

LEFT *Equating sorrel with sophistication is certain to attract ridicule from some quarters. However, by adding lightness and unity to this combination of buttercups and oxeye daisies, this is exactly what the russet flowers of the common sorrel,* Rumex acetosa, *bring to the composition. Behind these natives, the exotic* Photinia villosa, *from Japan and China, has been pruned to give the effect of a deluxe hawthorn tree and should thicken out and improve year on year.*

RIGHT *There is nothing subtle about* Lobelia *'Kompliment Scharlach', with its dazzling scarlet flowers. However, it does not look out of place in a naturalistic planting when it is toned down by a surrounding wash of self-seeded double feverfew flowers.*

trated weeding we are rewarded with a trouble-free, almost labour-free sea of flowers for a further four or five months—an area that is never exactly the same from one year to the next and which, unfailingly, reminds me of those glorious displays of Cretan wild flowers.

Natives and weeds

Certain native plants or 'weeds' such as meadow buttercup (*Ranunculus acris*), pink campion (*Silene dioica*), hawkbit (*Leontodon autumnalis*), ox-eye daisies (*Leucanthemum vulgare*) and orange hawkweed (*Hieracium aurantiacum*) are encouraged to grow in moderation in the Cottage Garden, especially towards the edges with the adjoining traditional English wild-flower meadow, where their presence helps to blend the two gardens together. Moderation and these named 'weeds' are not words which sit comfortably together and you have to be aware of their extravagant lifestyle when in mixed company, or, for a trouble-free life, leave them to colonize a piece of ground entirely. Ox-eye daisies, particularly, carry a resonance of flower-filled meadows of childhood memories and it is wonderful to see them adapting to modern life by colonizing road verges and spreading by these arterial routes. This is more obvious in the USA, where you can follow the progress of orange hawkweed (or devil's paintbrush) and ox-eye daisies, both introduced species from Europe, along the highways in places such as New England.

I try to leave ox-eye daisies in the garden wherever I possibly can, but they are not the easiest plant to manage in a mixed plant community. Show them some bare soil and they will try to fill it with their seedlings and so vigorous are these that other species hardly get a look in. It is strange that in the wild Swiss hay meadows, ox-eye daisy is a perfectly well-behaved companion in the richest plant association in the alpine belt, just dotting its beautiful white daisies among the floral tapestry. It is possible that this well-behaved Swiss ox-eye is a dwarf alpine variant, rather like the smaller version that has evolved in response to the windswept conditions of the Lizard Peninsula in Cornwall. If this is the case, then it would be a plant well worth bringing into cultivation. Exactly the same applies to the common lady's mantle, *Alchemilla mollis*, a restrained constituent of the understorey in the same Swiss meadows, but turning into a vigorous, self-seeding megalomaniac in our gardens.

With both of these plants there may be a case to be made for omitting them from the initial seeding or planting of a new meadow-style area and then introducing them when your other meadow flower species are well established. In this way they get less of a sight of bare soil into which they can seed.

Ox-eye daisy alternatives

An alternative, especially on better-drained soils, which I am trying under different conditions in several places around the garden, is to plant a less vigorous, ox-eye daisy substitute, namely *Tanacetum niveum*. This is a little more refined, with smaller, more numerous flowers carried in more elegant sprays for a longer time than those of the ox-eye daisies. On our naturally quite heavy soil, this tanacetum self-seeds very little and is not a reliable overwinterer, but judging by the number of seedlings of it that appear on the sands of the African Garden here it may well be a very different story on lighter soils, both in its profligacy and its persistence.

An easier option, although it is not as refined as *Tanacetum niveum*, is to allow the feverfew, *T. parthenium*, to seed around. This plant does not seem to be particular as to soil and self-seeded young plants are quite amenable to being moved. I started by planting out a few named forms of double-flowered feverfew but, as with the aquilegias, they have since spawned a whole range of flower shapes from mostly singles, which I prefer in the wilder settings, through to the original double forms. In most new plantings of perennials I tend to allow the feverfew to come up wherever it wishes, providing as it does an informal wash of delicate white, softening my planted groups and any heavy-looking individuals, such as *Lobelia* 'Kompliment Scharlach' (see opposite).

Delphiniums

This capacity of feverfew to lighten plantings was really emphasized when I visited a nursery to buy some delphiniums for planting out in the Walled Garden, since these plants had been such a feature when we first came to the Garden House.

Delphiniums, as most people are only too well aware, are probably almost at the top of slugs' hit list. Mr Fortescue would have us conscientiously piling ashes on top of their crowns every winter and then watering them with a soluble slug repellent; you could walk around the garden in winter and tell exactly where the delphiniums were planted by the piles of ashes that had accumulated on top of them over the years. Even then, more often than not, as we uncovered them in the spring we would find that the shoots had been eaten off 10–15 cm (4–6in) below ground. As much as I like their stately blue spikes I did begin to wonder whether the trouble of growing them was really worthwhile.

The field beds of delphiniums at the nursery were magnificent, with colours ranging from pinks and whites and smoky blues to the more conventional electric blues we associate with this species, but undercarpeting the whole field was a wash of white from countless feverfew plants. I loved the majestic spikes soaring out of the sea of white, daisy-like flowers, and came home fired up by the challenge of using this most traditional of garden plants in a wilder setting.

The area I chose to try this was the Spring Garden, which had been planted up with spring-flowering shrubs, mostly evergreen azaleas, kept trimmed if necessary to about 1 m (3¼ ft) in height. When they are out of flower, these shrubs form tapestries of green which I felt could be spiced up with a bit of later colour. The plan has been to plant delphiniums in varying shades of blue in small groups and as individuals, with *Tanacetum niveum* providing the lower white foil in gaps created among the shrubs. The shrubs then help to conceal any low support the delphiniums may need.

I hope that by shortening the main stems of the delphiniums as they shoot skywards they will produce secondary, smaller flower spikes that will need less support. I have treated *Campanula lactiflora* in this way very successfully for many years and have found that if I cut back this campanula as hard as I like at any time throughout the early summer up to the time the first flowers are opening they need no additional support. By leaving some of the plants unpruned, staggering the cutting of others over fortnightly intervals, and varying the severity of the pruning I can also extend the flowering period of the plant by some four or five weeks. Because of their hollow stems, it remains to be seen whether this same technique will work as reliably with delphiniums, but if it does it will produce smaller, more numerous spikes rather than the traditional style of larger, fewer-flowering spikes.

I have planted these delphiniums on sloping ground, made up the soil with plenty of compost and then put a 10 cm (4 in) layer of sharp sand on top, which seems to act against slugs in the same way as the ashes used to. It is likely that as the nutritional potency of the underlying compost wears thin, the spikes of flowers will become smaller anyway.

It remains to be seen whether the delphiniums will be a success or not in the long term, but it makes little difference since it should be possible to modify the planting to include species that will give much the same visual effect while being a little easier to grow. I am thinking here of the monkshoods, *Aconitum* species, which would not be as dramatic as the delphiniums, nor have their colour range, but would definitely be easier to manage; I have seen both monkshoods and delphiniums growing wild at altitude in the Rockies of Colorado (see page 90), intermingling with other perennials between shrubs in just the same sort of environment that I am trying to create with the Spring Garden.

After flowering the delphiniums and tanacetum can be cut down, to be followed by other later-flowering upright perennials, such as purple loosestrife (*Lythrum salicaria* varieties), or any number of the herbaceous lobelias which have been planted between the delphiniums. These later plants continue the architectural spikiness in shades of pink, red or purple, once again set off and made to feel more natural by the calming influence of white feverfew. Since I have sufficient space I have indulged myself with a little excitement by planting *Salvia confertiflora*, whose narrow vivid scarlet flowers bring a certain pizzazz to the colour scheme, though this salvia will rarely overwinter outside here.

Hardy geraniums

I do not know why it happened, but this area of the garden where the delphiniums are now being tried is one of the few parts of the newer, more informal garden where geraniums do not feature. Generally I have used them extensively, from the larger growers such as *Geranium* 'Patricia' down to true alpines such as *G. cinereum*, with well over a hundred others in between. Some, such as *G. wallichianum* 'Buxtons Variety', are gentle sprawlers and only started to appear to be at home when allowed to scramble into neighbouring plants. Grown in this way, the white-centred, blue flowers of 'Buxtons Variety', which seem to get bluer as the season advances, will often hover among the supporting host's flowers, creating natural effects which are impossible to rely upon but are quite magical when they do occur.

A more vigorous sprawler is *Geranium* 'Ann Folkard', which I planted at the top of a 1.5 m (5ft) bank, hoping it would cascade down the slope in the same way as I had seen *Convolvulus althaeoides* doing in Crete. This it has done quite splendidly, but during its first year of establishment, I supplemented its effect by planting some large-flowered surfinias of exactly the same shade as the geranium on the bank. From a distance of 22 m (25 yd) or so it was impossible to tell them apart, but quite a few horticultural visitors lost interest when they got up close. Why should a geranium be *bona fide* gardening, but a surfinia somehow less worthy?

Geranium pyrenaicum 'Bill Wallis' is yet another sprawler with small flowers which is very useful for growing among other perennials. Small they may be but shy-flowering it is not, providing a constant diffuse cloud of cool lilac flowers. I love it for sprawling between taller plants where it gently sets off more flamboyant neighbours. On a much smaller scale, I can imagine the low-growing *G. cinereum* 'Carol' and *G.* 'Sugar Babe' looking fantastic planted in much the same way. You would need a sunny, open and ideally slightly raised bed, so that the drainage was adequate. Both of these fairly new varieties seem to be long-lasting and free-flowering, the flowers of 'Carol' veering towards red and those of 'Sugar Babe' more towards purple. Either would look good interplanted throughout a whole bed with blue grasses. Festucas such as *Festuca glauca* 'Elijah Blue' with its striking silver-blue leaves could be used towards the front, with maybe *Koeleria glauca* which is more handsome in flower in the middle areas, and then the slightly taller blue wheatgrass *Elymus magellanicus*, which is unbelievably blue, at the back.

Creeping along the ground among the festucas and geraniums at the front you could add the completely prostrate, blue-flowered *Pratia pedunculata*, which flowers for months from early summer onwards. This little lobelia relative can mound itself up over a period of years, but I have found you can cut it back to ground level in spring and it will happily green up again and flower as if nothing had happened. The advantage of doing this is that as long as it is kept tight, many spring bulbs will happily come up through the carpet of the pratia. I can visualize that dark red-purple flowers or campanula blue ones would be very dramatic when seen against this predominantly silver-foliaged, pink-flowered mini-landscape, preferably produced on plants that are architecturally spiky and standing no more than 45 cm (18 in) high—I might start looking among the alliums, roscoeas and adenophoras for possible candidates.

❖ ❖ ❖

RIGHT *The South African garden forms the foreground of a flower-filled Long Walk at the Garden House in early summer. Pale yellow* Potentilla recta *var. 'Sulphurea' weaves intricate and random patterns with white feverfews and orange Californian poppies. Further away the more solid white clumps of* Tanacetum niveum *and pale yellow evening primroses take the same colour combinations off into the distance. Although the colours are different, the same sort of basic colour distribution can be seen in the wild in the view of Langebaan on page 127.*

WHEN I LOOK BACK OVER the forty or so years I have been gardening, one of the most striking changes that has occurred is the vastly increased availability of perennial plants, such as geranium varieties, from the garden centres and nurseries that are everywhere to be found. In my father's era, herbaceous plants were difficult to buy over the counter and in our gardens they were gener-

ally confined to herbaceous borders, a traditionally labour-intensive way of growing them, what with the annual regimes of splitting, mulching, weeding, staking, dead-heading and cutting back. One reason for their current popularity, I am sure, is the trend towards less labour-intensive varieties which can look after themselves to a certain extent.

Growing perennials in a naturalistic setting, where we can enjoy them in a more relaxed way by welcoming their changing faces with the ebb and flow of the seasons, is perhaps just a logical extension of this less labour-intensive trend. Add in the ingredients of unpredictability and excitement caused by allowing self-seeding and not automatically weeding out native interlopers and

we can write our own rule books and, even more pertinently, free herbaceous perennials from the constraints of that old-style herbaceous border. Perhaps then it will be possible to view this group of plants as the beautiful individuals most of them are in their own right and we shall be able to grow them in as yet unimagined, exciting ways.

5 Meadow mixes

The dictionary definition of a meadow is a piece of grassland, especially one used for hay. Since no one looking at an unfamiliar field knows whether it is cut for hay or not, in general usage the term has come to mean any area in which wild flowers are growing in a grassy place. Indeed in common usage even the grass has been relegated in importance, since wild flowers in a stubble-field will still constitute a 'meadow'. It is not surprising then that Richard Mabey, a fount of knowledge on all things natural in the UK, described a meadow in the *Flora Brittanica* as 'now a "place of the mind" as much as a precisely defined ecological system'.

I think that what we mean by 'meadow gardening' depends on where we live. To a Briton, for example, it is likely to be an imaginary romantic fusion of a hay meadow with the wild flowers of arable land (two ecosystems that actually demand very different treatments), a verdant green carpet liberally sprinkled at flowering time in early summer with the likes of ox-eye daisies, buttercups, orchids, cowslips and blue scabious or bluebells.

Further south in Europe the grass element of the meadow is likely to diminish in importance, until you reach the Mediterranean region where the grass species are nowhere near as dominant. Here, for much of the year, a flower meadow would be predominantly brown and straw-coloured, with the architectural dried seed heads of long-gone spring flowers featuring, perhaps highlighted here and there by the brilliant blue of chicory flowers in summer.

American meadows

A general preconception held by British gardeners is that an American flower meadow is composed principally of a 1 m (3¼ ft) high matrix of mostly perennials, such as golden rod (*Solidago*), *Helianthus* species, *Rudbeckia* and michaelmas daisies (*Aster*) with a few grasses thrown in, flowering at the end of summer, and certainly a very different kettle of fish to the British version. However, it does not take much travelling around in the US for a visitor from the UK to realize that

there are scores of other meadow variations, all of which have possibilities for adapting to the British climate and garden settings.

The New England version

In New England, I saw, appropriately enough, natural variations on an English meadow where lesser hawkbit (*Leontodon taraxacoides*) is replaced by the more airy king devil, or yellow hawkweed (*Hieracium pratense*), which also turns out to be a European introduction. Together with the introduced ox-eye daisies (*Leucanthemum vulgare*) and orange hawkweed (*Hieracium aurantiacum*), they create an occasionally spectacular splash of roadside colour. This orange hawkweed is sometimes called devil's paintbrush from its capacity to spread so rapidly over a piece of land. A more sophisticated version seen in

southern Vermont (see left) has a lot more species present, notably the common fleabane, *Erigeron philadelphicus*, which adds a new colour in lilac blue, and would look very much at home under an English sky.

Lupin meadows

Altogether different and much more of a challenge to create would be another North American speciality—the lupin, or lupine, meadow. As any wild-flower enthusiast would be, I was aware of the spectacle of massed lupins from pictures of Texas blue-bonnets and from having seen for myself the desert and alpine lupines growing in the wild. All of these, though, are annuals and are quite short, so I was surprised to find naturalized perennial lupins reaching more than 1 m (3¼ ft) in height, covering acres in New Hampshire and becoming something of a local tourist honey-pot during early summer. Growing and flowering with them were silk weeds (*Asclepias* species), a very few tall grasses and a limited number of other perennials, some of which, such as golden rods, would have extended the flowering season later into summer.

The few reports I have read suggest these lupin meadows can be a little tricky to establish unless you have just the right type of soil, and handsome though they undoubtedly are in early summer I do not think I would want to replicate exactly such a planting in my garden. What might be more fun to make would be a modification based on these meadows. Instead of the capricious wild species apparently so dependent on the right soil type, you could choose one of the modern hybrid perennial lupins as the foundation planting, particularly one of the bluer varieties with a more open flower spike. I have grown several of the 'Gallery' strain and been impressed by how wild they look compared to the standard garden Russell lupins, but I am not sure that there are true breeding colour lines yet. There is no reason why the lupins all have to be blue and in the New England meadows there was the occasional pink plant, but a hotch-potch of colours is unlikely to look very natural. It

would be much better to restrict yourself to a single-colour lupin for the vast majority of the planting, whether it be white, yellow, red or the blue of the wild species.

The advantages of these modern hybrids is that they are easy to grow in a wide range of soil conditions and they flower for a longer time. By planting blocks and drifts of seed-raised blue lupins in an open sunny position, it should be possible to capture the spirit of the original on heavier soils that the wild species would not tolerate. This in turn might mean that in the gaps between the lupins you could grow a whole range of later-flowering perennials such as those associated with prairie planting—the golden rods, asters, rudbeckias, for example—to produce a late summer and early autumn wash of colour from the same site.

Californian meadows

The western side of the North American continent produces flower meadows of an altogether different type, sometimes in colour ranges that are not for the faint-hearted. Whole hillsides ablaze with brilliant orange Californian poppies (*Eschscholzia californicus*) in their native state is a sight not easily forgotten, even if it is a little short on subtlety. More refined than the wall-to-wall orange of the poppies in Antelope Valley in southern California are the flower displays in the Temblor hills, inland from San Luis Obispo, further upstate. The orange of the poppies is again the main constituent, but weaving between them are the frail yellow of tickseed (*Coreopsis* species), the blue of annual lupins, and patches of purple-pink owl clover (*Orthocarpus purpurascens*). It was this image, seen in photographs,

ABOVE *A meadow of naturalized perennial lupins in New Hampshire, USA. Flowering over a period of about a month, this meadow was just going past its best. However, in a garden setting, with a careful choice of other perennials, this flowering period could very easily be extended.*

that had me driving down every road I could find in the Temblor range attempting to find them, even though I knew we were almost a month too early. We could not even see the lush green growth of the emerging flowers that we assumed must be there if the meadows were going to flower in a few weeks time. Virtually all of the ground appeared to be covered in a low sward of closely cropped grass and we left, disappointed, to pursue the desert flowers further south which was the main purpose of our trip.

A week later we returned and were amazed to see the 'grassy' hillsides turning orange. What we had assumed to be grass was in fact the foliage of the plants we had hoped to see, which in an incredibly short space of time shoot up and flower. It was a real surprise to witness this explosively rapid growth, something that was very apparent again in Vermont at the lovely woodland garden at North Hill belonging to garden designers Joe Eck and Wayne Winterrowd. In their garden, all manner of lush perennials had made enormous growth by midsummer when just five weeks before they had yet to emerge from under the snow. In the relatively damp climate of the UK, plants tend not to be in any great rush as they have a very long growing season. I loved a description of the British climate by Geoffrey Charlesworth, an American gardening writer transplanted from Britain, as a 'long drawn out spring which sometimes never quite becomes summer and a winter of never-ending threats and promises'. It all serves as a timely reminder that the cosy situation British gardeners deem normal is anything but for many of the world's other gardeners.

The rapid growth of the Californian poppy meadows is not relevant to British gardeners but the close sward is, on at least two counts. First, it appeared on closer inspection that many of the poppies were reappearing each year as seedlings. This is important in that the plants do not have to behave as perennials, which they are not inclined to do in a climate with wet winters. Secondly, the hills on which they were often growing reminded me of the rabbit- and sheep-mown turf of coastal

and downland hills in the UK. Put the two together and if you are lucky enough to live on a coastal hill-top or have an area of ground which is sunny, open to the sky and well-drained you could create your own Californian poppy meadow. In a coastal site the orange of the poppies would look stunning against a blue sky (as they do in their homeland) and blue sea, both rather less common than I would wish in the UK.

A garden made in exactly the same way as the African Garden at the Garden House (see pages 62–3), with gentle sculpting of the beds and a thick layer of coarse sand, would adapt effortlessly to being a Californian garden. If I were making a Californian poppy meadow I would make the contours of the site much more gentle than I did for the African version, perhaps virtually flat as long as the soil was very well-drained. By clearing the ground first of all perennial weeds and grasses and coating the soil surface with 10 cm (4 in) of coarse sand you could produce an environment that the poppies would feel very much at home in.

Texan wild flowers—or not

In a diary I possess that features American wild flowers, there is a photograph of a flower meadow in Texas—an extensive area of large, rich red gaillardia flowers, with patches of pale yellow buckwheat *Eriogonum* species resembling cow parsley, and bright yellow evening primroses dotted among them. I was so smitten with this image that I would ask visiting horticulturists who might know something of North American wild flowers if they knew what time of year it might look like this. One of them, who has an encyclopaedic knowledge of plants in the wild, regarded the photograph with scarcely disguised disdain. Apparently these particular gaillardias are not North American wild flowers at all, and are more likely to be garden hybrids; he guessed they might have arrived there as a result of builders or landscapers meeting contractual obligations to sow wild flowers on roadside verges after some big development or other. He felt that the spraying of such seed mixtures was becoming

an ecological problem, diluting the purity of true wild flower populations—-an often-heard and valid argument against introduced species around the world, whether they be flora or fauna.

I felt disappointed at the time, thinking those Texan gaillardias were not after all eligible as a wild source for an idea, but now I feel I should trust my instincts. After all, what I am doing all the time is seeing something in nature, taking the essence of some part of it and re-creating what I can in my garden, often with bigger, bolder-flowered versions of the originals. There are in fact a couple of gaillardias native to North America, one of which, *Gaillardia pulchella*, is a red-flowered annual, so the principle of what I do is embodied exactly within that Texan picture. Our gardens are by very definition artificial, so a semi-natural landscape that has already been modified by human influence in some way just makes the business of envisaging it translocated to our gardens that bit easier. I now welcome ideas from any source, whether it be truly wild or not, and feel that being a purist will considerably limit the gardener's options.

Alien invasion

When, if ever, does an introduced species become accepted as a *bona fide* wild flower? There must be some point in the future, albeit a long way off, when those gaillardias, for instance, if they naturalize and spread, will be included among the native flora. The ox-eye daisies already have made this transition, as have such stalwarts in England as the sweet chestnut (*Castanea sativa*), holm oak (*Quercus ilex*) and horse chestnut (*Aesculus hippocastanum*), all of them introduced species—the last of which, with its place on the village green, is now symbolic of a romanticized rural idyll. It is quite a pleasant mental pastime to imagine which of the vast range of plant species introduced into our gardens over the last fifty years or so will make that leap and become naturalized into the country-side over the next few hundred years. Ecological purists will be seething but personally I welcome the added richness that these introduced plant species bring to the UK, as long as they are not categorized as native wild flowers.

However, in parts of the world with more equitable climates for rapid plant growth than the UK, such as South Africa, California and corners of Australia, this is a major problem. For example, Australian species of *Acacia* introduced to South Africa have completely swamped vast acreages of native, low-growing shrubby habitats, and alien annual grass species do enormous damage to the sensitive balance of flower-rich areas of the same country. The fantastic display of flowers in the images of Langebaan (see pages 59 and 127) were nowhere to be seen when I revisited recently, partly because the flowering is notoriously unreliable in any one spot, but mainly because of the rapid spread of the annual grasses swamping that delicate ecosystem.

The English wild-flower meadow

The standard advice on how to create an English wild-flower meadow is to strip off the topsoil and use the less fertile subsoil in which to grow the plants. I am sure this is very good advice, but it must also deter people from trying to make a wild-flower meadow in the first place. I already had a section of the field we were turning into the new garden where the lady's smock, *Cardamine pratensis*, was thick, especially in its semi-double form, so I thought we would adapt what we already had without reducing the last vestige of greenery to a passable impression of the front line in a World War 1 battle zone.

Our natural soil is quite rich, so I had to find a way of reducing the vigour of the more aggressive grass species to allow the other wild flowers space to grow. It is likely that the semi-parasitic yellow rattle would have achieved this over time but for a quicker result I chose to use a chemical aid, in the form of growth retardants. In the first year I sprayed the area of field I wanted to leave as the flower meadow twice, once in the summer and once in the winter, and this lessened the growth of the coarser grass species noticeably by the following year. Having reduced the overall vigour of the meadow I now spray the growth retardant once a year during early to midwinter. This is timed so that the spray halts the grass growth, allowing the flower species (which start growing a little later than the grass) a head start. It also means that any bulbous species, such as crocus, are still below ground when the spray is applied, as well as salving my conscience, as I reason that at this time of the year all the wildlife is either underground or has migrated for the winter. It is virtually the only chemical I spray other than the occasional herbicidal spray on the paths and personally I find no moral dilemma with an annual application in midwinter with the concept of a more natural approach to garden design as the results more than justify the means. In this area of meadow there are now more plant species and more wildlife generally, especially butterflies, than there were before, thanks almost entirely to this spraying regime.

I have used both maleic hydrazide and mefluidide and both have been very successful. The effect is almost like a chemical sheep, keeping the grass low and compact, which in turn gives the flowering plants elbow room to grow. Initially I sprayed the meadow during the growing season, when its effect is to stop the grass growing for six weeks or so. A significant side effect, especially after a few applications, is to weaken considerably the more dominant grass species. Yorkshire fog (*Holcus mollis*), a handsome but invasive species, all but disappeared, to be replaced over the next few years by brown top or common bent (*Agrostis tenuis*) and sweet vernal grass (*Anthoxanthum odoratum*). Both of these species are much to be welcomed in a flower meadow. Over a period of two years, with a single annual application of the growth retardant, the grass matrix

BELOW *One example of a fairly species-rich English wild-flower meadow, occurring on an acid soil in a high rainfall area. On poorer soils in drier areas the species count is often considerably greater.*

RIGHT *Alkaline soils are often better for the variety of wild flowers that occur on them. These flowers are growing on a narrow band of limy soil overlooking the sea in Plymouth, Devon, UK, where they occupy a steep bank. They form a taller matrix than the plants in the photograph on the previous page, with fewer grass species present, and are more akin to the Swiss hay meadows (see the photograph on pages 132–3).*

reduced in size from approximately 45 cm (18 in) to just over 15 cm (6 in) and wild-flower species such as hawkbit, meadow buttercup, yarrow, white clover, daisy and plantain all moved in to take advantage of the lack of competition. In addition this much shorter sward allowed me to plant any number of other species, such as blue-bells, cowslips, orchids, orange hawkweed and the dwarf blue *Camassia quamash*. Once the competition from the aggressive grass species has been reduced it is possible to start to have fun with the planting of a meadow, and I shall try the snake's head fritillaries and cowslips *Primula veris* for early colour, or maybe some exotic *Iris magnifica*, an easy Juno iris that grows in damp meadows in Turkestan.

On one occasion I was showing a professor of horticulture around the garden and mentioned I sprayed the grass with a retardant. He had been researching these chemicals for many years and told me that the same retardant effect could be achieved more cheaply and in a form more readily available for the general public by using a herbicide with the active ingredient of paraquat at a diluted rate. After one or two slightly embarrassing experiments I eventually worked out that paraquat does indeed work as a retardant if you use it in concentrations at least ten times more dilute than the recommended herbicidal use. One particular area I used this spray on, in late autumn, was the gently sloping banks of a little stream which had become overrun by couch grass where I was hoping to naturalize the tiny *Narcissus cyclamineus*. The following spring the couch was all but absent, the daffodils flowered and seeded prolifically in the thin moss cover, and, as an added bonus, were followed by a magnificent display of lady's smock (*Cardamine pratensis*), flowering in a place where none had been seen previously. It appeared the seeds of the lady's smock were there all along, waiting for a chance to germinate and grow.

The final procedure in the management of an English wild-flower meadow is the all-important annual cutting and removal of the hay. This is done either in late summer or early autumn, depending on how much you like the dried grass seed heads. In my meadow this was a major job in the early years, honing my scything skills and exercising little-used and consequently deeply complaining muscle groups, but in recent years as the sward has become lower and less thick a rotary mower has taken the place of the scythe, much to the relief of my abdominals. Once cut, it should be left for a few days for the seeds to fall out, and then the hay taken away. It usually takes about a month for the meadow to green up again, and I then keep it mown with a rotary mower to about 5 cm (2 in) until it is time to apply the retardant in early winter, after which it will not be touched again until late summer the following year. All this is very much in line with the traditional management of the original hay meadows. In these, the grazing animals will be excluded from the field between early spring and early to midsummer, when the grass is then cut for hay, and the stock brought back to graze the land until the following spring.

Swiss hay meadows

My existing English wild-flower meadow, although not large, does command that lovely view over the church in Buckland Monachorum, but was rather too rectangular in shape for my liking. It occurred to me that by reducing this area by half to a central, elongated, roughly kidney-shaped zone and then planting up the edges with a modified version of a Swiss hay meadow I could solve several problems at a stroke, as well as gaining a constant reminder of Switzerland. First it would break up that linear outline and secondly, planted to flower from late spring to midsummer, would extend and enhance the flowering of this area.

As in the Cottage Garden, I raised these peripheral beds by between 15 and 23 cm (6 and 9 in) to drain a little of any excess water, having first 'burnt off' the area to be converted with a herbicidal spray. I was not looking for a complete kill, since if some grasses survive to push their

way through the raised bed above, all well and good. Having said that, I did not have any anti-social grass species here in the first place—couch grass, for example, is not welcome anywhere in my garden.

The slopes in and around the village of Mürren in Switzerland, which are cut for hay every year in midsummer, were a wonderful 60 cm (2 ft) high mix of white silene, blue campanula, pale pink bistort, yellow and orange hawkbit and cerise-pink campion to name but a few (see left). The species diversity was really quite amazing, and I would guess it makes for very nutritious and tasty hay for the contented-looking cows, each with its own distinctively chimed bell hanging around its neck.

Unlike British wild-flower meadows, in the Swiss version grasses are all but absent, allowing for a greater diversity of broadleaf flowering species. To the average Briton a wild-flower meadow is 90 per cent grass and 10 per cent flowers but to a Swiss person, I suspect, it would be 90 per cent flowers and 10 per cent grass.

The plan was to use species we had seen in the Alps which I knew from previous experience grow well here, such as *Trollius* (globe flower), *Centaurea*, *Alchemilla* (lady's mantle) and *Chaerophyllum hirsutum*, together with plants native to both the Alps and the UK, such as buttercups, ox-eye daisies, campion, common rattle and hawkbit, to form the core planting. Added to these were garden selections of Swiss natives such as the variety 'Superba' of the common bistort (*Persicaria bistorta*), or the dark purple-red form 'Hadspen Blood' of the masterwort (*Astrantia major*), and smaller numbers of a whole raft of other plants, some of which arrived by themselves. This Swiss meadow requires different maintenance to an English meadow, needing to be cut down immediately after flowering to simulate the annual cutting for hay—the Swiss cut many of these meadows while they are still in full flower, thus allowing rapid regrowth in their short summers for subsequent regrazing. The objective here was to produce a virtually grass-free flowery mead with a Swiss flavour.

LEFT *This is part of a hay meadow in Mürren, Switzerland, with blue campanulas, yellow hawkbit, white bladderwort and pink clover predominating. Compare this with the photograph on page 129 of what is now considered a reasonably typical English wild-flower meadow, and the number of flowers in the Swiss version is obviously much greater. Grasses are present but as a minor constituent part, allowing the broad-leaved flowering plants space to proliferate. Perhaps in bygone times, before the widespread use of fertilizers, meadows such as this were more common in England, but as a template for a version in the garden it has a great deal of potential.*

ABOVE *This planting was loosely based on a Swiss hay meadow. Among the planted astrantias and geraniums, gaps were left for the pink campion and others to seed into. In full flower during early summer, everything will be cut down in mid-summer, similar to the mowing these meadows receive in the Alps.*

RIGHT *Another part of the garden inspired by the Swiss meadows. Here the spikes of bistort mix with blue centurea, ox-eye daisies and a lilac form of campion, all Swiss natives.*

Dark colour accents

There are similarities between certain plant communities of the Swiss Alps and the Rockies (compare the image right with that on page 90), which was brought home to me by the monkshoods (*Aconitum* species) of Shrine Pass, in Colorado, where they were growing in places in open meadows. The colours and species are obviously very different, but the general balance and effect are similar. The monkshoods however add a colour contrast and tall elegance missing from many of the Swiss versions I saw. Being married to an artist who likes to paint wild flowers, as I am, does concentrate your mind on how certain plants and colours in an ecosystem stand out from the crowd. Dark bluish-purple is one such colour, especially when you link it with the elegant form of the American monkshoods, but most dark colours have the same effect, making the lighter colours contrast even better. Among British native plants, even the humble ribwort plantain, *Plantago lanceolata*, called hard-heads, among other things, because of its small, dark flower heads, fulfils this contrasting role in a very demure way among our meadow flowers. It is the same principle as my clashing colours of cerise and orange that was mentioned earlier; a small amount of either a clashing or strongly contrasting colour makes all of the colours sing a clearer, brighter tune. I feel that it would be good idea to plant some monkshoods in a flowering meadow, although quite what I will plant with them is still not decided.

Camassias at home and abroad

The same contrast and structure produced by the monkshoods is provided in the Swiss meadow by the bulbous *Camassia leichtlinii*, with its dark blue flowers on 1.2 m (4 ft) stems in the early summer. This camassia is a major constituent of the display to be found on Yellow Island, off the coast of Washington state, in late spring and early summer, but in the wild growing rather less

tall. Here it forms a patchwork of dark blue, weaving its colour among the red of *Castilleja hispida* and the yellow of *Ranunculus montana*. Dotted among this extravagant carpet can be found smaller amounts of other flowers, including the nodding bells of the yellow form of *Fritillaria lanceolata* (see page 136).

This camassia is a great favourite of mine and is an important feature in other parts of the garden here in late spring, self-seeding itself around prolifically. When we arrived in 1978 there were just a couple of isolated clumps, one of creamy-white and the other of dark blue, but in the intervening years they have spread and the colour range has extended to include pale blues, pinks and every colour in between, always tall, refined and elegant. In contrast, *Camassia cusickii* is paler, less elegant, earlier and with much heavier basal

ABOVE *Great swathes of this particular area of Switzerland were covered by this yellow-rattle, turning the whole mountainside yellow. Yellow rattle,* Rhinanthus minor, *is semi-parasitic on grasses and as a consequence helps to reduce their vigour. For this reason it is extremely useful to plant it if you want to grow flowers among a grassy meadow.*

RIGHT *Yellow Island, off the coast of Washington state, USA, is a riot of dark blue quamash, red paintbrushes and yellow* Ranunculus montana, *creating their own sunshine. This species of quamash,* Camassia leichtlinii, *can grow to 1.5 m (5 ft) in gardens, but I have also seen it flowering at just 23 cm (9 in) in harsh conditions in southern Oregon, USA.*
(Photo: courtesy of Dan Hinkley)

ABOVE *Among the blaze of colour of Yellow Island are the more discreet hanging bells of the yellow form of* Fritillaria lanceolata.
(Photo: courtesy of Dan Hinkley)

leaves. I grow them both, but there are no prizes for guessing which one will be the first to the bonfire heap if space ever becomes a serious problem. No such difficulties exist with the smallest of the bunch, *Camassia quamash*, with its frail grassy leaves, dark blue flowers and a height of only 45 cm (18 in), which I use in the English wild-flower meadow as a wonderful colour contrast to the yellows of creeping and meadow buttercups.

Grassy-leaved perennials for meadow effects

Another of these grassy-leaved plants that look so good in a meadow-style planting is the perennial, white-flowered *Paradisea lusitanica*, growing up to 1.2 m (4 ft) high at flowering time in early summer. It is described as tender, a trait that it has shown no tendency towards in the good many years we have been growing it. It seems to relish moist soil conditions, so it has been an obvious candidate for planting out in my Swiss meadow as a substitute for the Swiss native St Bruno's lily, *Paradisea liliastrum*, which I have found to be nowhere near as easy to accommodate. It may make the purists grind their teeth in despair, but it makes no sense to me when trying to capture the richness of a Swiss hay meadow to persevere with an authentic plant that just clings onto life when there is a perfectly good look-alike from another area of the world that is easy to grow in the conditions on offer.

Another good substitute, flowering at half the height and not quite so refined, is *Anthericum ramosum*. This has very similar-looking flowers but on branching stems. I have grown it for years in our nursery, where it appears to need a bit of elbow room for its rather coarse leaves. Since it is lovely in flower I keep meaning to move it into a mixed community in the garden where its foliage may be semi-obscured, but it comes up so early in the winter that it is always too late by the time I get around to it.

Damp sites

Damp sites and permanently moist soils need not be a deterrent for a flower meadow. I have seen beautiful flower displays in alpine damp meadows with yellow trollius, the white-flowered *Ranunculus aconitifolius*, and countless spikes of rich purple orchids. Closer to home, one of our drier counties, Norfolk, is not normally associated with damp meadows, but some of the best I have seen were in the abandoned gravel workings of Pensthorpe, near Fakenham. These were full of meadow sweet, *Filipendula ulmaria*, yellow rattle (*Rhinanthus minor*) and ragged robin (*Lychnis flos-cuculi*) and would very easily adapt to a garden situation. I have read of damp hay meadows in Iran where wonderful displays of soft blue *Scilla persica* grow with blue-black *Bellevalia paradoxa*, orchids and, rather surprisingly, purple gladioli. I have been told of similar meadows in Eastern Europe and on the north-western Pacific coast of the US on Yellow Island, and I have also listened, green with envy, to intrepid souls telling me of huge drifts of yellow and purple candelabra primulas, *Primula sikkimensis* and *P. secundiflora*, growing in the Himalayas. I can imagine all of these and many other variations making lovely garden compositions.

My imagination lusts after 0.5 ha (1 acre) or so of low-lying ground with boggy soil, interlaced with small brackish ponds, seeps and meandering drainage streams. Here you could introduce a mix of favourite plants from one or many of those natural variations that are so numerous and varied in the wild. I fancy planting great drifts of yellow candelabra primulas following the water courses, intermingled with pinky-lilac *Cardamine raphanifolia*, or its paler, more elegant hybrid with *Cardamine pratensis*, *Cardamine* 'Buckland', which arose in the garden here, all of them occasionally fanning out to form pools of cool colour. Behind them I can envisage extensive patches of that camassia mix from Yellow Island with drifts of trollius running through them. Breaking the uniformity of height I could

ABOVE *A granite stone stands sentinel over the buttercups in the English flower meadow at the Garden House. Around the edges, the buttercups gently infiltrate the Swiss meadow beds, helping to blend the two areas. The hope was to augment the blue* Camassia quamash *with the pink spikes of orchids dotting the turf, but a fox 'ploughing' the whole area in search of grubs one winter caused a change of plan.*

have pockets of lower-growing plants around some of the smaller seeps, places where the orchids would thrive and look sensational among the sphagnum moss. Around the edges of these lower areas I could build up into the Iranian *Bell-evalia* and *Scilla* mix, and towards the periphery of the whole garden I could plant enormous drifts of *Filipendula* and some of the more elegant *Persicaria* such as 'Summer Dance'.

Weaving their haphazard way among this meadow would be paths following what dry ground there was available or supported on a board walk. The totality of this meadow would provide wash after wash of differing colour combinations from spring through to early autumn and it could be magnificent.

❖   ❖   ❖

JUST THINKING OF THESE NATURALLY occurring plant communities makes me realize how minuscule my knowledge of plants in the wild is, and reminds me of how much I want to see them with their enormous cache of gardening possibilities waiting to be unleashed. We need to get away from the restricted view of meadow gardening that we currently have in order to open up fully the possibilities and interpretations of wild meadows. Meadow gardening is undoubtedly a concept whose time has come, a concept that conjures the alluring possibility of recapturing the flower-filled fields of yesteryear and of reclaiming the idealized sentiments of a countryside lost in our childhoods. It is a phrase that plays on the consciences of gardeners wanting to do their bit for the environment—but more than all this, it is an exciting, untapped and beautiful sphere of gardening just waiting for us to explore.

LEFT *Foxgloves and ox-eye daisies rise above a carpet of* Geranium × oxonianum *in another part of the garden.*

6 Prairie, scrub and grasslands

In exposed parts of the UK, many plants become shaped and sculpted by the incessant assault from the prevailing south-westerly winds. Under such a heavy bombardment there is often only one possible direction the plant can grow, and that is downwind. In some ways I think it is reminiscent of our attitudes towards gardening in this country, with the weight of historical tradition being so great that we either go with the flow or have our creative new shoots obliterated by the gales. So long have we been blown along by these forces we have lost sight of the fact that there may be a different way. Even if we only blew in from the south the slight change of angle would open up previously unseen possibilities, and the further east and north we swung around the more exciting and unforeseen these opportunities would become.

I mention this now because I feel that to unlock the full potential of grasses we need to look with fresh eyes and from new directions at their uses. With grasses in particular there needs to be a re-education process in our minds that says our gardens do not have to be all green, with our lawns that impossible emerald shade the advertisers of fertilizers would have us believe is perfection. For many, perhaps most, of us this will still be the ideal, but let us open our eyes to the beauty of other colours as well. This is especially relevant in areas with sparse summer rainfall and high temperatures, where I marvel at the incongruity of little green oases around so

many hotels when I know how much water and effort it takes to keep them like this. Even at the Garden House, where in some years it seems to rain from beginning to end, the closely mown grassed areas will take on that tell-tale greyish cast that presages imminent and rapid decline when the temperatures hover around 28°C (82°F) for more than a few days. Yet green is what we must have, and so we slave and toil, and throw every available resource we can muster into achieving it.

A highly intelligent acquaintance of mine and keen amateur gardener, whom I know to be generally happy with my more naturalistic style,

admitted he found it difficult to grow excited by the ochre shades and bleached colours of dried stems and seed heads in gardens, and wondered if it was perhaps indicative of an advanced stage in a gardener's development. He may well be correct, but I think this attitude has more to do with our general and traditional perceptions of what a good garden should look like, as the same person is very familiar with how extraordinarily beautiful the combinations of wild flowers and landscapes are in South Africa, a place where green is not the overriding colour.

This preoccupation with the past is not actually as entrenched with grasses as it is with many other plants, partly because in gardening terms they have only become fashionable in the last twenty years or so, and gardeners are not quite sure yet how best to use them. Landscape designers are starting to warm to them for their year-round attributes, ease of cultivation and maintenance, and classic simplicity planted en masse, when set against large expanses of hard-surfacing or mown grass areas. Garden designers, too, are accentuating the potential of grasses for complementing architectural features, as is exemplified in the Sculpture Garden at RHS Rosemoor in Devon, where they are planted in stark contrast to other bold-foliaged plants and the linear lines of the sculptures themselves. They are good like this, too, but to my mind more in the category of modern art and minimalist living environs than the plant-rich gardens I prefer.

In real gardens, as opposed to amenity spaces where grasses have temporarily found their home, I get the impression that gardeners want to use them but are uncertain how to. They have become associated with imbuing a garden with a sense of wildness, but it takes more than the addition of a few grasses to make a garden more natural-looking. Substituting grasses for some of the blocks and drifts of herbaceous plants in a traditional, Jekyll-style planting is one manifestation of this, which has been perfected in Europe by Piet Oudolf in particular. It seems to me that if we look to the way grasses grow in the wild and in what type of combinations, we might find an exciting range of gardening possibilities.

As you would expect from a plant group that covers a larger part of the planet's land surface than any other, grasses are adapted to a bewildering variety of conditions and climates. They are the ultimate in wind-adapted plants, with all their reproductive mechanisms being wind complicit, from pollination to seed dispersal. From a gardener's point of view, they bring that elusive quality of movement onto the stage, as well as adding a general delicacy and lightness to the proceedings. So well adapted to windy conditions are they that grasses are often the dominant plant species of open, exposed places, covering

huge tracts of ground on the savannas, steppes and prairies in different parts of the world, and blanketing the upland fells and hills where little else is adapted to grow in our own country. This, of course, is all rather academic unless you garden in such conditions, but occasionally you come across grasses growing en masse in the wild in such a way that they create a beautiful picture in their own right.

The American southwest

The dried seed heads of the Indian rice grass, *Oryzopsis hymenoides*, are a wonderful foil for the sage-brush and pines in New Mexico and Arizona (see opposite). One of the commonest grasses we saw in the American southwest, it was once an important food grain for the Native Americans living there. I loved its delicate and airy flower heads and can imagine it forming the basis of a low planting in a section of garden, but I have a horrible suspicion that it would not take to our wet climate. Still, I shall see if the variety

ABOVE *Looking somewhat like a ghostly firework display frozen in time and now drained of colour, the seed-heads of the foxtail barley,* Hordeum jubatum, *demand a closer inspection.*

OPPOSITE *The bleached, almost white, seed-heads of the Indian rice grass billow through the brown stems of a long-finished flowering plant, and, together with the sage-brush and pines, form a suitable foreground to the awesome spectacle that is the Rio Grande in New Mexico.*

'Nezpar', selected for cold hardiness, will succeed if it is planted in the sand-topped beds of the African Garden here.

I hold out some hope for the Indian rice grass succeeding with us because growing with it along the roadsides of New Mexico was the foxtail barley or squirrel-tail grass, *Hordeum jubatum*, which grows beautifully for us, provided it is given an open position. This hardly produces enough seedlings on my heavy soil but where I have top-dressed with sand it seeds itself prolifically and is apparently a major pest of irrigated fields in some of the western states. Although this can be perennial in well-drained soils, more often than not it behaves as an annual. Fabulous as it looks for a couple of months from when it starts to flower, in late summer at the Garden House, the foxtail barley does become quite

untidy later, so I prefer to use it as a dot plant, or at least in small groups, among low-growing plants, rather than as the main constituent of a planting scheme.

Flowering from September and growing to about 1 m (3¼ ft) in height, the pink muhly grass (or, more descriptively, the pink hair grass), *Muhlenbergia capillaris*, has flower panicles that open pink and fade to light buff, creating a spectacular gossamer-fine haze. The clone 'Lenca' was selected by Ron Gass of Mountain States Nursery in Arizona for being especially good in this respect, as well as for displaying greater cold-hardiness. I think it unlikely that it will prove tolerant of my much wetter climate but it may still perform in the drier eastern parts of the UK, and if so, it could have a great future in grass-dominated garden schemes.

BELOW *The myriad radiating, needle-thin stems of* Nassella trichotoma *gradually pale with age and, with the grey-brown flowers producing a cloud all around the dome's extremities, create a memorable feature.*

Grasses and companion plants

A similar effect can be produced on a smaller scale and earlier in the season by planting *Nassella trichotoma*, one of the needle grasses. This looks singularly unimpressive in its first year, with pleasant enough very fine-textured, fresh green but rather anonymous foliage. Being at rather a loss as to where to plant it, I stuck it in on one of the quarry banks behind the creeping thymes as one of the transition plants leading from the prostrate alpines into the slightly taller shrubs and herbaceous plants beyond. This position proved to be perfect. The following year, in early summer, it made a 45 cm (18 in) high dome in flower, a delicate hazy cloud of silvery grey. In full flower it reminds me of one of those fibre-optic tablelamp decorations that were so popular during the 1970s.

The trump card was played however by the self-seeded arrival behind the *Nassella* of the pale yellow evening primrose, *Oenothera stricta* 'Sulphurea'. It is amazing how good this evening primrose looks with a whole range of grasses. For a short while after the flowers had gone and the seeds dropped from this grass, I would look at it occasionally on a summer's evening and tell myself I should clean off the flower stalks, but as it was only a single plant and rather a long walk back to the house to pick up my secateurs, I never quite got around to it. This was very fortunate for me again, because these spent stems gradually faded to a bleached white and remained looking good all winter, with the plant eventually getting tidied up as the stems started falling off the following spring. A grass that looks good all year is always welcome but one such as *Nassella trichotoma* that changes so dramatically with the seasons is even more valuable as it enables the gardener to alter the mood and colour combinations of that part of the garden through the year.

Nassella trichotoma could easily be a major element in a low swathe of grasses for a garden on a well-drained soil. I can envisage it planted on 30 cm (12 in) high banks creating hazy, silvery grey, transparent clouds on either side of a meandering dry valley, about 1.8 m (6 ft) wide, which is planted with pink and purple creeping thymes, or the equally prostrate, blue, summer-flowering *Pratia pedunculata*. This little snaking valley would be simplicity itself to make by digging out the dry 'water course' to perhaps a depth of about 23–30 cm (9–12 in) and spreading the excavated soil on either side to make the low 'hills'. Scattered among the grass we could grow the pale yellow *Oenothera stricta* 'Sulphurea' with its maroon stems and butterscotch faded flowers that bloom all through summer. The purple-leaved biennial *Angelica sylvestris* 'Purpurea' would provide contrast in colour and texture from early in the spring and look sumptuous later in the summer with its delicate, cow-parsley heads of dusky pink flowers dotted among the evening primrose. Add in the gracefully arching grassy foliage and wand-like flowering stems of the dieramas, from the diminutive 45 cm (18 in) high *Dierama dracomontanum* on the headlands to the 1.8 m (6 ft) high wands of *Dierama pulcherrimum* in the background, and perhaps you can see the beginnings of a grassy naturalistic garden beginning to take shape.

Between these foundation plantings I could add any number of other plants in small numbers without disturbing the overall balance, a little like adding seasoning to a culinary dish. Nor need this garden look spartan in the early spring, as the *Nassella* retreats to a neatish clump after the flowering stems are removed in late winter, which would create space between the individual plants for spring bulbs, especially if I mulched the raised beds with a 5–10 cm (2–4 in) layer of coarse sand. The dwarf tulip species, *Anemone blanda* and crocus could all look good early in the year, to be followed by the pale yellow *Gladiolus tristis* in late spring, with perhaps the 60 cm (2 ft) reddish-violet heads of *Allium pulchellum* and the similar but rich purple-red *A.* 'Purple Sensation' enhancing that colour range in early summer.

A steppe garden

All of the grasses I have mentioned so far could equally be the star billing of a similar garden to the model I have just described. The Mexican feather grass, *Stipa tenuissima*, has already proved its popularity, producing its pale ochre flowers on arching clumps, and I know from personal experience it looks fabulous when planted en masse in exactly the same sort of combinations as the *Nassella*. It is, however, a slightly bulkier grass and would lend itself more to perennial combinations than to a bulb and alpine mix. At Lady Farm near Bristol, owner Judy Pearce and her friend and garden designer Mary Payne have used it just like this, creating what they call their steppe garden.

This garden is a wonderful mix in the early summer, with the stipa loosely scattered over the whole site, producing a soft, 60 cm (2 ft) high matrix punctuated by the odd taller plant. It has a feel as if all of the plants are huddling together for protection from an incessant imaginary wind. In the large gaps left between the grass clumps run drifts of apricot irises and tall red hot pokers (*Kniphofia*), both of which have bold, grassy, blue-grey foliage when the flowers have faded. This slightly grey foliage is picked up by further clumps of silver-leaved achilleas and eryngiums, which in their turn will bring flower colour of soft yellow and silvery blue to the palette. Yellow-flowered *Coreopsis* and the occasional bright orange splash of Californian poppy (*Eschscholzia californica*) will extend the flowering season into the summer, the *Stipa tenuissima* tying the whole thing together with a pale straw-coloured wash from its drying flower stems.

Even in the depths of winter there will be genuine beauty here with hardly a touch of green to be seen anywhere, from the now bleached stipa flower heads, the occasional arching dome of the bronze-leaved grass *Carex comans*, the dried flower heads of some of the perennials, the silvery-blue leaves of artemisia and lamb's ears (*Stachys lanata*), and from the mulch of warm

Prairie style

ochre pea gravel that has been spread over the whole site. In essence, it has the same sort of atmosphere as Lauren Springer's garden in Colorado, without the benefit of harmonizing quite so exquisitely with the surrounding countryside. I loved it, and in the sincerest form of flattery promised myself that one day I would create a similar garden, putting my own spin on their design to suit my site.

As it turned out, Judy and Mary came down to visit me a few months later and went away determined to make a new part of their own garden based on some of what they had seen here. Hopefully, as more and more people attempt the naturalistic approach, it is just this sort of exchange of ideas that will help to make this new naturalistic style even more exciting.

Alongside the steppe garden at Lady Farm, Judy and Mary planted their version of a prairie garden. This grows much taller than the steppe garden, and many of the grasses used here are upright growers, such as *Miscanthus* varieties and drifts of *Calamagrostis* × *acutiflora* 'Karl Foerster'. Between these they have introduced some genuine prairie species, such as orange heleniums, yellow rudbeckias, golden-rod (*Solidago*) and the Joe Pye weed *Eupatorium maculatum* 'Atropurpureum', all of which will flower as the summer gives way to early autumn. Earlier in the season crocosmias have been added to the mix to give the same orange, yellow and red colour contrasts but still maintain the grassy theme.

ABOVE *Part of the Prairie Garden at the Garden House. Clumps of white-flowered* Selinum tenuifolium *and drifts of self-seeded* Verbena bonariensis *add a splash of colour to the dominating grasses—in this section, mostly* Molinia *and* Miscanthus *varieties.*

OPPOSITE *This is exactly the same view as that above, but the photograph was taken a few minutes later, emphasizing the magical effects of a setting sun on the grasses.*

ABOVE *A lowering sun illuminates the flowers of* Miscanthus sinensis *'Kleine Fontäne' and gilds the stems of the verbena. The prairie aster,* Aster turbinellus, *completes the picture.*

RIGHT *By planting the grasses on raised banks, the effects of sun through the flowers can be appreciated all through the day. Here, the midday sun brings a little magic to the flowers of* Aster ericoides *varieties and the miscanthus.*

At the Garden House, I had for some time been toying with the idea of planting grasses in one particular area of the garden that is illuminated by the setting September sun. Grasses backlit by such special light are transformed, as is a Christmas tree when its lights are switched on. The other factor of this chosen site was the trunks of the thuja trees which soared skywards, like mini versions of the conifers in the Rockies. I landscaped the site to create steep banks so that one would be able to walk below the grasses whatever time of the day and catch the light coming through their flower heads. Even a novice geographer knows the prairies are flat, so I justified it to myself by mischievously pretending it was where the prairies meets the foothills of the Rockies and compounded the deceit further by growing small-flowered michaelmas daisies (*Aster* species) among the grasses, which do actually grow in the Rockies. The important factor here is, having taken the initial idea from photographs of the prairie, the scheme evolved to suit my vision of what would best suit my particular site. I felt that backlit grasses of about 1.2 m (4 ft) in height planted on the sloping banks, with the paths occupying the sunken space between them and washes of pink and blue small-flowered michaelmas daisies growing among them, could produce a very memorable part of the garden.

I wanted lighter-textured grasses and companion plants than are typically associated with prairies, so that any breath of wind produced maximum movement. Heleniums and rudbeckias, which are lovely in other schemes, such as at Lady Farm, were too heavy and stiff for my purposes here, where I preferred to use the more lacy delicacy of the umbellifer *Selinum tenuifolium*, the refined foliage and elegant flowering bottle-brushes of *Cimicifuga*, the gracefully arching stems of widely spaced flowers on the prairie aster, *Aster turbinellus*, and gently seeding through it all the upright *Verbena bonariensis*. Towards the back, but still catching the light from the sinking sun, I found places to plant the giant oat *Stipa gigantea* and the tall *Macleaya*

microcarpa 'Kelway's Coral Plume', whose buff-coloured flower stems are just as good when the flowers have finished. Since the site is at the bottom of the valley and as a consequence as well protected from winter winds as we can provide, I used some of the later-flowering eucryphias as background trees. *Eucryphia moorei* is arguably the most elegant of a very refined genus but also one of the less hardy. Here I am able to grow it with one of its hybrid offspring, *Eucryphia × hillieri* 'Winton', which is altogether hardier and has grown to 9 m (30 ft) on an exposed north slope in another part of the estate. Their slightly grey-green evergreen foliage and mass of white, sweetly scented flowers in early autumn are a perfect foil for the sunlit grasses growing in front.

Of all the naturalistic areas we have created here, the prairie garden has been the most wild-looking, and partly because of its setting one of the most atmospheric (see pages 146–8). However, such a garden still requires time and effort spent looking after it, as there is a very fine line between a magical wildness and just plain wild.

Pampas grass

One plant I was keen to incorporate towards the back of my prairie garden was the much-maligned pampas grass (*Cortaderia*). I like the challenge of taking a slightly unfashionable plant and seeing if, with a little lateral thinking, I can give it a slightly different image and there may not be a plant that more symbolizes middle-class, 1970s, suburban England than this. Even the *Encyclopaedia Britannica* describes it as a 'lawn ornamental'. My wife Ros, normally the epitome of fair-mindedness, just cannot distance herself from her dislike of this plant and its associations. It is true that it is lumpy and not the most elegant of grasses, but I am a firm believer in there being very few bad naturally occurring plants, just unimaginative gardeners who have not yet discovered a use for them, and pampas grass is quite definitely a wild plant, once covering vast areas of Argentina. In the only pictures I have seen of this grass in the wild it was growing in an utterly featureless plain, so I would say it is not high on my list of travelling destinations, and the picture is not a great help on the ideas front either. Perhaps the standard pampas grass, *Cortaderia selloana*, would lend itself to a large-scale dry garden, with rocks and sun-bleached driftwood where not a blade of manicured lawn is in sight, but even here the more elegant, loosergrowing *Cortaderia richardii* from New Zealand would be a better choice.

I planted the varieties *C. selloana* 'Pumila' and 'Sunningdale Silver' in my prairie garden towards the back with the intention of planting others further into the view beyond at widely spaced distances. This plan may still be put into effect one day, but developments in this area are temporarily on hold. Maybe it will not be possible to better the drift planting of pampas grass and other grasses with the coloured gravel mulch that one sees occasionally on municipal roundabouts. This is clearly going to be an ongoing challenge to the imagination.

Grassy foregrounds

Ideas for a garden design can come from the most unlikely sources. The superficially similar, omnipresent woods of New England come with three trims of foreground. The standard, economy model of the north, with dried grasses and scrub as foreground; the more prosperous de-luxe version with verdant green pasture to set the trees off; and finally the more sporty cabriolet model with water as foreground. All three would be perfectly good role models, but the last two are versions that British gardeners would already be familiar with.

The classic example, I would guess, of the use of manicured grass as a foreground for autumncolouring trees would be the acer glade found at Westonbirt Arboretum in Gloucestershire and perhaps the best exponents of using water to set off autumn colour would be the Japanese in their traditional water gardens. It was, however, the

economy model, with its dried grasses and scrub, that most impressed me.

In much of the north of the New England states, the countryside is not prosperous and for mile after mile the autumn colour among the conifers was set off not by green fields but by bleached dried grasses and scrubland. Initial disappointment that the countryside was not matching my stereotype gave way to an increasing appreciation that the golds, oranges and reds

ABOVE *As with the photograph on page 141, the soft neutral tones of the foreground and the dark conifers in these northern Vermont woods, in the USA, perfectly complement the spectacular fall colours.*

of the woods set among the almost black-green of the conifers was being perfectly complemented by the foreground of gold-brown ferns, silvery-white grasses, red vacciniums, dark green heathers, scarlet sumachs and the low thicket-like rejuvenating stems of maples and birches. The key element to this neutral foreground was the bleached flowering stems of the grasses, and I wondered if I could modify this natural scrub to incorporate a version of it into my acer glade.

Romanticized scrubland

The acer glade at the Garden House was planted in 1992. I adore Japanese maples, and Weston-birt is one of the best places in the UK to see them producing their autumnal pyrotechnics. So popular a destination has it become in the autumn months, though, that rather than joining in the annual scrum I thought I would plant my own version. First planted in 1992, it started life with a central grass glade along its entire 183 m

(200 yd) length, but over the years, especially since my return from New England, it has been revised into three distinct zones, each one capturing for me the different foreground types found over there, which is to say mown green grass, water and scrub.

In the middle area I hope to capture some of the feel of those northern scrublands with a low planting of grasses and dwarf shrubs, interspersed with the occasional taller shrub that will not object to being cut to the ground annually. The idea here is to replicate some of the colour of the maples and background evergreens in the low foreground planting but fill much of the intervening space with the golds and browns of ferns, grasses and low deciduous twiggy shrubs. The grasses I have chosen in this instance have been fairly low-growing and fine-foliaged because the site has been broken down into relatively narrow sections by paths. I also wanted grasses to complement the delicate, feathery leaves of the Dissectum maples and the naturalized diminutive daffodil *Narcissus cyclamineus*, which already grew along the banks of the tiny stream, rather than overpowering them.

Two of the sedges from New Zealand seemed to fit the bill perfectly, producing domed, cascading clumps of narrow leaves 30–45 cm (12–18 in) high, silvery green in the case of *Carex albula*, and bronze-coloured with *Carex comans*. I raided other parts of the garden, where they had very gently seeded around, to lift clumps as big as I could find, and ended up with rather more of the bronze *C. comans* than I would have liked. As this turned out, Lady Luck must have been smiling on us again, because the form and colour of this particular sedge mimics the shape and shade in miniature of some of the surrounding Japanese maples, especially in the spring.

A similar bronze colouring is found in *Chionochloa rubra*, the red tussock grass, again a native of New Zealand, but this time on a taller plant. At the time of writing this has yet to flower, and even if it is not the most ornamental grass it is at least supposed to have feathery upright flower spikes, which is more than can be said for either of the two sedges, both being spectacularly uninspiring in bloom apart from their Velcro-like capacity to attach their seeds to your legs, a memorable if slightly painful experience when wearing shorts. I am trying this chionochloa with the royal fern, *Osmunda regalis*, which reliably turns a good clear yellow in autumn. I hope the fern will grow to only 1–1.2 m (3–4 ft) high in the slightly drier spot than is usually recommended for it, so that it will not overwhelm the grass. In the sands of New England the autumnal golds and yellows of the ferns were a major element of this scrub vegetation, but the same *Onoclea sensibilis* which in E. A. Bowles's words turns a 'pleasant foxy-brown' shows no inclination to do so in my garden, so the royal fern is an attempt to improvise on my part. The British native lady fern, *Athyrium filix-femina*, also normally turns a good clean, light yellow in the autumn, then darkens to a rich chestnut brown, so with its delicate, lacy, fresh green foliage for much of the summer is an excellent companion for the maples throughout the year—albeit one to use sparingly and towards the back, as it can be a bit too much of a good thing.

Many of the deciduous grasses become bleached or drained of colour in the autumn, which is very nice in its own right, but not many turn a positive autumn colour, which was a feature I also wanted in order to complete my New England scrubland effect. Among the lower-growing grasses found at the Garden House *Hakonechloa macra* is lovely in this respect, forming cascading mounds, 30–60 cm (1–2 ft) high, of yellow-orange at this time of year. We are more accustomed to meeting this Japanese grass in its bright yellow striped form 'Aureola', which has become a staple of container planting for shady courtyards. I have tried a small patch of this variegated form on the periphery of my scrub planting because it turns a particularly clear yellow every autumn, but generally in this semi-wild setting I have limited myself to the green-leaved species. Considering that the green-leaved form is, in the opinion of Rick Darke, a noted author on grasses, 'more sun tolerant, drought tolerant,

LEFT *The annual hare's tail grass, Lagurus ovatus, seeds itself in the African Garden and stays looking good for months. Self-seeding, even in the receptive sands of this part of the garden, is surprisingly erratic with not as many plants as I would wish in some years and an absolute plague of them in others. Even in times of plenty, however, they are extremely easy to weed out of the sand.*

cold-hardy, faster growing and much easier to propagate', and still 'turns exquisite copper-orange tones', it is surprising that it is not seen more commonly in cultivation. To add to this impressive list of virtues, I can testify that prior to taking pity on it and transplanting the clump to this new part of the garden, I had grown *H. macra* on the edge of an especially unkempt part of my meadow and, in boxing parlance, it had gone the distance with that Mike Tyson of weeds, creeping buttercup, so it is clear that it possesses tenacity as well.

Bringing the colour of the maples down into this low matrix, I have planted the low-growing evergreen shrub *Leucothoe* 'Scarletta', which turns a rich red in the autumn, as well as small groups of the multicoloured *Pseudowintera colorata*, a shrub whose rounded evergreen leaves, silvered beneath, give an overall impression of reddish-bronze and ochre as the temperatures start to drop. This lasts through the winter, producing a colour contrast very much in keeping with the grasses. This New Zealand shrub is normally a woodlander, and in the form usually encountered in the trade changes its leaf colour to a jade green, lightly flecked with maroon, during the summer months. It is not completely hardy, so its place in this exposed section of the acer glade is a bit of a gamble. Should it succumb, I may well try the other form of this same species, 'Elliott's form', which is lower-growing and has smaller, more lanceolate leaves edged more distinctly with maroon. Although both forms of this *Pseudowintera* have lived quite happily outside at the Garden House for over 15 years, 'Elliott's form' is definitely hardier and more colourful in the summer, whereas the larger leaves of the typical trade form make more of an impact when coloured through the winter. I happened to have quite a number spare of the larger-leaved form so thought it was worth the risk. Time will tell whether it will pay off.

The main point of the exercise with this scrubland experiment was to provide a complementary foreground for the autumnal spectacle of the maples' leaves, so flowers are not really

LEFT *Even without a setting sun backlighting its flower-heads as here, the cheat grass, Bromus* tectorum, *adds a contrasting delicacy of form to many plantings. This grass should be rigorously avoided in parts of the USA where it is a real menace for the rapid way it seeds itself about, but in my wetter climate it seems a little better behaved. Even so, I have taken to weeding all of the seedlings out of the borders in the autumn, and potting up just a few to replant the following spring, exactly where I want them to grow.*

OPPOSITE *Eragrostis* airioides *produces a hazy cloud of gossamer-thin threads in the early autumn, which, as they age, turn a beautiful parchment colour. Here it is growing in free-draining sand and merits, even probably needs, an open position with no immediate neighbours to fully show off its graceful form.*

part of the equation. The exception to this is provided in this part of the garden by the odd flowering plant of species michaelmas daisies, such as *Aster cordifolius*, which dots the area in autumn with a delicate lilac blue, hovering over and between the neutral colours of the grasses and ferns. In order to prevent these asters becoming too tall and out of scale with the rest of the low planting, they are periodically cut back through the season.

There is no reason why flowers should not contribute earlier in the season, but I would limit myself to those whose leaves have either died away completely by autumn, or those with delicate ferny leaves or architectural dried flowering stems. Bulbs and spring woodlanders among the grasses are an obvious candidate for the first option and compact perennials such as *Sanguisorba* 'Tanna' with its maroon flower heads or *Serratula seoanei* with its late mauve thistle-like flowers that dry to a silvery-tan colour both fill the other criteria. Once again, the choice is just a personal interpretation.

Grasses on the B list

In all the options talked about so far, the grasses are the main ingredient with other flowering plants having significant but more transient walk-on roles. The reverse, of course, could equally be done. Look at any meadow and you will see this in practice, with the grasses scattered to a greater or lesser extent throughout the mixture. A flower-rich meadow may not have many grasses in evidence when the bulk of the dicotyledonous plants are in flower (see pages 130 and 132), but even if there are flowering grasses present there will only be one or two species. This is important if you want to use grasses naturally in a garden setting; it is better to limit your choice in most mixed plantings to just a very few grass species and dot and drift them through the entire scheme. This is probably the nearest I could come to producing a cardinal rule for mixed planting, which is a style that prides itself on a lack of constricting parameters, and it is especially relevant to grasses with their emphasis on architectural shapes.

The annual hare's tail grass, *Lagurus ovatus*, illustrates the point. This is a grass that seems to revel in a sunny well-drained soil, so when I bought a packet of seed the only place I had available in the garden to please it was the African Garden. I mixed the seed with one or two other annual species of flowering plants and sowed it direct onto the sand, and the few *Lagurus* that came up that first year looked pretty good. They self-seeded themselves and within a couple of years were liking the conditions so much they had produced a nearly continuous cover of young seedlings over the whole site in the winter. I had to weed out well over 90 per cent of them, leaving a scattering of individuals or small groups over the entire bed. As you can see from the photograph on page 153, they bring a lightness and textural counterpoint to the surrounding blaze of colour and are one of the plants that hold this eclectic mix together. This particular grass has an enormously long period of beauty, with its flowers opening pink in mid to late spring above compact clumps of blue-grey leaves, and still looking good in late summer when its now straw-coloured stems and flowers show a remarkable capacity to remain upright.

As the hare's tail grass finally loses the will to remain vertical, I hope the baton in the African Garden will be taken up by other grasses revelling in this sandy soil. Now is the moment in the year when the foxtail barley, *Hordeum jubatum*, is at its sensational best, gradually turning from a pink and grey symphony (see pages 143 and 158) to wonderfully contrasting straw colours. It is of relatively short duration in the beauty stakes so I do not employ it as a foundation plant. This role is filled by a much neater grass, *Eragrostris airoides*, which starts to flower in the second half of the summer and continues well into the late autumn. The supporting stems to the tiny flowers are incredibly fine, so as the plant dries to the usual buffs, it appears as if there is a little cloud of gossamer threads floating on the ground, like a three-dimensional dome of a spider's web 30 cm (12 in) high. The effect once again, via a different route, is to lighten and unify the whole planting.

The balance of grasses to flowering plants

During the early years of the Cottage Garden (see Chapter 4), when many of the photographs shown in the book were taken, I was deliberately excluding grasses from the beds in this part of the garden because I wanted to make naturalistic plantings without adopting the formula of 'border plus grasses equals naturalism'. The gardener's role in the management of this area is to balance the wild flower/exotic species ratio, and if for any reason this adjudicating influence is reduced for a season or two, it is almost invariably the native species that triumph in the rush for land domination. We had just such a period of time when we were unable to put as much effort as we would have liked into the weeding of the Cottage Garden and it was the autumn hawkbit, *Leontodon autumnalis*, which was quickest to the draw on colonizing. The only remedy was to restrict this and the almost equally prolific pink campion, *Silene dioica*, to small specific zones and to plant up the gaps where we had removed them with non-delicate species, and for this some of the grasses were perfect. Species such as *Calamagrostis brachytricha*, the Korean feather reed grass, are able to rise above the perils of any native plants recolonizing the exposed soil and still manage to remain neighbour-friendly and refined by forming upright, arching clumps. The 1.2 m (4 ft) flower spikes which appear in late summer remind me of pampas grass, only infinitely more delicate and graceful, and are pink tinted on emergence before fading to silver-grey where they remain handsome for much of the winter. The multi-faceted *Stipa tenuissima* is also tough enough to cope with a few weeds provided the soil is well drained, and its straw-coloured faded flower heads provide a wonderful contrast for the dried stems of the other flowering plants in the late autumn and early winter.

The stipa and calamagrostis are, barring mishaps, now fixtures in this part of the garden and helped to soften my attitude towards grasses

ABOVE *The bells of Dierama pulcherrimum vary in colour from white to a rich shade of plum-purple and flutter in the faintest breeze.*

in a mixed planting, but it has been a couple of annual grasses which have really opened my eyes to the possibilities. More ongoing removal of seedlings left patches much less densely planted than I would like, so with hare's tail grass spare by the barrowful, I planted some in the gaps and it has looked terrific. The same could be said for a long-awned grass I had admired on the edge of Lauren Springer's sun-soaked Colorado garden, at that time in midsummer already bleached and handsome, with copper overtones. I could not remember the name she gave me at the time, but the seedlings came up with a speed and vigour

unbecoming of such a graceful grass and were almost showing flower bud before I had time to pot them on.

I very quickly decided it was not a *Stipa* species, as my faulty memory had thought, but an annual, and planted them in gaps wherever I could find space, so that I could at least show Lauren that I had looked after the seed she had given me when she visited later that summer. It turned out to be cheat grass, *Bromus tectorum*, and she had, in fact, strongly advised me against growing it, as it is a major weed in the southwestern states. At least in the short term, this is

ABOVE *Everything about the wand flower,* Dierama pulcherrimum, *is elegant and romantic, from the neat, grassy foliage, its arching habit when in flower, right down to its alternative vernacular name of angels' fishing rods.*

ABOVE *From the moment the foxtail barley,* Hordeum jubatum, *opens its first flowers in mid- to late summer to the time the flower-heads eventually disintegrate in the autumn, this short-lived grass is a joy. It gently self-seeds on my heavy soil, but on lighter soils it can be prolific. It is native to a large area of the north and west of the USA.*

another case of serendipity since although they are individually rather frail, these plants have produced a gentle, almost transparent haze of silver-grey lightness, which turned to bleached, copper tones later in the summer even under our grey skies. It looked lovely, but I have this gnawing, leaden feeling in the pit of my stomach about overriding Lauren's advice.

Blending the zones

It is not at all surprising that the naming is confused in another group of grass-like plants, the dieramas, as like the aquilegias, if you grow more than one of these plants together they will hybridize shamelessly about. One of the general guidelines that I have found very useful to blend different parts of the garden is to plant one or

two species in both areas. The dieramas are particularly good in this role since, planted along the length of the Long Walk here, they have found conditions very much to their liking and have seeded themselves all over the place. In this way there is no stark transition as you walk from one area to the next.

Also in the Long Walk, among the many hundreds of different plants growing there, I have loosely scattered repetition planting of, for example, birches, *Erica vagans*, and the pale yellow evening primrose *Oenothera stricta* 'Sulphurea', along its 182 m (200 yd) length. They have helped to blend seamlessly at least four completely different areas of the garden, so that when they are viewed from either end these different gardens all join together to become one.

Dieramas

The flowering of the dieramas is an undoubted eye-catching highlight of the midsummer garden. This group of grass-like flowering plants would probably top the list of my all-time favourites. Although technically probably described as bulbous, this mostly South African genus looks grass-like in foliage, and it seems slightly odd to call a plant that usually keeps its 1 m (3¼ft) long evergreen foliage all year a bulb. They look more like herbaceous perennials in flower and are arguably the most graceful and beautiful plants in the whole garden at that time.

The most commonly encountered species and the one that has been in cultivation the longest is *Dierama pulcherrimum*, which takes my vote for the plant with the most romantic vernacular names of 'angels' fishing rods' or 'wand flower'. The wiry flowering stems grow up to 1.8 m (6 ft) high in early summer before gracefully arching over with the weight of the 5 cm (2 in) bells which emerge from silvery-pink calyces. These flowers, usually pink but variable from white to plum purple, are attached by thread-like stems and flutter in the faintest breeze, accentuating that grassy connection. Even when in seed they remain architecturally graceful.

It is not just the naming of dieramas which is confusing, as one writer will tell you they require moisture and the next will say drainage. Both aspects of this conflicting advice may well be right, depending on where you live. In the drier climate of the eastern counties of the UK dieramas may possibly be best in a damper situation, whereas in our deluged Devon they definitely prefer a more free-draining spot. I plant them in our ordinary moisture-retentive soil on sloping banks if I can so that surplus winter moisture drains away, as they are more likely to succumb to cold spells if their bulbs are in damp soil. Prolonged cold winter winds can also defoliate dieramas and this often reduces flowering the following season, but this is no reason not to try them since they usually shoot again from below

ground the following spring, and these same gales in this garden will finish off a whole range of evergreens we normally reckon to be hardy in southern England, such as helianthemums, cistus and ceanothus.

When I first came to the Garden House, Mr Fortescue had several established clumps of what was labelled *Dierama pumilum*. With that first winter being so cold, these plants were all but killed, and I moved the remnants to a fresh site where they eventually grew into clumps 60 cm (2 ft) high with flowering wands reaching up to double that height. I presumed this dwarf habit and the more widely flared flowers ranging in colour into more salmon and red shades were symptomatic of its differences to *D. pulcherrimum*, but since I can find no listing of *D. pumilum* in the garden's stock record book, I am beginning to doubt the veracity of my memory. He had tried several of the named Slieve Donard hybrids between the two species so I wonder whether this would explain the colour range but whatever their name they were very attractive.

Smaller still and flowering earlier in June is the other frequently met member of the family, *Dierama dracomontanum*. This plant grows only 45 cm (18 in) high with more upright flowering stems and opens its dark pink flowers from chestnut-brown calyces. We also grow a more terracotta-red form of this species, which was collected in South Africa by Robin and Sue White of Blackthorn Nursery in Hampshire. Occasionally the flowering periods of this species and *D. pulcherrimum* will overlap and one year this resulted in a few beautiful hybrids produced among the many seedlings from the smaller parent. They are, in size and habit, very similar to those of *D. pumilum*, but with larger, more widely flared bells opening from brown calyces, this last fact discounting the theory these were just rogue *D. pulcherrimum* seedlings. These seedling dieramas provide a delicate counter-balance to the heavy exuberance of the massed poppies in the African Garden as well as breaking up the winter flatness of the dunes with their compact clumps of foliage.

With more and more of these mostly South African bulbous plants being introduced, the chances of interesting hybrids occurring are greatly enhanced. This year I flowered what is reputedly *Dierama reynoldsii*, which opened its blooms in mid-spring. Even lacking the grace of some of the other species, it may still prove to be useful in hybridization with its very large, very widely flared flowers and in extending the flowering season. These could be exciting times for dierama-devotees.

We shall probably name one or two of the very best of our dierama hybrids, but I feel slightly reluctant to do so in the light of the fate of the Slieve Donard named clones. In that case a large range of what sounded very desirable hybrids named by this Northern Ireland nursery have all but disappeared or been diluted beyond recognition by other nurserymen propagating these varieties by seed instead of by division.

Crocosmias

New varieties abound in another bulbous genus with a superficial grass-like appearance that gardeners treat as herbaceous perennials, namely the crocosmias. The same technique of growing winter wet-sensitive plants on banks, with a top-dressing of sand, works extremely well with crocosmias, which in our wet climate are prone to succumb to cold winters when planted on the flat in our ordinary soil. The only two that grew here when we arrived were the grey-leaved, soft orange-yellow *Crocosmia* × *crocosmiiflora* 'Solfatare' and the large-flowered, late-blooming *C.* × *crocosmiiflora* 'Star of the East', both of which would still be among my favourites despite the inundation of newer varieties.

I do not want to describe too many of the ones we have since grown as they are often superficially similar, but for creating pools of colour in midsummer they are wonderful. Worth special mention is a superb large-flowered, red variety with a dark flower stalk which we bought as *C.* × *crocosmiiflora* 'Mrs Morrison' but which is now

called *C.* × *crocosmiiflora* 'Mrs Geoffrey Howard'. Seek it out, because it is a class act.

My interest in crocosmias was fired up by the enthusiasm of Irish plant collector Gary Dunlop, who is coded as the single supplier for more than a quarter of the two hundred currently listed in the *RHS Plant Finder* book. He once showed me a photograph of one of his stock beds of crocosmias in full flower and I immediately vowed to grow mine together in one bed. My problem here was overwintering them in our wet conditions, but I got around this by planting them on a raised, 1 m (3¼ ft) high mound of soil which I top-dressed in sand. This bed in full sun has other grassy-leaved perennials such as hemerocallis, asphodels and bearded irises to keep the crocosmias company, with bluebells carpeting the whole bank earlier in the season, and this grassy theme imbues the whole area with a very natural feel before supplying the back-drop hot colours in mid and late summer for the African Garden alongside.

❖   ❖   ❖

IT IS NOT SURPRISING THAT GRASSES and grass-like plants such as crocosmias have become associated with natural-looking planting schemes, as to a greater or lesser extent you will see them contributing to a vast range of wild landscapes. Grasses have almost become, with some justification, the epitome of wildness, but important as they are in defining the look of a landscape, either because of their strong architectural shapes or because of their sheer numbers in the wild, we should not get carried away with the belief that grasses are the necessary mainstay of every naturalistic garden. Sometimes, as in the acer glade at the Garden House, the grasses are just in line for the gong of 'best supporting role', and in yet other schemes they may just have a small walk-on part. However big the role they are given, it is hard to imagine a well-balanced, naturalistic garden that contained no grasses at all, and I for one will continue to think of them as the very essence of wildness.

LEFT *Towards the top of the Swartberg Pass in South Africa, these and other* Restio *species created much excitement among the American members of the group I was travelling with, as in the USA they are becoming very popular plants for container-growing. Although generally not at all hardy, I still enjoyed this stand as much for its beauty as for the elegant template it would create for a garden design using other hardy grasses of similar shape.*

7 Inspiration from the wild woods

I know there are many areas of the world where trees are utterly dominant, but in my mind, autumn colour and New England are forever linked. Like millions before us, we travelled there to see the fall colour, fulfilling another life-long ambition. Not that I was harbouring any great hopes of finding many exciting ideas to inspire new areas of the garden at home — the extent of my ambition was to photograph trees that might look like a more natural version of Westonbirt, the world-famous arboretum in Gloucestershire. Beyond that we were there to stare, just like everyone else.

I had come with a preconceived image of the scenery of New England as large sugar maples, white wooden-clad farms and houses and small paddocks surrounded by rustic wooden fences. This is almost certainly as a result of growing up with a large poster of just such a landscape in my mother's kitchen, the overall rosy-orange effect accentuated by the length of time it had hung on the wall. There are of course many areas like this, but for the first few days the reality was somewhat different. The interstate for the most part carved a 91–183 m (100–200 yd) corridor through almost continuous and impenetrable forest—though that word may be slightly misleading as generally the trees

were not huge, the big specimens having mostly been felled over a century ago. However, while the trees did give the impression of mostly being regrowth and relatively young, what they lacked in height they certainly made up for in biomass. Almost all of the woods were so thick that if you walked into them for just 46 m (50 yd) or so and were then blindfolded and spun around a few times, I am sure you would have a hard job making it back out onto the road.

I never thought I would become bored with trees, but after a week of travelling through these impenetrable forests I was itching for a gap in them, even though the fall colour was in places breathtakingly magnificent. On a route such as

PREVIOUS PAGE *This wood in Toronto, Canada, shows how yellow autumn colour accentuates the shapes and colour of the tree trunks, as well as making the whole scene appear to be bathed in sunshine, even on a dull day as here.*

the popular Kancamagus Highway in the White Mountains of New Hampshire, for example, the convoy of cars would grind to a halt on almost every bridge, or any other gap in the trees, so that we 'leaf peepers' could take the statutory photograph of the woods with something, anything, in the foreground. So desperate were we all to have something to take a picture of that on one bridge, with the limited verge space already occupied, others were stopping a little further on to take a photograph of the people on the bridge taking photographs. I cannot say in all honesty that I would look forward to an evening of seeing some of these holiday snaps, but in truth, we were all guilty of it.

As unlikely as it might seem from the above description, an extremely important gardening lesson did emerge from this experience, because even with the background hills consistently covered by millions of gloriously coloured trees, it was the foreground and its composition that made the photograph (see page 151).

Then there is the sheer scale of these forests, which cover an area almost twice that of England, in some places with almost no roads to interrupt the trees. In one area which was quite typical, we could have travelled in the same direction for 32 km (20 miles) through this solid woodland without crossing another road. It certainly altered my attitudes towards hunting in such places; anyone who can even find wild animals in such forests, let alone shoot them, has probably earned their right to fill their cooking pots as far as I am concerned.

Shrubby understorey

In western Maine, in the Grafton Notch State Park, we passed through magnificent woods of paper birch with a rejuvenating understorey of deciduous shrubs (see opposite). A picture I saw of a birch wood in China, with short-cropped grass around the trees, had hybridized in my imagination with native stands of birches I had seen in Kent and Hampshire in the UK, where shrubby undergrowth grew among the trees, to form the basis of my own garden version at the Garden House. Here in New England, my hybrid garden version was made manifest in the wild. Visiting the New England birch woods first would have cut out the middle man in my thought processes.

By the time I saw those wild paper birches in Maine I had already planted birches in tight groups of three to eight individuals at widely spaced intervals along both sides of the Long Walk at the Garden House, and in one section these had been extended to create a fairly open birch wood. Under the light canopy that birch trees provide, I intended to plant groups of deciduous azaleas and to a lesser extent groups of species rhododendrons and *Kalmia latifolia*, the calico bush, which we had seen growing on the edges of fairly dark woods in Massachusetts and Vermont, to all intents and purposes like holly in an English wood. I envisaged a very similar blend of trees, shrubs and perennials as in the birch woods in Maine, but with drifts of bluebells, primroses and the like growing between the widely spaced shrubs and trees. However, it took nearly nine years for the birch trees to grow tall enough to be able to start creating this understorey effect and in the meantime the plan has inevitably become modified. I am now thinning the understorey of shrubs to leave the deciduous azaleas with more space to grow into, but some of the evergreens, planted to provide shelter, have grown so well that I know I will not have the heart to pull them out. The Chilean *Berberis valdiviana*, for example, with its polished

green leaves and 10 cm (4 in) long drooping racemes of golden yellow flowers in mid-spring, has already reached nearly 4.5 m (15 ft) in height. Likewise, the Himalayan *Viburnum cylindricum*, with its waxy coated leaves on which, the story goes, messages could be written by the indigenous population, has also flourished. You certainly can write on the leaves but the speed at which this plant is growing suggests that very long arms and very good eyesight would be needed for this to be meaningful, as it is rushing to be a tree.

Single species copses

I have also planted single species copses of other characterful trees, such as the maple-like sweet gum with, for a change, an almost descriptive Latin generic name of *Liquidambar*, although its specific epithet of *styraciflua* rather spoils the illusion of a botanist with a romantic streak. The variety 'Worplesden', which I have used, takes the award for the plant with the longest autumn colour display at the Garden House, being consistently the first to start to turn through yellow and orange-red phases to a shining, glossy burgundy red, flushed with scarlet, which is still hanging on when all the other maples have finished. It is, however, a tree that needs an acid soil to do well and freedom from excessive winds as it is a little brittle.

When I first left school I worked at a nursery where the boss, a man named Charlie, would substitute *L. styraciflua* (of which he had masses) for the field maple, *Acer campestre* (which he did not grow), when landscape architects ordered the latter. It may seem like sharp practice but they were getting a very good deal and I have always carried a wonderful image of motorway verges covered in sweeps of New England-style fall colour, all courtesy of Charlie's bolshiness and opportunism.

Charlie was an honourable man for those who played straight by him but cared not a jot for social niceties or status. He was just as likely to

OPPOSITE *This wild birch wood in Maine, USA, appears almost garden-like as it stands. A straight substitution of deciduous azaleas for the rejuvenating understorey in the photograph with a path added to meander its way through the middle would make an extremely pleasing garden.*

double the price if he saw you had arrived in a Rolls Royce and had a pushy character to match. One grand lady, expecting him to hurry around after her like a puppy, got much more than she bargained for when he told her to go away, in vernacular terms you would not utter in front of a bishop. I admired his honesty, as this must be a sentiment secretly whispered by thousands every day who have to deal with awkward customers. The ensuing letter, starting 'Dear sir, You are quite the rudest man I've ever met . . .', became one of his most treasured mementoes. Nearly ten years later, when Charlie called in to visit us at the Garden House, he produced this very same well-worn, now parchment-coloured letter, which, on opening, fell into four neat pieces and fluttered down onto the kitchen table in vintage Hollywood style. It was the last time I ever saw him, but what an exit.

A dogwood glade

The centrepiece of the Spring Garden at the Garden House has not changed since I first thought of it. It was always my intention to have, rising above a 1 m (3¼ ft) high shrubby matrix in various shades of green, a central group of *Cornus controversa* 'Variegata', or wedding cake trees, planted to form a glade where I envisaged I could one day sit in the middle with the sunlight streaming down through their leaves.

Generally, I think if you create a group of any single type of plant you accentuate the individual characteristics of that species, and when the plant involved is a tree with its larger scale the effects are magnified. I am not a big fan of variegated plants as variegation and a natural approach are not easy bed-fellows, but this cornus is one of the most charismatic plants I know; its creamy silver-variegated leaves in late summer become imbued with the same maroon tint of the twigs, and all through the year its strongly tiered habit attracts attention.

I have always loved this dogwood since I first saw two majestic specimens growing in Bath

Botanic Gardens when I was very young. I remember clearly thinking then that they were the most amazingly beautiful thing I had ever set my eyes on, and my views have not changed much over of the years. I have seen a photograph of a single specimen of this most aristocratic of variegated trees that was in excess of 12 m (40 ft) in height and almost as wide, growing in southern Ireland. Sadly the tree is no more, but that is the stuff of heavenly dreams, and I would happily make a pilgrimage right across Europe to see a mature group of these plants

LEFT *A group of* Cornus controversa *'Variegata', often called the wedding cake tree, rises above an underplanting of* Rhododendron *'Fabia Tangerine'. I planted these five trees so that when mature, and viewed from the central clear space in their midst, their branches will intertwine, creating abstract silhouetted shapes against the silvered canopy of the foliage.*

Favourite trees

Another acid-loving tree which I have group planted is the golden larch, *Pseudolarix amabilis*, from China. This larch has an aura of indefinable aristocracy about it, being fuller foliaged and with a better habit than the superficially similar common larch, as well as unfailingly producing glorious autumn colour of rich orange-yellow. It is not a very common plant but one I have coveted since I saw my first specimen. In the absence of good seed, *Pseudolarix* is a difficult plant to prop-

agate, so when one year our good friend Vic Pawlowski rooted a small batch, I very quickly bought them all. I became so possessive of them that I could not bring myself to sell any, and was relieved in the end to be able to plant them out as a group in the garden here. Fortune smiled on me that day, because not only are they growing up to produce a beautiful copse but they are also a living memorial to one of Britain's great propagators. Vic was another honourable, disarmingly honest man, willing to share his considerable knowledge with any enthusiast with the time to

listen and constantly learning and questioning himself. Even as he was succumbing to the illness which finally brought him down, he was planning his next year's grafting. He cultivated an aura of magic around propagation, so it is fitting that this golden larch copse nestles around the northern side of the granite standing stones we call the Magic Circle.

A plant that I have always thought would look lovely growing in association with *Pseudolarix* is the Brewers weeping spruce, *Picea breweriana*. You would need a heart of stone to walk past a healthy, mature specimen of this spruce, as can be seen at Westonbirt Arboretum, and not be moved by it. The main branches sweep down and out in gentle curves, but it is the secondary branches that hang down vertically underneath to lengths of more than 1.8 m (6 ft) that give this plant a larger-than-life, other-worldly quality. The needles adorning these fine trailing branches are of a green so dark they are almost black, and have that wonderful capacity to trap fine water droplets, transforming the whole into a magical light show when sun catches a mist-laden tree. I have heard criticism that a group of these trees would paint a rather sombre, melancholy picture, but I think not, preferring instead to imagine they would create a truly memorable, atmospheric, if slightly spooky wood.

You have to be patient, though, with *Picea breweriana* as it is very slow; the seedlings I bought about fifteen years ago are still only 1.8–2.1 m (6–7 ft) high, although I must admit to not giving them a lot of attention. Nevertheless, the final space for these twenty-five trees has been allocated, although I am afraid it is likely it will be posterity only that will reap the true visual benefit. It is a rare tree in the wild, confined to a few locations in the Siskiyou Mountains in California and Oregon, so it was very surprising when one of the foremost plantsmen from that part of the world did not immediately recognize other healthy specimens of this spruce we had in the gardens here. He had of course seen these trees in the wild but said they bear no resemblance to cultivated plants, being very tall and

devoid of lower branches in their natural stands. It is a piece of information that will no doubt save me disappointment when I pay my own homage on my first visit to the Siskiyous. Clearly, my suggestions of borrowing ideas from the wild should be taken in the broadest possible context, allowing for the concept of occasionally romanticizing nature.

Japanese maples

When space is limited, as it is for most of us, thoughts of single species woods constitute no more than wishful thinking and we might easily dismiss the process as irrelevant. Yet in so doing, are we pigeon-holing our perceptions of what a wood may be ? When, for example, does a shrub become a tree? A hawthorn (*Crataegus*) rising from the ground on a small number of distinct trunks is still a tree to my mind, no matter if it is overall only 3 m (10 ft) in height. Among the shrubs and trees that would fall into this crossover category, the Japanese maples (*Acer palmatum*) reign supreme.

The Japanese maples are one of the few groups of shrubs that I can imagine creating a beautiful, naturalistic garden all on their own. I

ABOVE *The glorious autumn colour of* Acer palmatum *'Osakazuki' (red) and* Acer palmatum *'Sango-kaku'. See how the trunks stand out more distinctly against the yellow leaves.*

OPPOSITE *The autumn colour of Japanese maples almost defies belief. The top tree is* Acer palmatum *'Heptalobum Elegans', while that below is A.* palmatum *'Osakuzuki'.*

RIGHT *Part of the acer glade at Westonbirt Arboretum in Gloucestershire, UK. This group marked one end of the glade, and it is a fitting altar to a shrine for maple-lovers.*

RIGHT *Sooty, one of our ten Burmese cats, is totally oblivious to the beauty of the spring display of the* Acer palmatum *'Corallinum' above him.*

have planted such an area, the maples growing on steep banks surrounding a stream and small ponds, with the intention of allowing the ground surface beneath the acers to become completely covered by moss. It is, if you like, another hybrid creation between photographs I have seen of Japanese temple gardens and my idealized image of how these plants might grow in the wild.

There is no time of the year when such an acer glade would not look sensational. All through the winter months their beautiful tracery of branches looks magnificent coated in hoar frost and snow, or more commonly bedecked in myriad tiny water droplets hanging beneath the fine twigs. To see the perfection of a soft, low winter sun illuminating such rain-soaked maples is like looking at a magical copse studded in diamond fairylights.

Many of the Japanese maples have purple twigs, which, combined with older branches of usually grey-brown and a trunk often striated

with darker lines, makes for a striking winter appearance. Looking down the acer glade here during the winter months, where there are over seventy different varieties of Japanese maple planted, it is hard to single out one variety among the large range of varying twig and bark colour, but *Acer palmatum* 'Sango-kaku', commonly known as the coral bark maple, is exceptional with its coral red twigs and young branches. It is one of the taller-growing varieties, eventually becoming vase-shaped at maturity but without the graceful arching elegance of many. It is one of the first to start colouring in the autumn and holds its soft orange-yellow leaves for longer than any other variety we grow, often for six to seven weeks. *A. palmatum* 'Aoyagi' is a green-twigged variety, turning clear yellow for a relatively short period late in the season.

Altogether much smaller is *A. palmatum* 'Corallinum'. Here in a climate very amenable to maple cultivation it has reached almost 3 m (10 ft) in nearly thirty years. It is much twiggier in its growth, which makes it especially handsome through the leafless months with its purple-red twigs. However, it is for the spring colour of the young leaves that 'Corallinum' is famed. Many maples have lovely spring colour from the emerging leaves which usually only lasts for a couple of weeks before they gradually fade to their summer dress, but 'Corallinum' is exceptional in producing an amazing display of vivid shrimp pink to red leaves for about six weeks before fading to green in the summer. After such a performance anyone would forgive it for not colouring in the autumn, which unfortunately is the case. Other *A. palmatum* varieties such as 'Beni-komachi' and 'Chishio Improved' are very similar, if a little shorter in duration of spring colour. Slightly taller than *A. palmatum* 'Corallinum' but equally impressive in the length of its display is *A. palmatum* 'Beni-tsukasa', with young leaves of a softer pink bordering at times to orange-pink, but once again no autumn colour.

Good spring and autumn colour are not mutually incompatible, but as a general rule of thumb, those maples with particularly vivid spring hue will not colour well in the autumn. In more natural plantings, maples with slightly more restrained spring coloration are much easier to place, especially those with a graceful, rounded overall shape. *A. palmatum* 'Chitoseyama' and 'Matsukaze' are both very similar, with striking brown-purple young growth gradually changing to green by summer, brilliant red seeds, an arching habit and reliable bright scarlet autumn colour. *A. palmatum* 'Autumn Glory' goes through similar spring and summer foliage changes before living up to its name with a pumpkin-orange finale in the autumn.

The deeply divided, seven-lobed leaves of *A. palmatum* 'Omurayama' emerge green and turn orange and red in this garden in the autumn. When well established and happy (mine took nearly ten years to reach this stage of development), this variety grows so fast in the spring that the soft shoots are incapable of supporting their own weight, and consequently hang almost vertically downwards, like the shoots on a weeping willow. It was a photograph of this variety in J. D. Vertrees's wonderful book *Japanese Maples* that made it top of my first 'wanted' list of maples. Later in the season, as these shoots firm up, they raise up and finish the year arching gently downwards. The arching, graceful habit of these maples almost demands a location where they can be seen as individuals, so they would be perfect for a position on banks surrounded by moss or in the traditional Westonbirt-style acer glade surrounded by grass, in both of which sites they have been planted at the Garden House.

The 'Linearilobum' group

The narrow, lobed leaves of the 'Linearilobum' group have a rather different habit. Generally they make upright, twiggy shrubs without the beautiful arching shape, but over the years I have been growing them their year-round qualities have elevated this group ever higher in my personal league table of favourites, especially if shortage of space were to be an issue. The typical plant of this group would be *Acer palmatum* 'Linearilobum', which in ten years has reached about

ABOVE *The acer glade
at the Garden House.
The mounded shapes of
the Dissectum maples
are grouped in this area,
echoing the gentle
undulations of the ground
itself. The grass here has
since been removed and
ornamental grasses of a
cascading habit planted
to further emphasize the
soft curves.*

3 m (10 ft) here. From the moment the leaves burgeon into a soft milk-chocolate brown, a colour which the plant seems reluctant to give up even through the summer months, to the fall finale of orange with a dash of red and pale yellow, this plant demands attention.

The variety *A. palmatum* 'Kinshi' has the lobes reduced to thread-like dimensions, but against the odds the plant is remarkably robust and wind-tolerant—although I would not recommend this variety for planting in really exposed positions, which no Japanese maple would really appreciate. My acer glade is on an exposed north slope, but deliberately sited on a part of the property where a mature field hedge and neighbouring trees on the southwest side provide shelter from that direction's damaging winds during the sensitive summer months when the maples are in leaf. Even then, in the early years, I grew as many large evergreen shrubs as I could find around them to act as 'nurse plants' which are now, after eight or nine years, being removed to leave the maples in glorious isolation. The leaves on 'Kinshi' emerge in the spring as a wonderful, vibrant, fresh green and their delicate, lacy nature makes them irresistibly tactile all through the season until the plant turns orange-yellow in the autumn. A general rule of thumb seems to be that the more purple in the coloration of the young emerging leaves of a Japanese maple, the more red the autumn colour will be. Those varieties with vivid fresh green spring colour will almost certainly turn clear yellow in the autumn. Consequently, it is no surprise when the variety 'Villa Taranto', which is unable to make up its mind whether to have green- or brown-suffused young leaves, has autumn colour which reflects such indecision, turning pale straw yellow in

some seasons and orange-red in others, but more often all of these at the same time. These suffusions of colour are a hallmark of this variety from early spring to late autumn, and, coupled with its twiggy growth, broadly vase-shaped habit and height range of 1.2–1.8 m (4–6 ft) at maturity, make it perfect for smaller gardens.

I can imagine a closely planted grove of any of these forms of linearilobed maples looking wonderful in a tiny garden. They would provide perfect shade for any number of woodland perennials and bulbs and as they grew the very lowest branches could be removed, transforming them into a fabulously natural-looking copse, your very own woodland garden in miniature. If you used 'Villa Taranto' as this core planting, it is likely that you would need to scale down the size of the woodlanders growing underneath to keep the proportions of the whole scheme in unity.

Pine woods

Pine trees are my favourite conifers for creating natural effects. All through the northern hemisphere they are the backbone of so many natural plantings in the wild, influencing and contributing to a wide range of different landscapes. In hotter, drier areas than the UK, such as the Mediterranean and the southwestern states of North America, it is not just their visual impact but their all-pervading, resinous smell which is so redolent of these hot, sunny climates. Wherever they grow, their rugged trunks, distinctive habit and dark green foliage provide a perfect foil for whatever the vegetation surrounding them may be. I remember being breathtaken on first seeing the English Lake District, as I still am on each subsequent visit. Maybe the lakes and fells are mere puddles and molehills to our American

ABOVE *The view from the top of the acer glade at the Garden House. The bridge, which now acts as a focal point, was built to carry the pedestrian right of way, and the ground below it was dug out to enable a path to pass beneath the bridge and so link a further area of land to the glade.*

RIGHT *Scots pines are seen here silhouetted against the calm sea of an early Scottish morning on the island of Skye. The strong shapes of these trees, their glorious setting and the magical light encapsulate the romance that pines always carry for me.*

LEFT *A commercial planting of larch trees has been sympathetically thinned to leave a natural-looking wood on Dartmoor in Devon, UK. The free-range ponies and sheep keep the turf closely cropped and imbue the trees with a certain Tolkienesque quality.*

and Canadian friends, brought up on gigantic waterfalls and mountains, but to me they are a symphony of harmonized subtlety with exquisite dimensions and the specimens and groups of pines are an absolutely essential ingredient of this landscape.

Natural Tolkienesque woods

Woods of golden larch (*Pseudolarix amabilis*) and Brewers spruce (*Picea breweriana*) are dream-like, fantasy creations, almost straight out of the pages of Tolkien's *The Lord of the Rings*. Even ordinary larch woods which are familiar from forestry plantations can at certain times of the year possess something of this other-worldly quality. The serried ranks of a commercial planting do not inspire any gardening ideas, but when they are sensitively thinned and become mature there is an undeniable quality to the space provided beneath these trees. In one spot around Burrator Reservoir on the south side of Dartmoor, larch trees widely spaced at 15–18 m (50–60 ft) and cleared of their lower branches for half of their height preside over an area devoid of all shrubs and undergrowth and carpeted with short, sheep-mown grass. In the autumn, with their ramrod straight trunks rising from this emerald sward, and with a blue sky peeking through the pale yellow of the foliage canopy, the scene makes me think of the golden wood of Tolkien's Lothlorien (see previous page).

I can easily see this recipe being reproduced in a garden setting, albeit necessarily scaled down in size, to give a very simple but restful area. Many of the birches could be grown in exactly the same way to produce a similar sort of result. It would be a genuinely relaxing part of any garden, a place for contemplation and care-free strolls on sunlit evenings, freed from the visual intrusions of all those gardening jobs we should have done weeks ago.

I have a suspicion that the aspens I fell in love with in Colorado might be even more Tolkienesque when bedecked with trembling yellow autumn colour. The aspens I saw were muscular of frame, with clean, smooth trunks of creamy olive-grey counterbalanced by that fabulous, famous quivering foliage of dainty heart-shaped leaves. They were, without doubt, the star of the vegetation on our visit to the southwestern states, and the feel of those rustling aspen woods is something I would love to replicate if only I can sort out a suitable substitute that will grow for me—unfortunately the American aspen, *Populus tremuloides*, does not grow very well in the UK. Birches, once again, especially the rather heavier Himalayan species, might offer the best hope.

Magnolia copses

I am not sure where I first found the idea of a tightly packed copse of magnolias underplanted by spring bulbs. It may have been from Sissinghurst, with its spring display of bulbs and woodlanders under the tightly controlled, multi-stemmed hazel bushes of the Nuttery, or from the preponderance of blue and yellow spring flowers under shrubs, especially magnolias, that grew here at the Garden House; perhaps it was from the closely planted magnolia stock beds of a local nursery, or from the wild option of the blue-bell-carpeted, coppiced hazel woodlands of Kent. I could convince myself that any one of them was the most significant but as likely as not it was a combination of all four.

What these different locations share is the silvery-grey trunks of the trees. The trunk colour on the majority of magnolias is a wonderful silver grey, and is often surprisingly neglected when the attributes of these aristocratic plants are listed. In many cases its appeal is almost the equal of a birch tree, and aside from their flowers is their main attribute as far as I am concerned. In our damp but generally clean air of southwest England, magnolia trunks develop excellent lichen growth, which accentuates their wonderful sculptural qualities.

Wherever the idea drew its first breath, the plan was to put twenty-five to thirty magnolias in an area of about 20 sq m (24 sq yd), normally the same space allocated to a single specimen, and then allow them to grow where they wanted. A few years down the line, as they grew up, I intended to gradually remove their lower branches to leave an informal thicket of architectural trunks, surrounded by spring flowers and topped by clouds of exotic white flowers. I must admit the plan was influenced at this point by the availability of twenty-five to thirty young, scrawny and therefore unsellable *Magnolia* × *soulangeana* plants in dire need of a home.

That was all a few years ago now, so, did it work? The short answer is a simple 'yes', judging by the diminishing number of complaint notes left by visitors at the gate, telling us 'your shrubs are planted far too closely'. It was not a quick fix idea, anyway, but with the magnolias in such poor health to start with it became even slower. Once a young magnolia, as with quite a few other plants, receives a major check on its growth for a period of a couple of years or so, it finds it very hard to engage gear and get growing again, a point worth remembering if you are contemplating buying a sick-looking magnolia at a bargain basement price. They were not helped by an assault by rabbits who seemed to single out the magnolias for special treatment, a problem that was eventually solved by the building up of our cat population.

The close planting had a practical advantage in that the group as a whole seemed better able to withstand strong winds than single specimens, which are prone to split in exposed positions. As for the planting underneath, you will need to decide from the outset what you would like to grow there and plant early, as earth moving when the trees are established and have infiltrated every inch of the soil with their roots is not practicable. Once wood anemones, chionodoxas, primroses and erythroniums, for example, have been introduced to such a site they should seed themselves about without the need for any further soil disturbance.

Eucalyptus woods

Eucalyptus is a genus which I feel often looks out of place in an English landscape. In the UK these trees are usually planted as single specimens and more often than not, when mature, they appear to be 18 m (60 ft) of trunk topped off with 3 m (10 ft) of foliage. To my eye, they nearly always look slightly incongruous. There can, however, be safety in numbers and if you plant a group or grove of eucalyptus, it should be possible to capture the emotional spirit of a little part of Australia or southern California.

I have still to see the 'gums' growing in their native country, but I have come across them in the Golden State and South Africa, where in both cases they have found conditions very much to their liking and become a bit of a pest. There is a wonderful richness and quality of light from the cool shade of these Californian gum woods. Then, of course, there is that distinctive eucalyptus smell, not to mention the textural carpet of long bark strips, so dry you are almost frightened that static electricity from your clothes might spark off a raging inferno. A Tasmanian visitor told us of the amazing speed at which these fires can travel. When his property was threatened in a bush fire, the fire officer doused the house with water, brought the family into the garden and, judging the speed of the flames' approach, shouted to them exactly when to hit the deck and lie, face down, on the ground. After a few minutes the fire had passed, leaving them all unscathed—-a story that also shows a touching faith in the fire brigade on their part.

Mixed woodlands

Lovely as it is to see single species woodlands, the majority of natural British woods are mixed, as are most of the woods I have seen in other parts of the world. In the northern New England states and in Ontario, Canada, it is the evergreen spruces and pines which act as both foil and

ABOVE *In one part of Yarner Wood on Dartmoor, England, the trunks of the trees are of strongly contrasting shades. The busyness of the trunkscape is balanced by the simplicity of the bilberry ground-cover.*

contrasting shape to the glorious fall colours of the maples, birches and other deciduous species. I remember my father quoting the only other ornamental gardener (as opposed to a vegetable gardener) in the village where we grew up, who had told him that to achieve a good year-round garden there should be 75 per cent evergreens, particularly conifers. My father adopted it as a general principle and I followed suit, but now, with so many choices complicating life, I am not so firm in my belief. In a more traditional garden vista that uses trees and shrubs as its basis, such

as the Long Walk at the Garden House, I think it probably still holds good, although the percentage of evergreens perhaps should be closer to 40 per cent. However, I can visualize fabulous, more nature-inspired gardens where the evergreen element will vary from 0 per cent to nearly 100 per cent, so on that basis I am finally jettisoning that long-held plank of my gardening education.

Despite the name, western oak woodland is mixed, and is actually rare in Europe, being primarily restricted to the western UK and Ireland. Yarner Wood is a wonderful example and is part of a National Nature Reserve near Bovey Tracey on East Dartmoor. One of the designated paths takes you through a large section of quite open woodland with a striking combination of trunk colours and understorey planting (see opposite). The trees are mostly mountain ash (*Sorbus*), with silvery-grey trunks, and oaks covered in moss that turns almost black in the spring. This silvery-grey and black combination is set off by an almost continuous fresh green understorey of bilberry (*Vaccinium myrtillus*), forming gently undulating hummocks, and by the russets, ochres and verdant greens of the emerging leaves overhead. It is simple, restful and quite magical when the sun comes out. More importantly, it is eminently translatable to a garden situation. It would be relatively easy to produce an open wood with contrasting trunk colours and this was the rationale behind my own birch wood, but it would take a strong will to restrict yourself to just two or three tree species.

Birch trunks

I had already planted the birch wood here before I saw the more sophisticated version hinted at by the trees of Yarner Wood, or the paper birches of Maine, so mine is a cosmopolitan mix. Birches can provide a wide range of trunk colours apart from the whites we normally associate with them. The gardeners' classic white-trunked birches are *Betula utilis* var. *jacquemontii* and *B. papyrifera*, but in both cases buying a plant under these names does not automatically mean you will have a white-trunked tree eventually, as there is considerable species variation in the wild. If white is absolutely essential, it would be best to look for selected clones such as *B. utilis* var. *jacquemontii* 'Jermyns' or 'Inverleith'.

Among the creamy-white birches, *B. ermanii* 'Grayswood Hill' is my favourite, not least because of its clear, rich yellow autumn colour. *B. papyrifera* 'Saint George' is a vigorous variety and takes the trunk colour into a rich orange brown with good yellow autumn colour as well.

In the ochre to pink range of trunk colours, the hybrids *B.* 'Conyngham' and 'Hergest' lean towards the former colour, and the seedling of *B. utilis* selected here at the Garden House and named 'Buckland' is much more pink. All three show very little in the way of autumn colour and if forced to choose just one, I might just opt for 'Conyngham' for the lovely fresh green of its young leaves and the long catkins of flowers in the spring.

A rich cinnamon-coloured trunk is the hallmark of some forms of the very striking *B. utilis*, being the same colour as some of the strawberry trees (*Arbutus* species), or like a vigorous, non-peeling paperbark maple (*Acer griseum*). Darker still is *B. utilis* 'Fascination' which, although still very young in our garden, shows every sign of being exceptionally dark and a suitable candidate to represent those black-trunked oaks of Yarner Wood. A couple of years ago I might have given this job to the river birch, *B. nigra*, which develops its shaggy dark bark as it matures, but surprisingly is as smooth as a silk-stockinged leg when young. The group of river birch I had planted here shot up to about 7.5 m (25 ft) in no time and was a big hit all round, then the trees suddenly started to lose their lower branches at an alarming rate. I have since read that the 'Heritage' clone of this birch is a better 'doer'.

I could imagine any number of pairs of these birches looking good together, perhaps 'Grayswood Hill' with a cinnamon-trunked *B. utilis*, or the slightly lighter-coloured trunks of *Prunus maackii*, the Manchurian cherry, or maybe 'Conyngham' with 'Fascination'. I cannot think of a better understorey planting than the *Vaccinium myrtillus* at Yarner Wood. The fresh green of its foliage and its low, domed habit of growth is a perfect foil for showing off the trunks without blocking the vistas between them, yet grows high enough at about 1 m (3¼ ft) to provide wind protection for low woodlanders, and an element of surprise by obscuring the paths. In the much hotter, drier climate of southern Utah, in Bryce Canyon, we saw low *Arctostaphylos* bushes providing exactly the same sort of role as

RIGHT *Part of the birch wood at the Garden House. As smooth as silk when young, these river birch,* Betula nigra, *become increasingly shaggy with age. The balance of birch canopy to understorey and scrub foreground is very similar to the wild Maine woods shown on page 164.*

understorey planting beneath the dark pines, so it would be easy to imagine this idea working equally as well in a dry climate.

Good trunks are not just confined to the birches. The paperbark maple, *Acer griseum*, is really too slow-growing for a full-scale version of a trunk copse, but it would be perfect if you wanted to have the effect in miniature. I have a couple of groups of this maple, each with five or six planted very close together and allowed to grow where they want. I first saw the paperbark maple growing this way in a nursery where an open ground row had grown too big to transplant and had just been left to produce an informal group of shrubby trees. They looked charming at almost any time of year, but became especially so in the fall with the clear yellow autumn-coloured leaves of the climber *Celastrus orbiculatus* trailing through the red and scarlet colour of the maple leaves, and between them producing an extremely natural wild effect.

❖　❖　❖

WHEN YOU REALLY START LOOKING at woods you begin to appreciate the amazing diversity among them. It is all too easy to be so overwhelmed and humbled by the sheer scale of these magnificent plants that you are literally not able to see the wood for the trees. Delve a little deeper and you may start to notice the shapes and variety of the understorey, the sounds and smells, the colours and textures of the trunks and the quality of light imbued to different woods by the forms and types of various leaf canopies. Some open, majestic woods make me feel as insignificant as a grain of sand in a desert, and still others induce in me a sense of being overlarge and intrusive, like Alice in Wonderland. Yet, with just a little ingenuity and a dash of lateral thinking, it should be possible to harness some of these emotional responses in smaller plantings of our own and, in the process, ignite a little of the power and the strength of those original recollections in our gardens.

8 Shaping plants for effect

The Chinese, and later the Japanese, have been celebrating their wild landscapes for nearly two millennia through, among other things, the art of bonsai. By the creation of a single, relatively small, natural-looking, specimen 'tree' they are able to evoke the wider, wilder landscape. The same principle, on a bigger scale, can work equally as well in our gardens where the 'trees' grow not in containers but in the ground. It is not surprising that one of the commonest plants used by bonsai practitioners, both as the specimen itself and as the wild role-model, is the pine tree. Mature pines, especially those bent by the wind into fantastical shapes, have character of form, texture, colour and contrast. What more could you want? However, unless you are blessed with a mature pine, or several, already existing in your garden, you will have to improvise and down-scale to replicate the form of the wild.

In a moist climate, many of the taller-growing species will romp away too quickly, very easily destroying the balance of smaller schemes. In this instance it would be more sensible to plant slower-growing pines, such as the mountain pine, *Pinus mugo*, or be prepared to selectively remove strong, skyward-growing shoots on more vigorous species such as the black pine, *P. thunbergii*. Even *P. mugo* can grow too big in Devon, so I annually prune some and shape them to keep them the size I want. As you can see from the photograph on page 185, they are starting to produce perfect miniature trees. They will provide a wonderful, in-scale backdrop should I wish to change the foreground at some point in the future from grass to low, grey-leaved shrubs, for example, perhaps to introduce a more Mediterranean-style planting.

Creating miniature pines

The technique for creating mature-looking pine trees in miniature has been perfected by the Japanese in particular for centuries. Of the two pines shown on page 185, the one on the right was planted upright with its very lowest branches removed and the one on the left on its side and placed slightly deeper in the ground so that its lowest branches could be staked up to form a multi-trunked specimen. I tied slim metal poles, about the thickness of my little finger, to the undersides of each of the branches I wanted to keep. (The Japanese use bamboo canes for this purpose, which would be better on smaller branches.) All of these branches were then eased down to be about parallel with the ground and held in place tied to metal poles driven into the

ABOVE *These* Malus transitoria *seedlings are kept deliberately short to emulate the hawthorn-dotted paddocks of my childhood, and so that they do not spoil the view.*

earth. They were kept in these positions for at least two years or until they remained in this pose when all the branch supports were removed.

The next stage was to cut off all twigs growing downwards below the line of the cane tied beneath the branch, and shorten back those growing upwards to no more than 15 cm (6 in). Shoots wanting to go sideways were all left alone.

At this stage the trees were looking very sorry for themselves, but things got worse before they got better: all needles growing down below the line of the supporting cane were plucked off. The reason for this is that on a mature tree, all of the branches will grow up and out to catch the light, and by and large not downwards. The final humiliating touch was to make long cuts with a knife down the main trunk to speed the process of the trunk getting thicker, a bit like the splits on the Incredible Hulk's shirt as his body expanded. Not surprisingly, when I first tried this, I did all the work in the evening when the visitors had left for fear of being thought dangerously strange. You are a stronger character than me if you attempt this on a specimen in your front garden.

The following spring, the plants produced their young shoots on the upper side of the branch and these had to be pinched back to leave about 1 cm (½ in) of new growth. Far from being

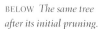

RIGHT *This* Pinus mugo *was planted on its side and, rather riskily, it was also planted very deep. Fortunately it survived, and created several trunks as a result.*

BELOW *The same tree after its initial pruning.*

a chore, I have always found this very therapeutic if done before the shoots become longer than about 7.5 cm (3 in). When new and soft they snap off very easily and satisfyingly between thumb and forefinger, but once they start to harden you will need to cut them, and then it becomes a bit of a bore. It is a process that needs repeating every spring and is no great hardship in the early years, but becomes reasonably time-consuming as the plant reaches the size of those in the picture above. Every shoot pinched back will produce three or four more the following year and the needle size will gradually diminish to give that authentic look. I console myself through this process with the thought that trees such as this in Japan become the main constituent part of a complete garden design and can cost five-figure sums to buy.

Turning shrubs into trees

Growing *Acer griseum*, the paperbark maple, as a short-trunked, multi-stemmed bush tends to blur the distinctions between trees and shrubs.

In this instance I have turned a tree into a shrub, but it works equally well the other way around.

Nearly all of us have shrubs in our gardens, which, with a little judicious pruning, can be turned into beautiful specimen 'trees'. Instead of an area where shrubs are just filling the space and are hardly noticed from one year's flowering to the next, we can create interest and a source of pride in an otherwise unexciting part of the garden. I have used this technique on countless bushes here at the Garden House without once, to my eyes, failing to improve the overall effect of the shrub, and usually transforming the whole surrounding area.

These shrubs may be in grass, but if they are growing in a border, lifting the canopy allows for more planting spaces underneath, a not insignificant inducement to plantaholics. Not all shrubs are suitable and with all due respect to such stalwart plants as forsythia, deutzia, hydrangea, philadelphus and kerria, no amount of pruning will turn them into elegant, natural-looking specimens—their bone structure is just not right. What is required is a bush with a pleasant outline; rounded or domed shapes are good, as are

RIGHT *The habit of these oak trees is fairly typical of native trees on Dartmoor in Devon, England. If you can mimic a similar shape with trees or shrubs of any variety, then you bring a little of the essence of these moorland locations back into your own garden.*

loosely columnar ones, especially if linked to arching or weeping outer branches. I have used this method successfully on a whole range of shrubs including conifers of all sorts, magnolias, azaleas, rhododendrons, camellias, leptospermums, viburnums, pieris and others. Size is not important—a mature evergreen azalea, be it 1.5 m (5 ft) or 60 cm (2 ft), will look excellent standing clear of smaller plants when pruned like this, provided it meets our other criteria. At the other end of the scale, I have shaped a 6 m (20 ft) high photinia to equally good effect.

The key factor in all these transformations is the main trunk or trunks. Just because the principle is to produce a specimen that ends up looking like a small tree it does not necessarily mean it should have a single trunk, although sometimes it will. Look for distinctive multi-branching low down, preferably at ground level, with trunks that run along the ground for a short distance before turning upright being especially prized. Upright trunks can also be good, particularly if linked to slightly weeping or arching higher branches. The bark of the main stems will also crucially affect the finished result. A trunk with an unusually rough, smooth, or flaky texture or one of unusual colouring is much to be preferred to a rather bland, ordinary-looking one. A good way of judging if there is a good specimen to be had in any given shrub is to look at it, if possible, when it is being strongly backlit by the sun. Very often you can see the main trunks in silhouette and imagine what the overall shape of the plant would be if some lower branches were removed.

Having decided on your victim, with saw and secateurs at the ready, your best plan is to proceed slowly. From a few steps back, look at every branch before you cut it off. Starting at the bottom, remove lower branches whose foliage is resting on the ground by cutting them off flush with the trunk, and then gradually, very gradually work your way up. As a general rule of thumb, I remove the branches up to a third of the overall height of the finished 'tree'. Cut off dead, weak or crossing branches with the idea of allowing light to penetrate into the centre of the bush—

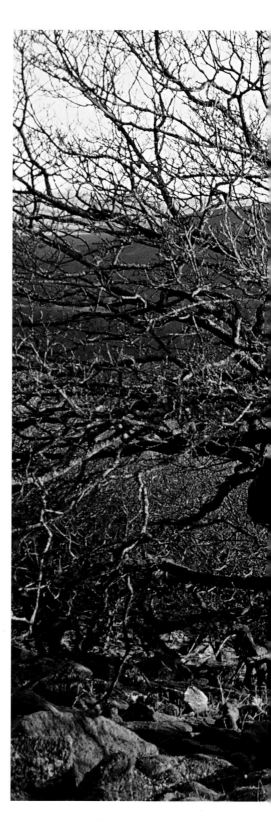

the effect of the dappled light striking the newly exposed trunks is definitely one of the bonuses of the whole process.

The final stage, and the one I agonize over longest, is the thinning of the crown itself. Occasionally it will not need any, but if it does, it is a question of balancing right and left, not necessarily symmetrically, top and bottom, while still allowing glimpses of the inner trunks. It gets easier with experience, but to be truthful not that much easier, so just take your time, and if you are not sure, leave it alone altogether and come back to it at a later date. I stop when I feel comfortable with the shape, this not necessarily being the same as my initial idea of how far I would go. It is, I imagine, a little like being a sculptor, when the shape of the sculpture itself (or the 'tree') takes over, and there comes a point, if you allow yourself to become sensitive to it, when you know you should stop. If you are in the least unsure, it is better to stop anyway and live with the shape for a while.

Shaping shrubs in this fashion has given me enormous pleasure and has undoubtedly contributed character and structure to the garden here, but I know from comments from visitors that results can be mixed. Some have told me, rather accusingly, they had to scrap the plants they were trying it on, as if it were my fault. I liked best one professional gardener's description of his ceanothus, which ended up looking 'embarrassed like someone caught with their trousers down'. Rather more have been successful and many have, very kindly, told me it has equally transformed their gardens, so with the caveat of 'slowly, slowly', I suggest you give it a go.

Low-level magnolias

It is difficult to know with some plants, such as *Magnolia stellata*, whether they should be treated as a shrub or a tree, but a little judicious pruning can swing the effect either way. You sometimes read that this plant looks especially good under-carpeted with blue-flowered spring bulbs such as

Scilla sibirica 'Spring Beauty' or *Anemone blanda* as they flower at the same time as the magnolia. This is true, but the shape of the magnolia will have an important effect upon how good they look together, since if it is grown as a tree, the white flowers will be up aloft and the blue flowers down close to the ground, only in your same eye-line if you are standing some distance away. Even in shrub form, there is often some distance between the flowers of the magnolia and those of the bulbs.

I have got around this problem by planting a young, small magnolia of this species among the bulbs, and then pruning out any upward-growing shoots above approximately 45 cm (18 in) from the ground. By taking out or shortening back annually any shoots that grow skywards, I have found that the magnolia has thickened up and grown sideways, producing compact, low-growing bushes no more than about 1 m (3¼ ft) high, covering themselves in flowers that, most importantly, are in very close proximity to the bulbs beneath. I like to think of them as plant floor-cushions among the bulb meadow.

This pruning experiment has worked out beautifully for me, and in other parts of the garden I have now trained and shaped magnolias against walls, over roofs, and into rounded and columnar small trees. However, in our excellent growing conditions for magnolias I am able to prune them as and when I wish, which may not be feasible in a less amenable climate. If in doubt, err on the side of caution and lightly prune first to see how the plant responds before embarking on major surgery.

Training for naturalistic effects

Straight-trunked trees, often growing to an immense size, are a speciality of the southern Rockies, but on Dartmoor, by contrast, I would almost guarantee that any straight-trunked trees, as with those larches near Burrator Reservoir, have man's fingerprints all over them in their

development. In my area, multi-trunking and twisted, bent trunks are the norm for trees left to their own devices, and this is a characteristic which I have tried to introduce into my plans for the wilder areas as much as possible.

There are at least two ways you can achieve the multi-trunking effect. You can plant deliberately very close, almost in the same hole, in which case you should angle the plants slightly away from each other, but with modern nursery trees being grown in relatively large pots, it is not easy to get the individual plants as close to each other as is ideal. At semi-maturity they will give a multi-trunked effect, but I am too impatient and want the group to look natural immediately. A better alternative is to buy young plants, no more

than 75 cm (2½ ft) high, and preferably whips, which are trees in their first year of growth with leaves coming directly off the main stem. These are perfect because they can then be cut back to about 15 cm (6 in) from the base to leave two to four latent buds, produced in the leaf axils, which will then develop into new shoots. The other advantage with young plants is that they are often grown in smaller pots, which means you can plant several close together should you wish to make an even bigger group. This was the technique I employed on the birches seen in the photograph above.

Young seedlings can usually be cut back quite safely and will sprout again from basal latent buds, but if I were transplanting a young seedling

ABOVE This group of young Betula ermanii *'Grayswood Hill' was deliberately planted close together, and as small plants they were cut almost to the ground to produce as many trunks as possible from the resulting regrowth. After this, left to their own devices, the trunks will grow at different rates, producing over a period of time a very natural-looking group.*

bare root, I think it would be a sensible precaution to allow it to become established for a year before chopping its top off. Should you buy a specimen of 1.5 m (5 ft) or more and wish to cut it hard back, then do so only if you are prepared to lose it, as it would be a bit of a gamble—it might shoot again or it might not.

I have been able to create a very natural, windswept-looking hawthorn (*Crataegus*) as might be seen on Dartmoor from a standard garden centre tree 2.1 m (7 ft) in height. I planted it

with its trunk at an angle of about 30 degrees from the ground and staked it to hold it in place there. Branches growing towards the ground were removed and long, upward-growing ones were tied to thin metal poles along their length, then bent back to run as near horizontal as possible and held in place by supports driven into the ground. During its formative years there were critical comments from visitors who thought we simply did not know how to plant a tree, but with basic annual pruning of being allowed to grow

would have been as guilty as anybody else on this if we had not had a *Wisteria sinensis* growing in the Walled Garden as a free-standing shrub. The Fortescues had planted it on the outside edge of one of the terraces, almost overhanging one of the bigger drops in the garden. I am not sure whether they initially intended to train it along a framework of metal poles so that its flowers hung down over the edge, gracing the lower terrace, or if it was destined to be a standard specimen as can be seen at Knightshayes Court in Devon, with which they would have been very familiar, but when I first saw it the plant was veering more towards a standard.

Growing any wisteria well is not a job for a half-hearted gardener as they do require regular pruning and standards are no better or worse in this respect than those grown in more traditional ways. The shoots they produce from the very base of the plant where it exits the ground are particularly vigorous and can reach enormous lengths in a single growing season. Whether by design or by chance, I let one of these shoots growing away from the edge escape the annual cull. Over the ensuing years it grew into a low-level counterpoint to the semi-standard part of the plant perched on the edge of the terrace, and has now developed into a magnificent specimen (see page 193).

Patience is probably the name of the game in growing wisterias this way, since no special skills are needed by the cultivator. If you want to try one as an informal shrub, start by tying the main stems to a strong post (I use a metal one) after planting, and leave to grow. Once or twice a year, depending on how much you want to fuss, you will need to prune the plant. The standard advice is to do this twice a year, once in late summer back to four buds from the base of the shoot and again in the autumn, shortening to just two buds, which it is to be hoped will be flower buds. How-ever, to save time, I usually do this once a year, cutting back to three buds in the late winter. Any shoots twining around each other or the support-ing post need removing, as do the strong whippy shoots growing from the trunk's base, although

ever wider without growing upwards, it has made a very passable wind-sculpted specimen in only about four to five years.

Free-standing wisterias

We are so used to seeing wisterias climbing over pergolas or trained against house walls, for which they are sublime, that we shut out the possibili-ties for using them in any other way. I am sure I

you can leave one or two of these to develop into future trunks if you want a very broad specimen. In this case, each potential new trunk will need its own supporting post added. All the other long shoots will need shortening back. Most of the shoots will be cut back as already described, but where you want the plant to grow wider, you can leave the shoots up to 15–23 cm (6–9 in) longer than is normally recommended—in fact, you can leave them as long as possible, provided that they do not spring up into the air above a maximum of about 30 degrees from the horizontal after you have cut them. At no more than this angle, when leaves are produced in the following spring, the

shoot will lower themselves naturally under the weight of the foliage to approximately the desired horizontal level.

Wisterias grown as informal shrubs are just about the only plant I prune where I do not have a fixed image in my mind of what I expect the final shape to be. I prefer to let the wisteria tell me in which direction it wants to grow, and in this way no two plants are ever alike.

A mature wisteria grown in this fashion constitutes for me the perfect shrub with complete year-round qualities. These range from beautiful flowers, elegant summer foliage, lovely clear yellow autumn colour (if you plant a

LEFT *This wisteria is being grown as a shrub at the Garden House. It shows the fabulous silvered and gnarled trunks the plant develops with the passing of time.*

FOLLOWING PAGE *Buttermere in the English Lake District.*

W. floribunda variety), those gnarled silver-grey trunks and most importantly a lovely overall shape and habit. While all of this is just as true for a mature wisteria grown as a climber, as shrubs they can be seen as a glorious isolated specimen with no architectural distractions as well as providing first-class dappled shade for smaller plants, such as low woodland perennials and bulbs, growing beneath the canopy.

Wistman's Wood

A wood not far away from the Garden House, on Dartmoor, provided the natural inspiration for a garden development here that may just prove to be my ultimate fantasy. Wistman's Wood is an ancient, predominantly oak wood, perched high on the moor and kept unusually low and stunted, at about 3–4 m (10–13 ft), by the savage growing conditions there. With its boulder-strewn floor and lichen-infested branches, it is the sort of place where you might expect to find a coven of witches or sullen-faced elves sitting around a smouldering fire—very atmospheric, and the sort of place that stokes creative fires in me.

Rather than use oaks, which take for ever to grow into a wood with such a personality, I thought I would use wisterias, allowed to branch at or close to ground-level, growing as natural bushes. These will make a passable impression of an ancient woodland within the space of just a few years, although naturally it will improve in atmospheric quality the longer time goes on. I have planted them on 1 m (3¼ ft) high banks and sunk the narrow, twisting paths, so that the shrubs will only need to reach 1–1.8 m (3¼–6 ft) before it is possible to walk underneath their branches. The banks themselves will provide perfect growing conditions for a vast range of woodland perennials and bulbs, which should thrive in the dappled light and good drainage and provide a colourful low tapestry for months in the late winter and early spring. With the sound of running water introduced in the form of a tiny stream flowing down the hillside in a series of cascades beneath the wisterias, which are trained at this point to arch informally over the water, this could develop into the most romantic part of the whole garden.

part 2
The Garden Landscape

9 Shape and structure

There is beauty in the sensual curve of a path disappearing tantalizingly and mysteriously around a corner, the sinuous line of a trunk or branch, the arching growth habit of a wand flower, or even the contours of a bank or multi-levelled lawn— in fact there is beauty in shape all around us if only we train our eyes to notice it. Perhaps I am a sculptor at heart, because for me good shape is the cornerstone of a good garden. There are so many books and articles written on the surface frothiness of colour coordination and so little on the more fundamental concepts of shape, yet it is the only thing with us in our gardens all year.

I have always felt that if I can make my garden look good and sit comfortably in its setting before a single plant is put in the ground, then I am already half-way to success. Like most people, when I look at a successful scheme I am initially attracted by the flowers and colour, but in my case it is the overall composition and structure of the view that stir deeper feelings of well-being. It is this latter response which I am sure is present subconsciously in many of us that is almost entirely ignored in our gardens.

Until you have trained yourself to absorb the shapes of landscapes, whether they are 'wild' or in a garden, by far and away the easiest time to study them is when the distractions of flowers and colourful leaves are largely absent, which is to say during the winter months. For a few pre-cious months we can feed our creative appetites by evaluating the balance between the various structural elements in our gardens. I have never seen the need to create a specific 'winter garden', preferring to ensure that the gardens I create achieve a natural harmony between land form, the evergreen and deciduous ratio and the various colours of twig and bark, as well as the more obvious elements such as the shapes and sizes of plants, lawns and paths.

In nature, these shapes can often be rather unpredictable, surprising us with their illogical randomness. I have always loved the way in which on many heaths the paths seem to meander rather aimlessly, changing direction suddenly as if created by some drunken sheep, rather the worse for wear, on its way back from a good night

out. A large stone or fallen branch necessitates a rerouting of the path and this sort of infinitely varied detailing is what makes natural landscaping so wonderfully interesting. It is strange, though, that if you replicate this formula in the garden you lay yourself open to accusations of fussiness from horticultural traditionalists who prefer their paths, for example, to be 1.5 m (5 ft) wide with no unnecessary deviations. Where, I wonder, is their sense of adventure?

Wild templates

Identifying the spread, density and general type of trees and shrubs in any landscape is an important element in the process of capturing the essence of that scenery back in your own garden. In smaller plots, the choice of shrubs can dictate the atmosphere for the whole section of garden. In each of the possible examples of garden types discussed here, the shrubs you choose will provide the general ambience of the scheme, and the personal preferences for what grows between will be different for all of us. Tempting as it is for me to produce suggestion after suggestion as to the different effects that could be created, the main purpose of the exercise is to encourage you to interpret these natural landscapes for yourselves rather than to attempt to impose my vision upon you.

In a sunny location, with a well-drained soil, preferably sandy, you could have a romanticized version of the Californian sand dunes I saw north of Los Angeles, near San Luis Obispo, where blue ceanothus grows with the silver-leaved, blue-flowered, shrubby lupin *Lupinus versicolor*, backed in the hinterland by groves of eucalyptus providing some welcome shade and shelter. This is not a garden suitable for cold locations, for sure, but certainly it is one that is achievable along much of the southern counties of England, especially on the Hampshire sands. The pink-flowered tamarisks would consort really well with the Californians and all these shrubs would combine to give structure and shelter for the

palette of colour provided by spring bulbs, annuals and perennials planted between them.

A similar site would be equally suitable for a modified 'sage-brush' garden. The wild originals in New Mexico and Arizona consist of vast tracts of grey-blue sage-brush, with bleached grasses and stands of black-green small pine trees or junipers. The colours of those landscapes translated back into an English garden would provide a very sophisticated backdrop for flowers of soft blue, pink and creamy-yellow when surrounded by low, aromatic, often grey-leaved shrubs. The choice of which shrubs is dependent on your interpretation of the original landscape and your assessment of how the plants growing there would suit your own particular conditions. The pines are, however, a constant, and in this case it makes no difference if they are young pines or not since it is their foliage texture and colour that is more important than habit. The choice of the pines will again be dependent upon the particular climate where you live.

Another variation could be based on the Mediterranean maquis, with low-growing, pink- or white-flowered cistus and grey, felty-leaved phlomis species, usually with whorls of yellow flowers, forming the framework for the more exciting colours produced by the non-woody plants growing between. In this instance you could punctuate the low mounds of the shrubs with groups of the broad, grassy-leaved asphodels, such as *Asphodelus cerasiferus*, whose branching 1.8 m (6 ft) high flower spikes of white flowers have a delicate hint of pinky-brown. Just a little later in the year, the aristocratic foxtail lilies (*Eremurus* species) would produce the same result with flowers ranging from white or pink through rich oranges, salmons and yellows. Provided you choose plants that are compatible with the site orientation and soil type you garden on, the only constraining factor governing what may be planted between these framework shrubs is your imagination.

Had the quarry at the Garden House been in a significantly hotter, south-facing location, for example, I could have created a 'bush' oasis or billabong atmosphere by planting several examples of eucalyptus, clumps of spiky yuccas, some grasses and maybe grey-leaved tamarisk shrubs. The water already present on site and a few large pieces of sun-bleached driftwood would have completed the picture, while the added trapped heat of such a site would also have intensified the eucalyptus aroma.

The overall impression of some eucalyptus trees reminds me of the olive trees of the Mediterranean, although they don't quite have the gnarled charisma of the real thing. However, beggars cannot be choosers, and since we have no hope of growing olives in our area growing one of the hardier gums and then periodically pollarding it might be worth a try. Imagine five or six trees minus 1.8 m (6 ft) of the usual straight trunk so they branch from near ground-level, planted at 7.5–9 m (25–30 ft) spacings, with thin patches of low, dried grasses beneath, and you would have a fair impression of an olive grove.

Bringing the wildness home

In the New Forest in Hampshire it is the balance between the trees (whether they be beech, birch or Scots pine), heaths and pony-munched grass that gives the open glades their character. My mind has a typical image of the New Forest as a wide, central grass ride sited in a gentle depression, with a broad area of heaths and low bushes on either side. Breaking these low shrubs are occasional clumps of multi-trunked birches and, more distinctively, Scots pines. Flanking the whole area are mature woods of generally widely spaced oaks and beeches. For six months through the winter period the harmony between the verdant green of the grass, the mid-greens and russets of the heaths and ferns, the dark, almost black greens of the pines, the white trunks of the birches with their purple clouds of young twigs hovering above and the encircling grey browns of the oaks and beeches is a winning combination. Who would need a 'winter garden' if they could look out of their window at such a

colour scheme? It would be very easy to add summer colour into this equation without compromising the integrity of the original structure.

If you add a few 'sand traps' to this basic model you have a man-made landscape very familiar to many of us, namely the golf course. I enjoy watching golf more for its scenic value than for any sporting prowess taking place and always look forward to the television coverage of the Masters Championship at Augusta, Georgia, where in a normal season the woods surrounding the fairways have a planted understorey of massed azaleas and dogwoods in full flower, a sight that is six weeks earlier than would occur in

southern England. It was these two images that formed the original template for the general shape and composition of the Long Walk back at the Garden House (see page 197).

Shaping the land

Stepping effortlessly from the sublime to the ridiculous is a route some thought I was making in the early years here, as I moved away from the beautiful Walled Garden into the newer areas and started experimenting with shaping the contours of the ground itself. Using the occasional

ABOVE *The young leaves of* Acer shirasawanum *'Aureum' are a beautiful shade of soft yellow/green, among which the clusters of small red flowers can make quite a show for a short time.*

barrowload of spent potting compost to create or emphasize mini-ridges in the rough grass sections made more sense of the closely mown paths that meandered informally as they skirted around these raised parts. Equally, though, to some of our more traditional visitors, it just seemed a little odd. I well remember one notable personage politely enquiring what, or who, was buried beneath the barrows. Even on such a small scale, I still feel such earth-moving is justified as almost insignificant changes of level in short turf can give dramatic light and shade contrasts when viewed in low-angled winter sunlight.

Earth moving with mini-diggers

Over the years, as the engineering works became more ambitious with the help of earth-moving equipment such as mini-diggers, the amount of soil we were able to relocate became ever larger and the potential for earth-sculpting ever greater. By learning to become proficient at handling one of these mini-diggers I opened up a level of creative potential and enjoyment that I would not have thought possible previously. It also had the benefit of forcing me to observe landscapes in the wild more closely, noticing the minutiae of the land forms themselves with the awareness that they are a significant contributory factor to the spirit of the whole.

Moving thousands of tons of soil on a green-field site is not, I realize, everybody's idea of fun, but there are still good pragmatic reasons for considering this route. First, you are able to re-create more closely certain natural landscapes, and second, there are purely practical benefits of gaining shelter and privacy. Consider, for example, a flat, windy site. If you dig out a section of land 1 m (3¼ ft) in depth and mound up the displaced earth 1 m (3¼ ft) higher than the surrounding land on the side of the property from which you want protection from the prevailing winds, you will have created a 1.8 m (6 ft) high windbreak. Plant a series of wind-tolerant 1 m (3¼ ft) high shrubs along the top of this ridge and you will be starting to gain some real benefits from wind protection. It must be said that on a

lot of flat sites digging such a hole will create a deep pond, but the general principle is the object at issue here and it would certainly work on an elevated or sloping site.

Hidden benefits

Altering the natural levels has other advantages as well. It naturally follows that if a bank of soil can create shelter it can also provide privacy. Along the public footpath which runs through a section of the garden here, I have mounded up the soil by approximately 1 m (3¼ ft) along most of its length and planted shrubs of the same height on top, creating an almost instant screen.

Other effects are rather more esoteric. Sculpting the land creates interest and secrecy. A flat green-field site or one with a single slope can all be viewed at once from any given point upon it, or at least until the trees and shrubs grow up, which can take quite a long time. Dig out and shape the land and you create areas that cannot be seen, hidden corners and different slopes and aspects that will suit a wider range of plants— southern slopes, for example, for sun-lovers. In other words, you introduce the crucial element of surprise and diversity.

Lowering the paths relative to the surrounding land also introduces character and a sense of age to the garden, which is priceless in a new development. Paths used for centuries tend to become sunken, so by sinking them to start with, you will trigger that subconscious time connection. Sinking a path and piling up the soil on either side means that any plant growing on these banks automatically appears bigger in relation to the path, which again makes them appear older than they actually are. All tricks, I suppose, but I think it is only natural to want to create the effect of a mature garden as quickly as possible.

Using vistas

In the process of creating the Long Walk, the main vista running away from the house in the newer part of the garden, I piled up thousands of tons of soil in selected places to emphasize the view. By ensuring that the highest part of these soil mounds was at the end nearest to the main viewing point (that is, in front of the house) and that they then sloped gently down towards the intended focal point of the granite standing stones, I managed to create the effect of natural arrows leading your eye into the composition.

A second but almost equally important reason for their existence is their concealment of what lies behind them, emphasizing that element of surprise again. The visitor strolling along the Long Walk for the first time has no idea of what is about to come into view beyond the banks, just a few yards ahead. In this way, for example, I was able to hide the quarry which I had excavated behind one of these mounds, so increasing the sense of drama for the visitor upon first seeing it. To heighten the contours of these banks further, we planted along their ridges large groups of evergreen shrubs, such as hardy rhododendrons, camellias, *Pieris* 'Firecrest' and 'Forest Flame', and *Kalmia latifolia* seedlings, all of which I had in large numbers from our own nursery production. These evergreen groups are the structural ribs of the whole vista, quietly going unsung about their business all year, acting as shelter belt, screening and dark backdrop to deciduous plantings and perennials along the entire length of the Long Walk, before finally having their moments of glory in flower every spring. This was a very windy spot, fully open to the north, so it has been a complete revelation to me how fantastically well the camellias and pieris in particular have thrived in such conditions. It almost certainly helped that we had a series of wet summers for the first few years after planting, and the thick mulch of bracken we applied was especially useful in keeping their roots cool on these exposed banks.

Mulches as backdrop

Sometimes the details can be as important to re-creating the spirit of a place as the big picture. Bark mulches, for example, were firmly linked in my mind to the less sophisticated demonstration gardens of garden centres and flower shows. However, travelling around the western states of the US, especially southern California, made me re-evaluate my prejudice, since I saw bark being used with real creative gardening possibilities. For a start, it had bigger flakes than any that I had seen before, each individual flake being anything up to 15 cm (6 in) long by 5–7.5 cm (2–3 in) wide. Spreading a layer of this bark would immediately create the atmosphere of a coniferous forest glade even in a very small area. And as an additional advantage, the larger size of bark might well trap still pockets of air and act as an insulator for low-growing plants.

Then there is the colour of the bark mulch itself to consider. Having only ever seen a dark brown bark mulch before, it came as a surprise to me to see rich red bark chippings. It is not important whether this was a natural coloration from redwoods, or whether it was the result of the bark being treated; the surge of excitement I felt on seeing it was due to the creative planting opportunities this colour provided. The dark greens of pines, for example, took on extra vibrancy surrounded by this red mulch. The lighter tone also meant that most plants contrasted more noticeably, an invaluable consideration if using low-growing plants.

A bracken mulch is excellent if you want to grow mostly shrubs, especially if they are ericaceous ones. We cut the bracken from the nearby moor when it has made maximum growth, but before it starts to turn brown, usually around mid- to late summer. We get it baled as quickly as possible, bring it in off the moor and then ideally leave the bales to compost down for a year before using then. Cutting it green and baling immediately means the bracken heats up fast and thus rots more quickly. A 7.5–10 cm (3–4 in) mulch of this is a wonderful weed suppressant—lasting for years and eventually rotting down into a very desirable leaf-mould that improves soil structure—is far cheaper than bark and, just for good measure, looks good into the bargain.

Rotted bracken has been used here at the Garden House for over fifty years, either as a

One wonders how old this stunted shrub emerging from a crack in the rock in an area of very little rainfall in South Africa might be. It reminded me of one of those truly ancient 'driftwood style' bonsai specimens.

shrub mulch, layered into the dung heap to stretch the farmyard manure further, or rotavated into the ground where ericaceous shrubs are to be grown. We mulched all of the new beds with bracken in the newly broken field, and were amazed that the bracken appeared to suppress even such rampant spreaders as couch grass and sorrel which we could not totally remove from

the infested root-balls of countless shrubs moved into this new ground. I have since been told that bracken has a mild herbicidal effect when used as a mulch, and our experience would seem to support this.

Although mulching is invariably considered a good thing it is possible to make a mess of it, as I found out when I applied a 7.5–10 cm (3–4 in) layer of bracken to a bed of deciduous azaleas one winter, producing a dramatic reversal of fortunes for two other plants growing in the same area. The good news was for the Scotch flame flower, *Tropaeolum speciosum*, which had previously been languishing in this spot and suddenly became reinvigorated by the newly imposed cool protective blanket. It took off like bindweed, even managing to kill one or two of the large established azaleas supporting it. The bad news was for the thriving colonies of wood anemones, especially the large-flowered variety *Anemone nemorosa* 'Allenii', which were all but wiped out. The moral of the story here is not to mulch your wood anemones too deeply.

Hedges and banks

In the very large garden and park settings that Capability Brown created for many of his grand customers, it was the trees that were the main vegetative structural element of his plans. Not many of us have gardens coming into this category nowadays, but as you come down in scale it is the role of shrubs that increasingly rises in importance and dictates the structure and atmosphere of the garden. In smaller gardens, devices such as hedges, banks, and so forth can give a feel of a wild landscape when planting a beech copse is not an option.

When I was a child the most exotic location we ever travelled to on our summer holidays was the lush greenness of South Devon. There, the banks lining the small lanes are amazingly steep, with the untrimmed hedgerow on top often as much as 4.5 m (15 ft) above the road-level. These shady, precipitous banks are the home of massed ferns, primroses, wood anemones, celandines, wild violets and bluebells (*Hyacinthoides non-scripta*) in the spring, and late in that season are where you will also find one of the southwest's best flower spectacles, featuring a colour combination of pink, white and blue from campion (*Silene*), greater stitchwort (*Stellaria holostea*) and bluebells. Following on from those, foxgloves

(*Digitalis purpurea*), valerian (*Valeriana officinalis*), yellow toadflax (*Linaria vulgaris*), hedge-bedstraw (*Galium mollugo*) and stinging nettles can all be occupying the same stretch of roadside. It does not take a great leap of imagination to visualize a more romanticized version of this, creating a wonderful feature in a garden using the more colourful of the native plants, but supplementing them as necessary with some showier semi-exotics, such as Jacob's ladder (*Polemonium*) or larger-flowered species of geraniums.

Old, established natural hedges are often composed of many different species, and there is a rule of thumb that the number of woody species in a 27 m (30 yd) stretch equates to the age of the hedge in centuries. When this principle is translated into a garden setting, with several different varieties or species in the same hedge, the result is sometimes called a 'tapestry hedge'. Another style is the 'cloud hedge', a concept that has been around for a long time and is currently very fashionable. Cloud hedges are so-called because their informal, undulating outline is more reminiscent of fluffy, cottonwool cloud formations than the traditional ramrod-straight profile that is more usually aspired to as hedge perfection. The huge yew hedges at Powis Castle in Wales have been cut in this way for years, and at the Garden House I have given the same treatment to a large camellia hedge, albeit without describing it by the catchy name.

Spring-flowering banks

Given the right setting it would be good to combine the principles behind the tapestry and cloud types to produce a hedge which I have not seen done before. I arrived at the idea from the unlikely source of the ubiquitous and much-hated flailed hedges that have become such a staple of the English countryside. Around here and in Cornwall particularly, these tightly trimmed hedges occur on top of walled banks and are cut back annually almost down to hug the bank itself. Each spring, the banks are transformed into natural gardens, as a whole series of perennial plants come into flower with the twigs of the shrubs supporting them. You see the same mix of bluebells, white stitchwort and pink campion as are in the Devon lanes, and with yellow butter-cups flowering as well among the unfolding croziers of ferns and the russets, golds and greens of the burgeoning leaves of the hedge itself, there is a flower spectacle as good as anything the British flora has to offer.

A modified version of these hedges would make a wonderful feature in a garden, perhaps on a wide, sloping, raised bank. The first requi-site would be shrubs that did not mind being cut annually, and then the list could be narrowed down to include those with a range of different young growth colours in spring. If shrubs were chosen that displayed autumn colour as well you could have at least two periods of the year when this bank was looking marvellous, without con-sidering any flower effects or the architectural shape it could be trimmed into. In my wet cli-mate the list of shrubs which are content to be trimmed hard annually would be much greater than in areas with less liquid sunshine. I would choose shrubs of similar vigour and with similar leaf size, but aim for maximum variation of spring leaf colour and a mixture of evergreens and deciduous plants. Cutting would probably take place in late winter, shaping it into very gentle undulations with a hedge-trimmer, and I would plant robust bulb species such as bluebells or perennials in the lower troughs created by this annual trim. I can imagine a bank where the vig-orous *Euphorbia cyparissias* 'Red Devil', with its purple-stained young foliage, would grow between and below this low-cut shrubby frame-work, producing drifts of its frothy, acid-yellow flowers at the same time as bluebells and pink campion, and it could be sensational. A whole series of interlocking banks planted this way, with the path threading its way beneath them, could create a lovely framework for a garden, especially in a wind-challenged site.

The structural element of this idea would be enhanced even further if the banks were faced, as in the Cornish originals, with rough walling stone. The effect of this would be less gentle and undulating, but the stoned banks would impart far stronger definition to the whole garden, particularly in the winter months.

Sylvan similarities

Given their size, it is not surprising that trees, whether they be large or small, are one of the most important elements of the structure of most gardens. Generally speaking I prefer to plant trees in groups of single species when trying to produce a naturalistic effect. However, when space is at a premium, as it is for the vast majority of us, the temptation to grow as many different plants as possible is overwhelming. For example, since birches are nearly all superficially similar, I felt no need to stick to a single species in attempting to create a birch wood atmosphere, as a number of different species and varieties still provide an homogeneous whole while creating subtle variations of trunk, leaf and fall coloration.

I have used the same technique with all the main tree types employed in the newer garden, limiting myself, apart from birches, to just a few genera, namely the dogwoods, magnolias, maples and witch hazels (*Hamamelis* species), but planting all of these in considerable variety. It may seem a little incongruous to plant such apparently exotic genera and hope they blend with a quintessentially English landscape such as the Devon country surrounding us here but surprisingly they do, with the exception of the Japanese maples which I have planted together out of sight of the main views of the countryside. The reason they blend so well without being replicas of the native species is because the exotics chosen still have the feel of the immediate natural environment. Take as an example the flowering dogwoods, especially the Asiatic *Cornus kousa* and its varieties, which have a superficial similarity in flower and habit, when seen from a distance, to our native elder bushes, *Sambucus nigra*. Witch hazels have an uncanny

resemblance in leaf, trunk colour and habit to our native hazel, and magnolias are not dissimilar in habit and leaf to sweet chestnut and in their winter trunks to ash trees. So by using these tree species, together with the odd oak, mountain ash and beech, I have been able to replicate the core identity of the treed landscape all about us while introducing a range of more ornamental species. As a result of this, the garden and its surrounding countryside blend seamlessly and the garden itself is imbued with a larger-than-life naturalness. In this way I am accentuating the ornamental qualities of our landscape, or, if you like, romanticizing nature.

ABOVE *But for the cistus growing at their feet, these Cretan oaks would not look out of place on Dartmoor in the UK.*

10 Between rocks and hard places

There can be very few gardens indeed, whether traditional or naturalistic, which do not benefit from the twin needs of having a focal point and a strong structure, and nothing is better at supplying these than stone in all its various forms. Whether it be stone walls, scattered rocks or just some form of chippings or sand upon the paths or parts of the planted beds, by carefully introducing stone to our gardens we can add contrasting and complementary colour, and provide a new dimension in texture and form against which our plantings can only be immeasurably enhanced.

The area of England I most associate with rock and stone is the Lake District, in the far north of England. Here there is a unique harmony with the wider landscape, where stone is the constant unifying factor between fells, lakes, woods and man's imprint in the form of the walls and buildings. Such is the perfection of scale in this scenery that it appears more massive than mere altitude figures would seem to suggest. There is a romantic perfection here as well, in the balance between these various elements; in the same way that some Japanese gardens portray an idealized version of their own natural landscape, the 'chocolate-box' flawlessness of whole sections of the Lake District is just so complete it seems almost more contrived than natural, giving the impression of being the Almighty's attempt at creating his or her own divine Japanese garden. Look for a moment at the photographs on pages 233-49 of watery scenes from the Lakes; none of them would seem at all out of place in a Japanese garden.

From my point of view, looking for gardening inspiration from natural landscapes, it appears as if some dales, for example Borrowdale, are just gigantic living manuals of gardening inspiration. From the banks of Derwentwater, through the woods and following the becks up on to the fells, there are ideas everywhere you look. Aside from the water-related possibilities, which I will return

ABOVE *An old quarry at Castle Crag, Borrowdale, in the north of England. The combination of rock faces, stone rubble, mossy turf and sculptural larch trees could be re-created in a garden setting with a whole host of different planting options.*

PREVIOUS PAGE *A pair of greylag geese make it quite clear that this pond, just below Haystacks in the English Lake District, is their territory.*

to in the next chapter, these might involve more narrowly focused concepts, such as the shapes and curves of walls (see page 12), the distinctive feel of the open oak woods with their mixture of predominantly ferns and rocks below, or a wealth of micro elements from the plant inhabitants of the walls. All are capable of being interpreted in a garden setting.

Quarries

In the photograph above of Castle Crag, in Borrowdale, this old quarry seems to exemplify the point. I could have used the image to illustrate the shape of the trees and how this may be achieved in the garden, or how the larches create a quiet simplicity in this setting which I for one would be only too happy to live with. In fact, I include this photograph at this point because it is the stone itself I wish to draw attention to. Most

gardeners when faced with a site where stone is lying around might be tempted to clear the area first without giving much thought as to whether the stone itself could become a main feature of the garden. In fact, strictly limiting the number of plants grown among the rubble and congregating them in isolated groups would emphasize the qualities of both plant and stone and still give a strong sense of a quarry environment. If stone only is present the feel is that of a desert; plants alone are lush but dull and give no sense of place or setting; but use them together in moderation and you can allow magic to invade this space, with the strength, texture and colour of the stone acting as a perfect counterpoint to the soft delicacy of the plants.

The stone rubble lying in front of the trees might be a template for any number of dry garden designs. For example, substitute a group of eucalyptus for the larch and grow a few spiky, architectural plants among the stones and you

LEFT *Scots pines grace a typical English Lakeland view above Borrowdale. Tolerant of harsher growing conditions than many other species, it is the tree often found on these upland, exposed sites. More often than not, they are twisted and bent by the winds into highly distinctive shapes. As with bonsai specimens, emulating these characteristic forms in the garden can regularly remind you of the wild, rugged and windswept locations that Scots pines naturally inhabit.*

would have the basis for a garden with an Australian feel. Alternatively, replace the larches with dark-leaved pines and grow low grasses among the stones and you might catch the atmosphere of New Mexico or Arizona. Should you live in a damp climate, the same photograph could be used as a basis for a completely different planting with ferns and herbaceous plants growing among the stones.

I have always felt sad that Mr Fortescue filled in the one remaining small quarry that had been opened for stone extraction to build the house here. Quarries are such romantic places; I can almost hear the sharp, reverberating tap-tapping of ghostly chisels every time I walk into a disused one. The echoing sounds of one's own presence is a tangible reminder of the countless souls who toiled there in the past. All that prodigious manual effort in such harsh conditions is reduced to a hole in the ground, now softened as likely as not by the mirror-like surface of a lake of unfathomable depth, with the eerie squeals of nesting kestrels bouncing off the all-encompassing, plunging, vertical cliffs. There is nothing quite like an old, abandoned quarry to unite the past with the calm of a self-contained, imaginary world of the present.

Most farmhouse-sized country houses, built in areas where building stone is present underground, would have their own quarries nearby. If you are lucky enough to own a house with an old quarry in its grounds and want to incorporate it naturally into the garden, it will depend on its size and location as to how you might go about this. Many, perhaps most, that you see are found in wooded locations, presumably because after the stone extraction was finished the quarry and its environs became unproductive ground, and seedling trees were able to grow unmolested. In these sites ferns and foliage plants seem the obvious plant inhabitants, and I would attempt to restrict myself to green-leaved plants. More sunny, open sites give you more of a choice of planting styles. The soil in a real quarry is likely to be in short supply, so it is probable that some of the stone might need to be removed to add

something for the plants to root into. Where a quarry ambience is being deliberately introduced, the stones can be just added for effect, on top of existing soil.

The very enclosed nature of quarries means that you can develop a garden design from almost any part of the world, without it clashing with the surrounding countryside. My ultimate garden site would be an abandoned 0.8–1.2 ha (2–3 acre) quarry, surrounded on three sides by 6–9 m (20–30 ft) high cliffs and open with panoramic views on the fourth and south side. The quarry floor would be strewn with stone debris, broken up into smaller units by moraine-like hills which would in turn create some small ponds. In this version of gardening heaven, I could make different gardens based on natural landscapes, each with a flavour all its own, and none of them looking out of place.

The Garden House Quarry Garden

Stretching over a period of a couple of years at the Garden House, where I had started to extract building stone, quite a large hole in the ground had developed and the deeper parts of this had exposed some good rock faces. I thought I might be able to blend this small quarried area with the rest of the new garden by having large groupings of alpine plants on gently sloping raised banks with no rock to be seen, and this is exactly what I did, thereby bringing the Quarry Garden into existence (see opposite below and page 55).

The origins of this had come years before when I had changed a small shrub-covered raised border in the Walled Garden into an alpine bank. Since I had so few places to grow alpines I grew numerous different plants crammed into this small space. It was, in fact, a typical alpine enthusiast's alpine bank, fascinating to visitors who are very keen on those plants and deadly dull to those who are not. Over the next few years the planting gradually became increasingly simplified, either because the more difficult plants died during our wet winters or because they mysteriously disappeared. The result was that the groupings became larger, with easier-to-grow

plants predominating. The overall effect was much better, and it became a favourite part of the garden for many of our visitors. With the arrival of the Quarry Garden, I could try these same combinations on a much bigger scale.

One of my guiding principles in gardening is to have all the plants in a particular area of the garden flowering together and accepting that at all other times it will be mostly green, instead of trying to make each area flower for as long a period as is humanly possible. With this in mind, my intention was to make the Quarry Garden have a relatively short but spectacular flowering display, relying at all other times of the year more on its seductive shapes and calming, trickling rivulets of running water.

Creeping thymes (*Thymus serpyllum* varieties) form the basis of the planting, turning the ground throughout late spring and early summer into interwoven carpets in shades of purple and

white, as rich as any Persian rug. Between the thymes I have indulged myself by planting great swathes of *Rhodohypoxis* in variety. These start to flower in mid-spring and will continue for two months, or even longer if the soil is good, meaning that their colour combinations can be taken advantage of prior to the thymes. The easy alpine phloxes *Phlox douglasii* and *P. subulata* grow really well with them, as do some of the more compact alpine pinks (*Dianthus* varieties), especially *D.* 'Brymos' whose grey-green hummocks still look neat after the candy-pink flowers have faded. Linking this mid to late spring flowering together is the glaucous-leaved, white flushed pink-flowered *Sedum rupestre* 'Minus' which gently self-seeds around.

The thymes also happily self-seed into any vacant bare soil they can find, which has spread them much further than was originally my intention. As a result they have put themselves among the herbaceous plants and low shrubs of neigh-bouring parts of the garden, which in turn helps to blend the different areas together (see page 213 top). One such area of just a couple of square metres (square yards) had been planted with the low-growing *Dianthus* 'Brymos' and some dwarf, shrubby helianthemums and rhodo-dendrons. In came self-seeded thymes, the pink sedum and the pretty but invasive wild tormentil, *Potentilla erecta*, which grows all over Dartmoor (see below). I felt quite pleased with this little combination of plants, though I had no right to as it was so little to do with me.

Screes

To those of us who are constantly advised that a free-draining, moisture-retentive, humus-rich loam is the holy grail of soil types for gardens, it must seem a bit peculiar that alpine specialists recommend growing especially treasured plants

in a pile of stones and gravel—this being essentially the composition of a scree (see page 216). In general gardening parlance, the term 'scree' is used to describe any planting that comes through a surface mulch of pea-shingle or fine chippings, especially if it is on a slope. But this is too simplistic a definition.

A properly made scree will be at least 60 cm (2 ft) deep, with potato-sized stones occupying the lowest 15 cm (6 in). Since perfect drainage is the name of the game, you will need to choose a site where even the water percolating through to this lowest stone level can drain away, so this is easiest to achieve on a sloping site or in a raised bed, but can be done on level ground with a little ingenuity. The next 23–30 cm (9–12 in) above these stones should be made up with a mixture of good top-soil, leaf-mould, pea-shingle and small stones of 5 cm (2 in) diameter or less. I would use these in a ratio of about 25:25:30:20 but this is flexible so long as the mix is very sharply drained and contains nutrient-rich soil or similar, for this is the main root zone for the scree inhabitants. You can test whether this is draining fast enough by emptying a watering-can of water through its rose as quickly as you can onto the mixture. The water should drain straight through with absolutely no ponding. If it does not you need to add more pea-shingle.

Above this layer comes 15–23 cm (6–9 in) of 75 per cent pea-shingle to 25 per cent good soil or leaf-mould, and lastly, topping off the whole scree, comes a 7.5–10 cm (3–4 in) layer of pea-shingle. The whole construction is designed to make the plant send out its roots deep into this mixture, producing a wide-ranging root system that will remain cool at this depth, whatever the weather above, as well as perfectly drained, but with enough moisture remaining among the stones to need no watering once it has become established.

Just about every genus of plant, from vegetables to daphnes, has its fanatical devotees prepared to move heaven and earth for their chosen ones, and in most cases, aesthetic considerations as to whether the newly created environment blends with the rest of the garden are irrelevant. The beauty of a scree is that it will blend into any garden design provided a little thought is given beforehand. Not many of us, I suspect, will have gardens where the steeply sloped screes of the mountains will have a resonance, as you would need a sloping, rocky site for the 45–60 degree scree to look right. However, screes constructed on the flat or on gently sloping sites are extremely practicable. Wherever you choose to create one, the top layer of pea-shingle should match the colour of your local stone as closely as you can manage it if you want the scree bed to blend in with its surroundings.

Walls and colonizers

I am creating a garden of low tumbledown walls at the time of writing, but it is situated in a little too much shade to capture the feel of the stone walls of the Mendip hills which were so much a part of my childhood. I know that one day I will build a much larger garden based on those Mendip walls; I can picture it in my mind now. Although the occasional erratic turn would add surprises, generally the 1.8 m (6 ft) wide path will slope downhill, gently meandering from side to side. Raised slightly above the path (to give a sunken lane feel) and set back by 1–2 m (3¼–6 ft) on either side will be roughly built dry-stone walls about 1 m (3¼ ft) high. These sloping verges will be filled with an informal mass of herbaceous plants, intermingled with plenty of British native species such as campion, ox-eye daisies and buttercup—the whole planting mostly in the 60 cm (2 ft) range. There will be no variegated plants, the aim being to re-create the feel of those natural Mendip verges, but adding a little extra dash of colour. The whole thing will be a sea of summer colour with the stone walls affording both some protection and acting as a handsome backdrop to show off the flowers. The walls will frame the garden picture, making this 3.6–5.4 m (12–18 ft) wide feature a complete garden in its own right, especially since, ideally, it

will be located on the side or brow of a hill with wide-ranging views.

Dry-stone walls

I had a small dry run of this 'Mendip' version when I built the 'cottage' in the Cretan area of the garden. Instead of leaving the little 'ruin' standing in isolation, I extended the walls in one direction, gradually lowering their height until they disappeared below ground-level. A parallel wall, built 1.8 m (6 ft) away, creates a narrow approach path to the cottage, with both walls shaped to mimic the contours of the distant hills in the church view. The intention here was that visitors, on first seeing these walls, would subconsciously link the surrounding countryside with the garden standing immediately in front of them. Their construction gave me a lot of fun,

enough thought to analysing the conditions these plants are growing in. Walls can be wonderfully cool environments or spectacularly hot and dry, depending on their orientation obviously, but more pertinently on the proximity of a body of cool soil behind the stone façade in which the plants can root.

The overwhelmingly vast majority of free-standing dry-stone walls erected in the past are built with stone rubble packing the central gaps between the stone faces and then the wall topped-off with a coping stone course to prevent water penetration. In this way, the wall as a unit stays dry and therefore avoids subsidence. Established dry-stone walls in good condition are unlikely to be easy places in which to grow new plants. Often those that are already growing in them have got their roots deep down into the wall where soil and moisture are available, or else they occupy a little pocket of accumulated leaf-mould. Without an artery of rooting medium running into the core of the wall, it is very, very difficult for any introduced plant to survive without almost constant watering. Drought-tolerant genera, such as *Sempervivum* and some sedums, are possible, but even their success is not really guaranteed. The only sure way of having free-standing stone walls covered in plants is to build your own planting as you go.

When building my Cretan cottage walls, I used top-soil and spent potting compost to bed down my stones instead of the usual stone rubble. This should be vigorously rammed into the gaps, particularly behind the stones, to try to prevent large air pockets developing when the soil inevitably subsides. The handle of your stone hammer is good for this compacting, but this is not a job for damp weather when it becomes impossibly sticky to work with the soil. It will help subsequent planting a lot, too, if you angle the stones so that their tops are dipping down as sharply as you can manage towards the centre of the wall. This results in any rainfall running back towards the roots and helps to lessen the chances of soil washing off in heavy downpours. If you are well-organized enough to know at this stage what

and an opportunity to build walls specifically for growing plants in.

It is amazing how many gardeners have tried to cultivate plants in an established dry-stone wall and failed at this task. I think in part this may be because having seen plants flourishing and looking lovely in a wall somewhere, maybe tumbling from old walls in another garden or in the countryside perhaps, they have not given

LEFT *A hawthorn tree ekes out an existence on an enormous semi-stabilized scree in the English Lake District, its shape emphasizing the downward pull of gravity upon the whole hillside. The calm of Buttermere acts as a counterpoint in the distance.*

RIGHT *Behind the majestic spikes of* Rodgersia pinnata *'Superba' stands the old tower, dominating the lowest terrace of the walled garden. It is all that now remains of a sixteenth-century vicarage that once stood here. The leaves and stems of self-seeded* Campanula poscharskyana *dotting the masonry are red-tinged from the spartan conditions of its habitat, forming a fortuitously perfect complement to the harmony between stone and the pinks, purples and blues of the foreground.*

you want to grow in your new wall, it certainly is very much easier to plant things in stages as the wall is being made. In the finished construction, it is often only possible to plant small specimens.

Campanulas

Certain plants look so right growing in these walls, and a number of the alpine campanulas come into this category. I would imagine many of the harder-to-grow species would be quite at home in these conditions, but I have limited myself to the easy varieties. It is unfortunate the taxonomists gave a new name of *Campanula portenschlagiana* to a species whose old name of *C. muralis* (of walls) so accurately described where it looks so much in its element. Even after its soft blue flowers have gone over, the neat foliage hugging the interstices between the stones clothes the wall with fresh green leaves. I have seen this species growing out of hairline cracks in mortared walls, producing neat pools of colour in late spring.

C. *poscharskyana* is much more vigorous, almost rampageous. This harebell flowers later, in midsummer, covering many of the walls in the Walled Garden as well as colonizing any flat ground it can, where its sprawling flower stems can mound up to 45 cm (18 in) high, although they are more likely to flop over at this height. In drier conditions, as in the stonework of the Tower, the flowering stems and buds are quite noticeably red-tinged, giving a beautiful two-tone effect which complements the red and blue colours in the stone itself (see left). Its vigour demands I urge caution upon you before you plant it, but I would not want to be without the unifying wild naturalness with which it imbues the whole Walled Garden, when it is both in and out of flower.

Other wall-dwellers

The same effect is produced in the walls of the Cottage Garden by the pink and white, daisy-flowered *Erigeron karvinskianus*. This is the same plant that at one time covered much of the paving and low walls surrounding the pond near

the house at Great Dixter, Christopher Lloyd's garden in East Sussex. Its common name is the Mexican fleabane but I have heard it called the crazy daisy, for the rapid speed at which it can spread. I am happy to forgive its colonizing tendencies, as it flowers almost incessantly and is undeniably pretty. When I originally conceived the idea of a ruined cottage looking as if it had been reclaimed by the natural spread of an encircling luxurious garden, I could not have wished for a more perfect plant to help clothe the walls

ABOVE *The Mexican fleabane,* Erigeron karvinskianus, *completely obscures the wall it has colonized, deservedly earning itself its other vernacular name of crazy daisy. A self-seeded* Geranium palmatum *looks just right growing at the wall's base.*

than this little daisy. Unlike the campanula, its smaller leaves and finer growth habit means it is feasible to grow other plants with this erigeron, especially if it is periodically sheared back close to the stonework.

Another self-introduction to the cottage walls must have arrived from a seed in the compost which I had used in part to fill the central spaces in the walls. This was an *Epimedium* hybrid, with the evergreen, yellow-flowered *E. davidii* as one of its parents, judging from the foliage, and normally very much a cool-growing woodlander. It is pretty without being very exciting, and an unexpected success in the side of a wall. In this position the flower stems grow vertically on emerging from the stones so they are almost immediately standing clear of the leaves, which solves a minor problem some epimediums have of hiding their flowers among the foliage. On the other hand, *E. × versicolor* 'Sulphureum', which put itself in a similar site in the Walled Garden, does not send its flowering stems more noticeably skywards than if it were growing on the flat so trial and error, as always, will give the answer.

Other plants, beautiful in their own right on the flat, are transformed into an even lovelier sight when they are grown on their sides in a wall. When, for example, you see the Pyrenean plant *Ramonda myconi* flowering in such a position you know that this must be how it grows in the wild. The dark green, corrugated leaves form rosettes which hug the wall, with the flowering stems standing vertically like those of the epimedium hybrid, so you view the lilac-blue saucer-shaped flowers against the stone.

If the idea of growing plants on a vertical plane appeals to you but you do not have the time, money or inclination to build stone walls, you could use the idea of the hollow concrete structures that hold back steep banks on the side of a motorway or around supermarket car parks, for example. I adapted this concept to the hollow concrete blocks that builders merchants will supply for building cavity block walls in houses. Placed on their sides (rather than the way they are meant to be used) and angled slightly back,

each one provides two very nice planting holes. With no mortar required between the blocks, the wall is simplicity itself to build and it is a quick, cheap way of retaining a bank of soil. The standard concrete blocks are certainly not very pretty, but if you look around they do come in rather less ugly guises, sometimes in a pleasing ochre colour, with larger, easier-to-plant cavities. A north-facing wall I built like this grew the best petiolarid primulas I have ever cultivated, with the mealy-leaved soft yellow-flowered *Primula aureata* and the ice-blue *P. whitei* growing like small cabbages.

Wall dwellers for sun

Most of the plants mentioned so far are cool growers, best on the shady side of a wall, since the southern aspects can get very hot. However, there are suitable sun-worshipping plants for the sunny side and it would be very practicable to build a wall specifically for them.

If you have spent many an hour fighting with bindweed (*Convolvulus arvensis*), you may not feel too inclined to plant any other convolvulus in your garden. However, if you have a warm, sunny garden, you would be missing out on two lovely members of this genus. *C. althaeoides*, coming from the northern Mediterranean, is the hardier of the two, and is a really beautiful sprawling perennial. It runs by underground roots in the same way as its monstrous northern European cousin, yet barely enough in my garden. The beautiful, silver-marked leaves would be reason enough to grow it without the silvery-pink, funnel-shaped flowers which appear continuously as the stems lengthen. This, the more commonly encountered form of the species, is named *C. althaeoides* ssp. *tenuissimus*, and in Crete typically forms patches of 2–3 sq m (2½–3½ sq yd) on the road verges. More handsome in flower and considerably more vigorous, often covering great swathes of roadside banks, is *C. althaeoides* var. *althaeoides*, with larger flowers with a darker eye. The foliage is not as silver, nor is it quite as hardy, but I would try them both if I had some south-facing, soil-backed walls. In a similar position, the North African *C. sabatius*, with soft lilac-blue flowers, might also survive, being I would guess about as hardy as the more vigorous form of *C. althaeoides*. If the conditions suit them all of these refined convolvulus will run about among the stones of a soil-filled dry wall, popping up here and there.

I knew that the silvery-pink-flowered *Diascia vigilis* was capable of gently running when happy, so I planted it at the base of a southern wall by the cottage. Against the odds, it chose to grow up into the wall and proceeded to colonize this in preference to the border in which it had been planted. In the Walled Garden the grey-leaved, pale lemon-flowered trailing snapdragon, *Asarina procumbens*, rejected the semi-sunny site I had chosen for it and died, but not before it had produced a single offspring which put itself the other side of the path, across a bed, over the edge of the terrace and half-way down the retaining wall. It stayed there on this shaded wall for years and years, looking cool and classy.

Developing the wall as a planting zone

When experimenting with what will grow in walls, pleasant surprises such as this are not infrequent because it is a branch of gardening that has been insufficiently exploited in the last century. Gertrude Jekyll used the wall space as another planting dimension, having the benefit of working in collaboration with the brilliance of Lutyens-designed masonry, but since then, I can think of very little that has been done. This is not really surprising given the enormous physical efforts that are involved in building a wall coupled with the astronomical costs of stone. Building just a small section of wall about 60 cm (2 ft) thick instilled in me something approaching reverence for all the hard graft and skill of those stone-masons of the past. There are, though, areas where stone is cheap and readily available, and for those willing to make the effort or else pay someone else to, this is a sphere of gardening with enormous potential.

Think of the variations in dry-stone walls, and the different techniques necessary to build them. Within just a 3 km (2 mile) radius of the Garden House, I know of walls with the stones placed horizontally, others with vertical courses and moorland walls with random boulders. All of these, if built with plants in mind, would create a different atmosphere and would support different species. Multiply that by the variations around the UK alone and then throw in subtleties such as colour and how this affects the choice of plants and the subject becomes ever bigger. And why just stone? We could use logs to create walls or indeed peat blocks, if taken from areas of the world where there is no shortage of this increasingly endangered material. The choice of plants is varied enough in a free-standing wall with two aspects and a top to consider and becomes even greater when the walls are retaining walls, holding back soil banks. There is enough factual and creative potential here for an entire book on wall gardening alone.

Types of rock

The major importance of the type of rock on which the garden sits is clearly the relative acidity it imparts to the soils above, but it also has considerable aesthetic implications for the gardener. The most obvious of these will be the colour of the rock, with the soft orange-buffs of the stone in the Cotswolds having a very different visual effect on the plants nearby than the slatey blue of the stone here at the Garden House. Different colour ranges of plants may look better against one type of rock than another. As an example of this, the glaucous and silver-foliaged plants of Judy Pearce's steppe garden at Lady Farm, near Bristol, with its repeated use of orange flowers, is set off much better by the sparing use of an orange-buff pea shingle that complements the underlying red Devon sandstone. The same combinations of foliage and flower colours, with the same mulch, would not work so well in my south Devon location with our dark grey stone. Conversely, the rich greens of ferns and plants with lilac-blue and pink flowers are shown off to far

ABOVE *Autumn sun illuminates the granite posts of the 'Magic Circle'. These stones have echoes of ancient Dartmoor, the boundary of which starts by the mist-shrouded trees on the horizon.*

the effect of breaking the surface layers of rock into countless millions of smaller stones, thus creating shillet. Digging down just a couple of metres into the shillet layer and leaving this exposed to the elements results in a jumble of shards of stone that can make a very natural-looking surface around any outcropping bedrock or water feature. This same shillet also makes an excellent mulch for the beds and surface for the paths, and so there develops a common unifying thread to the whole garden. The stone, and the uses we have put it to in this garden, is the single most important factor at the Garden House for blending the very different elements of these 4 ha (10 acres) into a cohesive unit. I can see absolutely no reason why the same principles put into effect at the Garden House should not apply equally to other rock types, which, with their own distinctive colours and textures, will provide a different range of creative possibilities.

Granite

When we first came to live in Devon I played cricket for Tavistock, partly because I loved the location of the cricket ground. It is situated on the moor above the town, with panoramic views, and is called the Ring. Its name comes from the magnificent circle of granite standing stones that form the boundary fence. The club rarely had to mow the outfield as it was constantly being grazed by the local free-range ponies and sheep, but it did make diving for a catch somewhat of a hazard. I would have stopped playing years before I did in order to concentrate on gardening had it not been for the lovely location and that enormous circle of granites.

I become emotional about granite stones, with subconscious feelings beyond my powers of description that I experience with no other rock. I do not know whether it is their texture, as granite is a very tactile stone, or the way they weather so beautifully, for there can be few rocks that age so handsomely. New Agers might tell me that it is the internal energy of the stones themselves I am responding to—one visitor returned with dowsing rods to check the energy levels of the granite

better advantage, I think, against our stone rather than against that lovely pea-shingle.

The texture of your local stone can also exert an influence on the effects created in the garden. The stone we have here is very easy to break along planes of weakness. This makes it a wonderful material for wall-building, but it also has

Sandstone

standing stones that I had put in at the end of the Long Walk and told me in all seriousness there were very good vibes around them! Maybe it is because they age so well that granites exude a palpable sense of bygone times, for even when my 'Magic Circle' granite gate posts were standing in their freshly dug holes, propped up by forks, there were visitors asking us whether they had always been there. I did compound the myth a little by raising the soil around the base of the stones, something you see in the countryside where the animals are unable to get their feet in close while using the stones as a scratching post, and by scooping out the soil from the central area between the circle, as if centuries of maidens might have danced naked there on midsummer's eves and worn away the ground.

By contrast, sedimentary rocks can seem a bit dull—or at least that is what I thought until I visited Utah, where the overriding impression I came away with was of bright colours. It was possible to find, for example, a white hill on one side of the road and red outcrops on the other, with a black escarpment beyond. This was geology in the raw, with most vegetation scorched into submission under the unforgiving glare of the summer sun. It was not obvious territory for garden inspiration, yet even here there were places that suggested to me some gardening possibilities. Bryce Canyon was one such place. Magical, other-worldly, fairy-tale are all adjectives that spring to mind to describe these incredible pillars of orange-pink sandstone. The quality of

ABOVE *Sunlight bouncing off the pink rocks of Bryce Canyon in Utah, USA, floodlights the trunks of the pines. This simple grouping of trees is reminiscent of a Japanese garden and, in a location with a more reliable number of sunshine days than I'm accustomed to, would make a wonderful basis for a garden design. I, for one, would never tire of these warm, rich colours, the resinous scent of the pines and the sculptural shapes and dancing shadows upon the sand.*

light reflected back from the encircling cliffs as the sun strikes them in the early morning was phenomenal. We were told that earlier in the year the wild flowers in the canyon floor are lovely, but at the time of our visit in midsummer, the hummingbirds were having to work hard to find many flowers—not that any were needed to make it more beautiful since the tall pines, junipers, dried grasses and large clumps of low-growing, evergreen arctostaphyllos shrubs were a perfect contrast to the orange rocks and dark blue, cloudless sky (see page 208).

Similarly, the pinky-brown adobe walls so common in this part of the US make a wonderful foil for plants. Using coloured walls is currently almost de rigueur among British designers creating small town gardens and these can be very successful, but I wonder if, by looking at sympathetic natural harmonies of plant against coloured rock in places such as Bryce Canyon, the idea might be taken on a stage or two further. By manipulating the colour of the rock and choosing plants carefully it should be possible to evoke the characteristics of a particular landscape. Maybe concrete block walls, rendered with a cement wash and then painted an orange-pink colour, sounds like a recipe for disaster and set against the traditional green garden it probably would be. However, imagine the walls were surrounding a swimming pool, that most difficult of living spaces to incorporate successfully into a garden. With ochre-coloured paving, orange-pink walls, dark green pine trees, isolated clumps of low evergreen bushes, grasses such as *Stipa tenuissima* with its fluffy clouds of flowering stems and the big central block of brilliant blue from the pool itself, and you have all the elements of the Bryce Canyon landscape. Mulching the beds with orange-red bark chippings or ochre pea-gravel would only accentuate the impact of the dark green foliage.

I associate coloured rock with blue skies and dry or semi-dry landscapes, so it is hardly surprising that I think rock-coloured walls look best when associated with garden designs that are predominantly hard-landscaped. If you logically extend this line of thought, it then becomes an obvious choice for gardeners faced with a water-challenged climate. When Lauren Springer and her family built their house in the grassy foothills of the Colorado Rockies, she cleverly incorporated the house and garden into the landscape by building a series of 1 m (3¼ ft) high rendered walls and painting them the same colour as the surrounding natural rock. It was a masterly piece of design, giving just enough form and neutral colour to complement the informal, semi-naturalistic planting she wanted to introduce. The ochre colour she used is a perfect foil when the garden and countryside are both green in the spring and early summer, and just as good when the grasses within the garden and outside its margins assume their bleached summer dress.

Architectural landscaping with stone

When the old thatched summer house in our Walled Garden looked to be in imminent danger of collapsing, I took the opportunity of redesigning the small area on its north side, rerouting the paths to pass through the new building. This developed into the Ovals Garden on the western edge of the Walled Garden and I built it during the course of one summer in the early 1990s. The round stone seat at the lower end of this section of garden was built ten years previously. I was always very proud of my stone seat, sitting as it does like a giant ammonite on the corner of one of the terraces with views of the buildings and the lowest terrace below, but very few people actually came and sat in it.

I have always thought that if people are not drawn into any area of a garden then the design of the garden itself must be at fault. There should be no need for directional arrows to tell you where to go, for the garden should pull you ever deeper into its clutches and seduce you with its possibilities. This new section of the garden is only about 6 m (20 ft) wide and 20 m (66 ft) long, on a steep north slope and sandwiched between

tall conifer hedges, so I made dry-stone walls that boldly sweep from side to side, and up and down, forming as they go a sculptural figure of eight (with an additional section). These three oval shapes link to the existing round stone seat and their curves make this whole area seem much bigger than it is in reality.

In the little raised beds created by the high sections of the walls, I planted six *Cornus alternifolia* 'Argentea', whose horizontal branching accentuates the architectural elements of the site. This is a magnificent dogwood, the equal of the only other alternate-leaved cornus, the superlative *C. controversa* 'Variegata', but in a smaller form. Sometimes called the pagoda tree, *C. alternifolia* 'Argentea' can grow up to about 3 m (10 ft) but is more usually less than half that.

As the summer progresses the maroon colour of the twigs starts to show up on the leaves themselves, giving the whole shrub a pink tinge, and it is at this time they look so good with *Berberis thunbergii* 'Harlequin'. This variety of barberry lives up to its name, with shades of silver, pink and purple, but produces more soft pink and silver leaves if you give it a hard annual prune. I prefer to cut it back during the winter, using a hedge trimmer and picking the clippings up with a fork, in an attempt to avoid the barberry's savage thorns. With the soft pinks and purples of the berberis contrasting with the silver tracery of the dogwoods, the Ovals Garden can be spectacular in midsummer when the walls turn blue from the flowering *Campanula poscharskyana* which has made itself at home in them.

ABOVE *Looking down the Ovals Garden to the stone seat now under the canopy of a katsura tree,* Cercidiphyllum japonicum. *The swooping walls and curves distort perspective and make this area seem much larger than it actually is.*

ABOVE *One of the hybrid fawn lilies, Erythronium 'Minnehaha', nestles at the base of the cairn-like Shock Waves, built in the bulb meadow to add summer interest.*

RIGHT *Another stone creation I built just to add sculptural interest to an area otherwise given over exclusively to spring-flowering bulbs and woodlanders.*

I am proud of the way the Ovals Garden turned out, but its strong architectural qualities do tend to polarize visitors' reactions. There are a few who really cannot abide it and others for whom it is their favourite part of the garden. On reaching the Ovals, one member of a group I was showing around said he really liked the new naturalistic areas I had done and this part (that is the Ovals) would be all right when I demolished it. Gardening to me, and perhaps millions like me, is about passion and emotion, so I am only too happy if my garden reflects that, and I know full well that it will not appeal to everyone. I am more disappointed if the garden leaves the visitor feeling unmoved.

Sculptures in stone

Creating sculpture out of natural stone is something I would like to spend a lot more time doing. It probably would not be sculpture in the normally accepted sense of the word, being rather more a hybrid art form between the skills of the country stone-mason and modern simplistic sculpture. An artist whose stone skills I admire is Andy Goldsworthy; sculptures such as his are not just about the art itself, but also about how it fits into its setting. I love the simplicity of many of his stone sculptures and dry-stone wall creations and his clever fusion of these into the landscape has very clear links to the style of gardening I espouse. I thought the same sort of shapes would harmonize even better with the romanticized natural garden settings I was creating than the countryside itself.

I am slightly embarrassed to talk about my own constructions (see opposite) as if they were sculptures, but in all honesty I cannot think what else to call them and hope that by showing pictures of my simple efforts it might fire others up to produce something far more exciting. They are built in the bulb meadow, partly to create a focal point and change of texture and form amid the carpet of spring flowers and then, when the bulbs have finished flowering, to act as a point of interest among the gentle undulations of the ground itself. They have become a talking-point, with many suggestions put forward as to their possible historical uses. I suppose I was slightly put out at first that most visitors were not treating them as sculptures, but now I am rather glad they do not, with this blurring of the functional and aesthetic becoming an added dimension to the garden visit.

Andy Goldsworthy's Wandering Wall, which snakes its way in sinuous curves between the trunks of mature trees in Grizedale Forest in the Lake District, his sheep-folds on the hills of the Pennines, and his stone sculptures built totally or semi-submerged under water, have all given rise to ideas and projects in my own garden. Once again, Goldsworthy's initial ideas have been modified to suit my conditions and often what emerges is something so far removed from the original as to bear it no resemblance.

Adding some fun

Sometimes I wonder whether we are all a bit too serious about our gardens. A little fun occasionally might add a genuine element of surprise to a garden visit. On such a theme, I like the idea of making a clutch of four large 'dinosaur eggs', using our home-quarried slatey-blue stone—though, if I could justify the cost for a flight of pure whimsy, I would make them out of a polished grey-blue granite with its exquisite marbled patterns for preference. Each egg would be about 37 cm (15 in) long, and they would be carefully positioned in a slight depression among bleached driftwood twigs. By informally surrounding the 'nest' with the 60 cm (2 ft) high, bronze-leaved grass *Carex comans*, and siting it under the canopy of a large katsura tree (*Cercidiphyllum japonicum*), which has a slightly prehistoric feel, the whole composition would have an informal, slightly 'arty' feel to it. I think I would call it 'Deserted 2000 BC'.

The eggs could actually look good in their own right, a bit like the central feature in Shock Waves (see opposite top), or a smaller, neater version of one of Andy Goldsworthy's cairns, only

ABOVE *A granite boulder bathed in evening light on Dartmoor, England. Note how the moss and other plants are congregated in linear cracks along its top face, suggesting to me it should be possible to build a 'boulder' like this one.*

OPPOSITE *The narrow spikes of wall pennywort hug the stonework in a local form of walling where the stones are placed vertically to help drain away surplus water.*

made with little stones to make them more symmetrical. In this shady spot, moss would soon grow in the tiny cracks, especially if I gave them a coat of liquid cow manure after they were built. Collected fresh, mixed in a bucket with water and then painted onto stone or cement surfaces, this smelly mixture will soften the raw new look, not only by greening the colour but also by giving fungi and mosses something to feed on and grow, but it is not a job to undertake too soon after you have had your breakfast or lunch. With bulbs, such as the erythroniums which are already growing here, or short-lived perennials such as pink purslane (*Claytonia sibirica*) coming up between the grasses, it could form a genuinely pretty picture. Once again, as with the more traditional stone sculptures I have built, such as

Shock Waves, it would challenge the viewer's perceptions of the purely functional and the aesthetic, and add a spark of adventure to garden visiting. I would love it, as a quirky reminder of my bird's-nesting days of long ago.

Creating boulders

Dartmoor is covered in boulders, such as the one shown above. I especially liked this particular one because weathering had produced a 'ridge and furrow' effect across its entire surface, so that the moss and lichen had combined to create a banded, highly textural effect. I wish there were boulders like this one in the garden, but there are not, and we lack the financial resources to bring them in. Even if we did, the mere thought of the weight of this 1 m (3¼ ft) high rock makes my back ache. I reckon it should be possible, using the same techniques as in the Shock Waves cairn (see page 226 top), to build such a boulder *in situ*. The stones would be held together by mortar binding the unseen parts of the stones as one unit. In this central core I would substitute peat for part of the sand element in the mortar, so that the drainage was improved. In the constructed boulder, I would leave spaces of about 2.5–7.5 cm (1–3 in) between the vertically placed stones that are held in place by the central mortar. If these spaces were then filled with soil, or a more freely draining mixture, it would be possible to make an entirely natural-looking alpine garden.

The planting possibilities in this 'boulder' are almost infinite. I would go first for a textural, shady model, looking as natural as I could make it to remind me of the original, and would site it accordingly. This would entail limiting myself to just a few residents, such as sedums, small ferns such as the maidenhair spleenwort (*Asplenium trichomanes*) with perhaps wall pennywort (*Umbilicus rupestris*) growing on the sides, and allowing mosses to colonize the boulder as well. In a sunny location, I might opt for a variation on the glacial rocky outcrops we saw in the Alps, perhaps with the evocative white-flowered *Dryas octopetala* hugging the stone, with gentians, auriculas and even the odd dwarf shrub in deeper-rooting sections. An extension of this would be to use large stones to create a boulder with deep planting pockets which could be filled with a mixture to suit the royal family of alpine shrubs, the daphnes. Just imagine a natural-looking rock studded with the domed hummocks of heavenly scented *Daphne petraea*, for example.

Taking this boulder idea a stage further on, why not have several of them, of different sizes, loosely scattered in the same general area? They would, in effect, form raised beds with a difference, and they would potentially be much more natural-looking than gardens normally associated with specialist alpine growers, perhaps resembling

RIGHT *Limestone pavement in the Swiss Alps. Forming mats and prostrate cushions on the rock in the foreground is the mountain avens,* Dryas octopetala, *whose glistening white flowers with yellow stamens turn to track the sun across the sky throughout the day.*

the limestone pavements of the Alps (see right). What you cannot see from this photograph, however, are the vertical cracks and fissures in these rocks, called grikes and clints, that are caused by the erosion of the limestone by rainwater. In an area of limestone pavement in Ireland called the Burren, on an exposed part of the County Clare coast, the plants famously huddle out of the winds' fury by growing in the safety and shelter of the grikes. I have always liked the idea of re-creating a small area like this as I think certain plants would look marvellous grown in this sort of setting, but on a bigger scale it could be a devil to weed. My custom-built boulder garden would have some wider fissures in the rocks less than fully filled with soil, creating in the process my very own grikes.

A little more controversial would be to make your own 'rock boulders' using the same rendered blockwork approach described on page 224, perhaps as the centrepiece of a garden design based on one of those semi-arid landscapes. It would be relatively easy to make pillars of concrete blocks or bricks, shaped like granite gate posts or menhirs, and then render them with a cement wash to give a stone effect. If the aim is to achieve a semi-natural look, you could paint them with a dilute cow-manure wash. Adding 25 per cent peat to the mortar used for rendering the mosses will green the surface rather quicker, as well as giving a more textural finish, and a light brush down with a soft brush as the mortar is hardening up will accentuate the finished stone effect. You could add colour to the boulders either by rendering them with a cement wash made with sands of various colour, or by adding a dye to the mortar mix during construction. Painting with a masonry paint when finished is not likely to look very natural, and is not a course of action I would take. Coloured 'rock' menhirs could look wonderful rising out of architectural plants, surrounded by pea-shingle, and purely on a practical front would be much easier to build *in situ*, exactly where you want them, rather than trying to manoeuvre an extremely heavy real boulder into your garden.

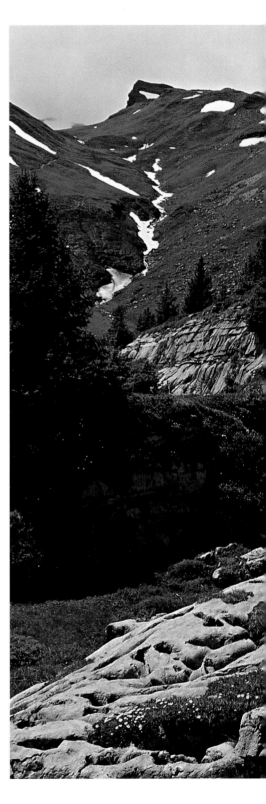

11 Going with the flow

If grasses are the soft landscaping element of a garden most likely to suggest a wild naturalness, then water must be the hard landscaping equivalent. Nearly any established body of water, from the grand sweep of a lake at a stately home to a tiny suburban fish-pond, will develop a natural equilibrium below the surface, but how we deal with its margins and surrounds will dictate whether that part of the garden as a whole has a natural feel. This chapter looks at how nature deals with water and its interface with the land and how, by sympathetic modification, we can create garden-worthy, natural-looking waterside plantings that can also be as colourful and spectacular as anybody might wish.

There was a regular exhibitor at Chelsea Flower Show in the 1980s who created the most magnificent natural slate gardens you could ever wish to see, with water cascading between lovingly constructed rock-work, all of which had clearly been minutely observed in the wild. I would always admire the attention to detail in the perfect hard landscaping while trying not to notice the dwarf conifers, immaculate fertilizer-advertisement green lawn and other plantings that made up the rest of the garden, all of which seemed a little incongruous against the rock-work. If only the same eye to detail had been applied to the plants surrounding natural streams and the selection of species adapted to suit the

garden design, the result would have been a harmonious natural water and rock garden.

The moorland streams that were the template for those masterly exhibits are as good a starting point as anywhere. In all likelihood it was the streams of the Pennines and Lake District that started to open my eyes to the whole concept of natural landscapes as a source of gardening ideas when I walked in these areas as a teenager. Interested at that time in training to become a landscape architect, I was very conscious of how the moods of these streams changed as you walked along them, depending on the surrounding vegetation, openness to the sky and the different forms that the water-edges assumed. Here the

RIGHT *The Japanese blood grass, Imperata cylindrica 'Red Baron', looks magnificent planted in a position where sunlight can stream through the red young leaves.*

PREVIOUS PAGE *Daytime colour drains away from Derwentwater in the English Lake District, leaving the lights of Keswick twinkling in the evening half-light.*

landscape was very obviously fashioned by the fast-moving water with the vegetation clearly adapted to the environment, all very different to the sluggish, seasonal flows we called streams in my corner of North Somerset. There is an effervescent *joie de vivre* in these tumbling cascades that is both exotic and uplifting, not to mention simply beautiful. It is hardly surprising that we would like to transfer a little of this spirit back into our gardens if we can.

A stream passing through any rocky landscape will produce an enormous range of different detailing. Rounded smooth stones can be left in the stream itself, varying from large boulders down to pea-shingle. The smaller the stones the more they will accumulate in the slower-moving sections of the stream, often creating tiny sandy beaches in the slowest eddies on the sheltered inside of the curves. The larger the stone the more likely it is to be found in the fast-moving sections of water. Pebbles the size of your fist can form shingle banks, again on the inside of the curve away from the strongest currents, sometimes accumulating parallel to the direction of the flow, leaving quiet slacks of almost still water on the stream-bank side. Almost any fast-moving stream will demonstrate these endless variations, many of which can be copied on a much smaller scale in a small stream in a garden. This busy type of stream, typically found near the origin of a water-course or where a larger stream or river crosses a rocky section of its floor, is not the template for adding contemplative restfulness to your garden but more for the drama and excitement that loud, brashy water can add. It is the equivalent of white water rafting in rapids rather than gentle family paddling down a quiet, slow-flowing river.

ABOVE *This Herdwick sheep, together with its brethren, is the likely cause of the closely cropped grass along the stream banks in the upper Buttermere valley in the English Lake District. The tiny pebble beaches and undulating profile of the banks have real garden potential, but it is probable that the erosion occurring on other parts of these banks led to the eventual fencing of this particular stream.*

Fast-moving water planting

To keep the emphasis on the water, the planting for this type of stream garden should be mostly low-key, with foliage plants that revel in the buoyant, moisture-laden air predominating. Ferns and mosses immediately spring to mind, whatever the aspect and shade levels of the stream may be, but in a more open site I would be tempted to add some grasses to the banks. The green-leaved *Hakonechloa macra* would look fabulous arching between rocks alongside the stream, planted with ferns and the occasional clump of green-foliaged hostas. If all this is rather too bland for your tastes, you could use variegated forms of the hostas and hakonechloa and still be partly true to the spirit of the wild—not the way I would go since I think it might look a little contrived, but it largely depends on the variegation. For example, the narrow white-margined leaves of the sedge *Carex siderosticha* 'Variegata' would look really good and still be quite natural, growing between the ferns and rocks. In a more sunny location, the variegated purple moor grass *Molinia caerulea* 'Variegata' would not appear at all out of place alongside the stream, planted either singly or in small groups, as it is another very soft variegation. The streamside is just the sort of location the purple moor grass grows in the wild, and the dwarfer, more refined variegated form would be very high on my list of grasses for this situation.

Another grass that could look sumptuous planted alongside the stream, perhaps on the brow of a little bank or at the top of a waterfall, preferably where the sunlight can shine through its leaves, is the Japanese blood grass *Imperata cylindrica* 'Red Baron'. For several months in the early part of the growing season this seems quite ordinary, with upright, rather nondescript leaves 15–23 cm (6–9 in) high, but from midsummer onwards they become increasingly red until they positively glow when backlit by sunshine.

All four of the grasses mentioned here exemplify the principles I follow: the shape, form and texture are similar to grasses you will see growing alongside natural upland streams, yet the varieties suggested are that bit more refined, exotic and colourful. Combine them with ferns, mosses and a few of the native flowering plants, such as primroses, wood anemones and pink campion, or with exotics giving the same sort of effect as these natives, and you have a green, naturalistic garden alongside your stream that is anything but dull to the eye.

Slow-moving water planting

The closely cropped grass of the stream-bank in the photograph on page 235, which is to be found above Buttermere in the Lake District, is typical of streams flowing through open, tree-less areas on many upland moors. It is often associated with deeper, slower-moving water and creates a

more tranquil atmosphere much more suitable for adaption to garden ponds and lakes. This sort of meeting of water and land can be seen echoed in garden settings where lawns sweep down to the water's edge, providing what many plantsman gardeners would think is a rather uninspired use of the water. Yet, with just a little bit more thought and effort, this same water and mown grass combination can be turned into something much more natural-looking.

In both nature and in gardens, you rarely find short grass joining the water without a little bank of some sort, partly because most grasses growing at water level would not survive if they were constantly waterlogged. As in the photograph of Buttermere, where the banks give way small beaches of sand or pebbles very often accumulate, allowing animal access to the water. The profile of the grass banks themselves is also virtually never flat, with gentle undulations being the

norm, and in some of the damper spots along these banks, dark green upright clumps of sedges are a common sight. If we were to incorporate some of these features with the lawns sweeping down to the pond or lake, we might achieve a very different result. By making the lawn profile less straight when seen against the water, creating access at water-level from the lawn with the addition of a mini-beach or two, and substituting those sedges for the odd clump of ornamental grasses or ferns, we can still have the simplicity of lawn against grass but in a less suburban form.

Marsh and boggy seeps

There are also garden possibilities to be drawn from that other stalwart of moorland standing water, the boggy seeps. Dartmoor, in particular, seems to be covered in these watery pitfalls,

ABOVE *Pines and rhododendrons grow together on an island on Derwentwater, in the English Lake District. The proportions of the plants here would look good however much this island was miniaturized.*

ABOVE *A dreamy mix of Campanula lactiflora, filipendulas and astrantias grace the lowest terrace of the Walled Garden at the Garden House with a spectacular midsummer display.*

looking almost identical to the mossy turf of dry ground all around until you sink up to your ankle in water. On the moors here, these bogs, found surprisingly often on the steep hillsides, are the home of sundews (*Drosera* species) and bog asphodel (*Narthecium ossifragum*), and would hardly be worth considering for garden adaption, but in the Swiss Alps this same type of marshy ground is a favoured place for orchids, which look charming growing with lady's smock (*Cardamine pratensis*), daisies and bog asphodel among other things.

Mossy bog garden

Imagine a typical small pond sited in an average garden at the end of a mossy lawn, with a ring of flat stones masking its edge. Nothing wrong with this, but you could create a new plant habitat by

digging out part of the lawn adjacent to the pond, placing a waterproof liner in this space at about 15 cm (6 in) below ground level, and then filling in with good soil or potting compost. In effect you will have made another pond and filled it to the top with soil, although you could leave a patch of this area slightly shallower so that it showed water in wetter spells.

Now comes the fun part—the planting. The traditional and safest option would be to plant standard bog plants, such as candelabra primulas, dwarf astilbes, small hostas and so forth, but that would not really make the transition from lawn to pond any smoother. I favour a more naturalistic approach, borrowing ideas from wild marshy areas from different habitats and trying to blend the lawn and the marsh plantings with the pond itself. The key element to this would be moss, and once this boggy area has become saturated, establishing moss all over it should not prove difficult. How quickly you want to make it look the finished article will dictate your next steps. If you follow the television make-over principles of 'must be finished in two days', then you would moss the whole area and plant everything else through it. If I were doing it in my own garden, however, I would set out the other plants, put some mosses in that would spread by spores, and leave the rest of the space clear so that I could keep it weeded for a year to help establish my introduced plants and give them space to self-seed, if they want to. By that time, the mosses should be beginning to cover the area.

You would expect marsh orchids to like such conditions, but I was genuinely surprised to see *Dactylorrhiza foliosa*, the Madeiran orchid, self-seeding into the moss on top of a permanently waterlogged clump of iris in Robin and Sue White's Hampshire garden. If this spectacular orchid took to a boggy seep, it would be a magnificent place to grow it, surrounded by moss, at the water's edge, and even if it did not, the marsh orchids would be a very worthy second string. Cowslips, primroses, bog asphodel and lady's smock could all keep the orchids company, with *Narcissus cyclamineus* and *Fritillaria meleagris* worth trying as bulbs for the spring and maybe *Anagallis tenella* 'Studland', a selected form of the bog pimpernel, creeping around amid the saturated moss. Perhaps the beautiful large-flowered butterwort (*Pinguicula grandiflora*) from south-western Ireland with its sticky, insectivorous leaves might be induced to grow here as well, somewhere close to the water and near enough to dry ground for 10 cm (4 in) high violet-blue flowers to be appreciated.

There are so many little treasures such as these that would love these conditions and yet we so rarely have the places in which to grow them. A boggy seep could provide an ecologically sound plant habitat and a nursery haven for young froglets, and when it has all finished flowering it might just look like a slightly richer green part of the lawn.

Bog gardening on a grand scale

On a bigger scale bog gardening is of course nothing new, but even here we still tend to stick to the tried and tested formulae. How many bog gardens must I have seen with large-leaved blue hostas, growing alongside some bright golden grass or yellow-foliaged meadowsweet. Candelabra primulas will margin the water channels, with the contrasting flower colours of astilbes, the coarse leaves of lysichitums, and, in a corner somewhere near the water, the inevitable *Gunnera manicata* from Brazil. 'Gunnera the Gargantuan', with individual leaves over 1.5 m (6 ft) across, is like an enormous rhubarb on steroids, a superhero of the boggy perennial world, undoubtedly impressive but also rather overblown and almost coarse. Individually I love all of these plants and can imagine bog gardens in which each one would look in its element, but somehow this total ensemble leaves me rather cold. It is colourful, for sure, but lacks subtlety. I yearn for an altogether softer, gentler mix of moisture-loving perennials, one I could at least pretend might occur in the wild.

I have in mind a large-scale planting like that in the lower walled garden here, where the darker pink *Filipendula rubra* 'Venusta' forms frothy blocks of colour with the lighter-coloured and finer-textured *Filipendula palmata* 'Elegantissima' (see opposite). Both of these meadowsweets will grow in permanently moist soil but do not actually demand it, which is why they are growing so happily on the bottom terrace here in the company of *Campanula lactiflora*, astrantias and sidalceas, none of which would welcome boggy conditions. For a good few years now, as funds and time permit, I have been modifying the shape of part of our side of the valley, moving thousands of tons of soil in order to create a series of dammed pools which may, one day, provide a setting for a bog garden of about 0.5 ha (1 acre). With the huge, ancient lime trees towering above and the deep, coombe-like atmosphere of the restructured, flooded valley to place it in, this part of the garden would have a wonderful 'lost world' ambience all of its own, which a

RIGHT *This small pond on the summit of Haystacks in the English Lake District is flanked on one side by a perfect rockery in miniature. The stone and mossy turf almost form a scaled-down landscape of their own, one mirroring the fells and larger landscape beyond.*

romantic sea of pastel-coloured flowers reflected from the mirrored surfaces of the still ponds could only accentuate.

Back to the Lakes

Although there are ideas aplenty from the plant combinations found in the Lake District, it is the rock and water that keep surfacing in my mind each time I think of this area. Walking on the fells, as in countless other upland or mountainous areas of the world, is a very humbling experience. Faced with these awesome panoramas, I feel uplifted, privileged and totally insignificant, in equal measure. From my own experiences, the Alps and the Rockies are very capable of stimulating gardening thoughts with the plants growing at altitude there, but the felltops of the Lakes have rarely triggered such a response in me. My obsessive preoccupation with all things gardening dissipates into the wind when I am confronted with this breathtaking hilltop scenery. However, the rock and water combination near the summit of Haystacks (see right) could be rolled up intact and displayed at Chelsea Flower Show to rave reviews. The balance of stone, water, and the relatively level areas between the rocks would make a fabulous garden in any setting. Substitute low alpines such as phlox or creeping thymes for the mossy grass carpeting the ground between the rocks, plant a few smaller, moisture-loving plants around the water's edge and you would have an easily maintained small rock and water garden to die for. Alpine enthusiasts could translate those level grassy areas of the wild version into small screes to provide homes for some of the more difficult treasures.

Valley floor and fellside

Gardening connections seem to bombard me from every direction when I am in the no less beautiful, relative intimacy of the valley floors and wooded fellsides of the Lake District. A stone-pebbled shoreline, as in the photograph of Derwentwater on page 242, is perhaps a more

common sight in Japanese water gardens than in western ones, although of course they do appear, especially in small urban garden water features. In larger gardens these historical national preferences become more apparent, with the Japanese wishing to create perfect, romanticized reflections of especially beautiful or meaningful parts of their countryside. The position and shape of every tree, bush, rock and pebble is an important element in achieving this aim. I was once told that among the army of volunteers who consider it almost their duty to maintain the Japanese temple gardens in this unreal state of perfection, there are those who are delegated to remove the pebbles from below the water surface of the ponds each day, polish them and then return them to their original positions.

Such communal effort and self-discipline is way out of our league, however much we may admire the results—though they may be a little too organized and static for some tastes. By contrast, western gardeners simply enjoy water more for the reflective qualities, cooling atmosphere and home for fish it provides. It is highly improbable, except in the case of a minute number of dedicated enthusiasts, that we can produce and maintain authentic Japanese gardens in the West, yet by looking more closely at natural landscapes and plant combinations we encounter in the wild and allowing a little more of that deeper oriental interpretation to insinuate itself, we might evolve a magnificent gardening hybrid between the two cultures—a hybrid of some of the structure, attention to detail and significance in design of the oriental model coupled with the plant-rich exuberance and laid-back enjoyment of western gardens.

Islands

My interpretations are, of course, very liberal, and the photograph on page 237 of an island on Derwentwater is not intended to suggest that copying it is a serious option—after all, the island itself is bigger than most gardens. Here the interest lies in the shapes of the taller specimens in relation to the understorey of rhododendrons. If

you scale this whole planting down by whatever ratio would fit your site and select plants to give the same effect as the trees and shrubs the result will be a very balanced island. Even on a tiny islet, just 1 m (3¼ ft) across, you could use the same format, substituting small specimen herbaceous plants with a similar upright arching habit for the pine trees, and lower, denser-growing plants for the rhododendrons. Maybe some of the umbellifers, such as angelicas or selinums, or alternatively some of the grasses, could do service representing the upright trees, with perhaps compact geraniums such as *Geranium sanguineum*, epimediums or low ferns such as the plumose oak fern *Gymnocarpium dryopteris* 'Plumosum' or *Adiantum venustum* providing the understorey. Equally, these two ferns, with their fresh, pale green leaves, would make an excellent

understorey to 'trees' created from dark green dwarf conifers, cleared of their lowest branches to produce diminutive trunks, like a smaller version of the one on page 182. The choices and options are endless.

The island seen in the photograph above is already garden-sized. In this case, the whole composition of rock and heather would seem just as much at home in a garden setting as it did on this remote felltop. This island must have made an absolutely wonderful nesting site for the pair of greylag geese swimming in front of it, whose territory this most definitely was. Isolated as this pond was, these birds made a friendly beeline for us as soon as we came into view and then followed us around the pond's margins, clearly recognizing walkers as being a good source of easy food. It was strange, and rather a privilege,

ABOVE *A small island such as this could easily be replicated in a garden setting. This particular one, being patrolled by the same greylag geese as on page 209, is covered with heathers, but the same principle of using a very narrow range of species to provide a sense of unity would apply whatever the size of the island.*

OPPOSITE *A heron stalks its prey in the millpond-calm water of early morning at Derwentwater in the English Lake District.*

to have such wild birds behaving like semi-tame muscovy ducks on a busy village pond.

Even though they would look wonderful, I do not advise using Japanese maples in these situations unless your island is at least 60 cm (2 ft) higher than the water-level, as they do not like standing in water. A viable option, especially if water is too valuable a commodity to squander on ornamental ponds, is to create islands in a dry 'water' garden. You can represent the water around the island either by water-worn pebbles or a flat rock platform, decreasing in stone size as you approach the land so the shores are fringed by sand beaches, or do it the other way around, with sand as the open water increasing in size towards the land. If you live in an area with numerous cats you might think the former option a more hygienic one. Even in areas where water is not in short supply dry water gardens can look good, and in these there would be no problems growing Japanese maples on the islands. I am not advocating a true Japanese-style dry garden, more of a loose adaptation, though if you are prepared to rake the sand into patterns at least once a day you could take a more strict approach.

Getting close to water

A large part of the fun of water is being able to get close to it. Whether we are just three years old or thirty times older, there appears to be a

LEFT *This stream has been photographed very close to its source and so almost gives the impression of being a seasonal flash-flood channel following a depression through a meadow. The long grass right down to the water's edge gives a very different feel to the closely cropped grass in the photograph on page 235.*

RIGHT *The cunning plan when I built this bridge was to bring the pond underneath it, so that the flowers on the far side would be reflected in the water under the bridge. It does work, as you can see, but you need to be about 15 cm (6 in) high to really appreciate it. Even so, the bridge does act as a focal point when seen from many directions.*

OPPOSITE *A large, simple granite slab spanning a tiny stream is perfect in this Dartmoor woodland setting in Devon, England.*

universal desire to get as close as we can to the wet stuff. It is a factor you ignore at your peril when designing any water feature, if anybody else is going to see it other than yourself. Easy-going alpine phlox or treasured marginals all will succumb to feet, both large and small, unless you make allowance for visitors to reach the water. Paths that cross the water surface are a good solution, allowing unhindered viewing of the mysteries of the deep, without compromising that valuable marginal planting space.

A simple stone across the water course (see opposite) is the easiest option if the stream is narrow enough, but gives plenty of opportunity for little ones to score a perfect six in the accidental double-somersault category. Even putting up a little fence alongside, as I have done in the Quarry Garden (see above), simply pushes up the degree of launching difficulty, allowing for two and a half turns before the inevitable close encounter with the newts.

For wider streams, rivers or ponds there are numerous wooden and metal bridge designs, from Chinese rainbow bridges through Monet's water-lily bridge to more functional constructions.

However, they do not seem as natural as stone structures, maybe because, however well-built, they are inevitably more ephemeral, although that argument is a bit spurious in relation to metal bridges. Perhaps it has more to do with the link between stone and water, which are a natural double-act, always acting in tandem, as fundamental as the sun and the moon. Nowhere is this more obvious than in the Lakes, where man's sensitive contribution has served to enhance the natural stone and water aesthetic. The low-arched bridge in Borrowdale (see page 249) is a typical example, and it is not too hard to imagine a scaled-down version enhancing a garden.

On Dartmoor, the stonework, like the hills themselves, seems almost primitive by comparison. Paths across fast-moving moorland streams and rivers are often no more than stepping stones, a nice idea for a garden, but one I have always felt slightly wary of. I am more comfortable with a solid lump of granite underfoot, and the clapper-bridge at Postbridge (see page 248) is more my style, a design which could easily be scaled down and used to make a crossing over shallow water, mostly planted with bog plants.

ABOVE *The magnificent granite clapper-bridge at Postbridge on Dartmoor in Devon, England. A much smaller, scaled-down version would still work in a garden of very modest dimensions, which is perhaps just as well when you think how heavy those top stones must be.*

Boardwalks

An elevated walkway through lush planting is the hallmark of the Jungle at Heligan, in Cornwall. It is my favourite part of the gardens there, mainly because of this enormous boardwalk. With the exotic vegetation growing all around, and the path changing levels to follow the steep contours of the valley sides, it almost gives one the feeling of being Tarzan in the treetops, but with the addition of comforting hand-rails and drops of no more than 1.8 m (6 ft).

I firmly believe that any bridge, or bridge-like structure, in a garden environment should have a clearly identifiable reason for its existence if it is to sit comfortably in its setting, and Heligan's boardwalk was built in order to protect sensitive root systems and a fragile eco-system from the trampling feet of this popular garden's many visitors each year. Nevertheless, it works wonderfully well as an aesthetic feature in its own right. I have seen photographs of other boardwalks serving this dual purpose, crossing equally sensitive sand-dunes or marshy peat bogs. Sometimes they are flanked by wooden hand-rails, and sometimes not.

In either style they can make good focal points in a garden design, particularly where the ground is partially marshy, as well as providing textural and aural elements to a garden walk. The slight sense of 'give' on an elevated timber-built walkway and the sound of one's foot-falls is an integral part of the entire boardwalk experience.

Omitting handrails from a raised walkway, however, not only adds a certain frisson of excitement and a wildness to the basic functionality, but also an actual increased risk if visitors are expected. With the increasing possibilities of litigation, perhaps all public gardens will have those corralling hand-rails one day anyway.

❖ ❖ ❖

I STARTED THIS CHAPTER with the suggestion that water might be considered to be the hard-landscaping equivalent of the very essence of a wild naturalness, and it seems right to return to it at the end of not only the chapter, but the book itself. Water has the capacity to complement every single element I have touched upon throughout, even in its enforced absence in semi-arid schemes where its effect can only be hinted at. It has the ability to elevate almost any planting or hard-surface element in a garden from the ordinary to the sublime, so it is hardly surprising that garden designers are so keen to incorporate it into their show gardens. In naturalistic gardens it is just as important, because this magical effect that it imparts is even more the case in naturally occurring wild landscapes, which it enhances often to jaw-dropping perfection. Its inclusion in our gardens should serve to remind us of these magnificent sights as well as ensuring that we keep our feet planted firmly on humble ground.

Epilogue

More than anything, this gardening style is about 'going with the flow'. In the newer parts of the garden here the effects change from year to year, with seemingly perfect combinations capable of disappearing altogether. One British gardener renowned for her tightly controlled colour combinations was mortified at my apparent lack of remorse when a particular grouping she had admired here one year had disappeared the next, but I am prepared to be flexible. I can look at photographs of most sections of the new garden and know what year they were taken by the distinctive unique combinations of the plants involved, and this very uncertainty is partly why it is so exciting.

I am convinced there is a revolution occurring in the horticultural world at the present time, a quiet, bloodless revolution that has been growing in strength over the years with the increasing awareness of conserving wild flowers and their habitats, coupled perhaps with a slight boredom with the regimented blocks of traditional gardening. It is a true people's revolution, in the best sense, coming from the bottom up where ordinary gardeners want to enjoy their plants in a more relaxed environment and to be able to put their own spin on their plots without fear of ridicule. I have written these chapters in the hope that you may catch some of the exhilaration that seeing plants in the wild and adopting this gardening style can generate and be inspired to have a go yourself.

Ultimately this book is not about my ideas but about freeing your own creative inner spirit from the straitjacket of horticultural tradition, about looking at natural landscapes with fresh eyes and interpreting what you see there in a way that suits you and your conditions. It is about confronting the challenges of your garden and having the self-confidence to implement possible solutions. I do not pretend to know all the answers to my own problems, let alone anybody else's, but I do know the questions I want to ask, and I absolutely know how much fun and pleasure

this journey has given me. Even if I never made a garden ever again, the thought processes and enjoyment involved in looking closely at natural landscapes has opened my eyes still further to the truly staggering beauty of plants and the countryside around us.

There will, of course, have been glaring omissions from what I have chosen to illustrate my points with, but I can only write from my own

LEFT Erythronium citrinum *carpets the ground below* Arctostaphylos manzanita *in southern Oregon, USA.*

experiences or from the limitations of my own imagination. One Australian group I took around the garden felt quite rebuffed that at that time there were no influences from their continent, and took some persuading that no national snub was intended. I have been told I should not apologize for gaps in my knowledge, but there are so many ideas out there that even the most travelled explorers could feel slightly fraudulent putting pen to paper unless they stress that their examples are just the tip of a very large iceberg. I hope that by writing of my own experiences up to this point in my life I may persuade others to set off on their own journeys of self-discovery, and if just one of you chooses to do so, then the extra pounds in weight I have added while writing this instead of digging my garden will not be too heavy a price to have paid.

Index

Page numbers in **bold** type indicate illustrations

Acknowledgements

I would like to thank everybody who has helped to make this book become a reality.

Special mention must go to my wife, Ros, whose unwavering support through thick and thin has helped to keep this dream alive and well. Also to our son, Tom, who showed remarkable patience whenever plants became involved on any of our holidays.

Particular thanks are also due to Anna Mumford at Timber Press for having the courage of her instincts to initiate this book, and then with with her diplomacy, good humour and dedication to make this project work by gently encouraging and teasing my tangled thoughts into something approaching a coherent argument.

Thanks also to Peggy Sadler for her brilliant work in designing this book and to Jonathan Hilton and Diana Vowles for their detailed editorial input. My thanks to Dan Hinkley for his foreword, managing in one page, with his seemingly effortless gift for words, to make all that follows seem rustic and unsophisticated—my thanks are through gritted teeth. Thanks to you all, you made this whole process become a pleasure.

Finally I would like to thank my fellow gardeners and all those, too many to mention individually, we have worked with in the creation of the garden, but especially David Milburn and, if you are looking down on us Tom, Tom Hooper, who both unquestionably bought into the dream that was the Garden House, as did so many of our visitors and the gardening press. Your loyalty and support kept the show on the road. My final thanks go to the trustees of the Fortescue Garden Trust for allowing me to carry on for so long despite their reservations.